Law For Dummies™

Cheat Sheet

W9-BWD-927

Important organizations and government agencies

If you're having trouble paying your bills and you want help negotiating lower monthly debt payments, contact the **Consumer Credit Counseling Service** (CCCS). The CCCS is a national, nonprofit organization that can help you get your financial situation under control. To locate the office closest to you, call 800-388-2227.

If you've been denied credit, employment, or insurance because of information in your credit report, request a copy of your report by contacting one of the following credit reporting agencies:

TRW
National Consumer Assistance Center
P.O. Box 2104
Allen, Texas 75013
800-682-7654

Trans Union
National Consumer Disclosure Center
P. O. Box 390
Springfield, PA 19064-0390
610-690-4909

Equifax
Office of Consumer Affairs
P.O. Box 105873
Atlanta, GA 30348
800-685-1111

If a mortgage lender denies you a loan or a seller refuses to sell to you and you believe that you're being discriminated against, call the **Department of Housing and Urban Development** (HUD) at 800-669-9777 to file a formal complaint. You must do so within one year of the incident.

If you believe that an unsafe or unhealthy situation exists at your place of work, you can bring the matter to the attention of your employer, or you can contact the **Occupational Safety and Health Administration** (OSHA) at 202-219-5000.

When you want to apply for Social Security benefits — retirement, survivor, or disability benefits — call the **Social Security Administration** at 800-772-1213.

If a telemarketer contacts you with an offer that seems to good to be true, call the **National Fraud Information Center** at 800-876-7060 to find out if the company is in the Center's database of fraudulent telemarketers.

The **Auto Safety Hotline** maintained by the National Highway Traffic Safety Administration provides information about auto safety and recalls for both new and used cars and other vehicles. Call 800-424-9393. In Washington, D.C., call 202-366-0123.

For a free fill-in-the-blanks living will that's legal in your state, contact **Choice in Dying,** a nonprofit organization, at 200 Varick Street, New York, N.Y. 10014-4810; 800-989-WILL.

The federal **Small Business Administration** has established a Web site — U.S. Business Advisor — to assist business owners. It tells you about the myriad federal rules and regulations you may need to comply with, and it allows you to download government forms and get information about government-backed loans and other federal assistance that you may be eligible for. Check it out at http://www.business.gov.

The **Federal Trade Commission's** Office of Consumer and Business Education publishes a wide variety of informative materials to educate consumers and businesses about their rights and responsibilities related to the laws administered by the FTC. Contact the FTC at its Office of Consumer and Business Education, FTC, Washington, D.C. 20580; 202-326-3650. Or you can go to its Web site located at http://www.ftc.gov. Here, you can find the text of more than 140 consumer and business publications.

For Dummies™: Bestselling Book Series for Beginners

Law For Dummies ™

Cheat Sheet

Requirements for making a will legal

State laws vary when it comes to creating a will. When you draw up your will, be prepared to meet the following requirements:

- You must be a legal adult — at least 18 years old in most states — when you write your will or when your attorney prepares it for you.

- You must be "of sound mind," which means that you must understand what you're doing: You understand your relationships to the people in your will; you know the nature of the property you own; you realize the significance of a will.

- You must be preparing your will because you want to, not because anyone is forcing you to or threatening you if you don't.

- Your will must be written, signed by you, dated, and witnessed, usually by two people.

Questions to ask an attorney you may be hiring

When you meet with a prospective attorney for the first time, ask the following questions:

- How many years have you been practicing law?

- What kind of cases do you handle most often?

- Approximately what percentage of the cases you've handled have been like mine? Of these, what percentage turned out successfully for the client?

- Based on what information you have, what do you see as the strengths and weaknesses of my case? How strong is it?

- How do you charge for your services? Will you put that in writing?

- How much should I be prepared to pay from start to finish if you take my case?

- Will I be consulted before you make any important decisions regarding my case? (You should be.)

- How long do you think it will take to resolve my legal problem? (If it's going to take longer than a month, ask if the attorney will provide you with a monthly written progress report.)

- Can I get an itemized bill? (You have the right to specify exactly what details you want included on your bill.)

- Who is actually going to be working on my case — you, another attorney, a paralegal?

For Dummies™: Bestselling Book Series for Beginners

Praise for Law For Dummies

"This book slices through the legal doublespeak and lays out your rights. It helps you resolve problems yourself and lets you know when to call in legal counsel. Whether you're a consumer, an employee, or a small business owner, John Ventura's easy-to-read guide will save you from making costly legal mistakes."
— Gail Gabriel, Senior Editor, *Home Office Computing* magazine

"*Law For Dummies* is just like having John as your personal attorney. His advice is practical, easy-to-understand, and it works!"
— Dan B. Flores, President, American Investigations & Security International, client of John Ventura

"John Ventura is an attorney who takes a simple, no-frills, no-nonsense approach to the legal system and has an overriding concern for the legal rights of the individual. In *Law For Dummies*, John Ventura has given you a valuable tool for improving the quality of your life."
— Max Betancourt, News Director, KKPS/KFRQ, Westlaco, Texas

"Simply Splendid. John Ventura has saved us a great deal of time and money. He has made the complex simple and the difficult easy. I feel as if I have been liberated from the shackles of a legal system designed by those who wish us not to understand. John, bless you! We now understand and we thank you."
— Francisco J. Hernandez, Ph.D., Vice Chancellor, University of California, Santa Cruz

Praise for Other Books by John Ventura

"If only one can be purchased, choose Ventura's, which is more focused and better written."
— Library Journal on *The Credit Repair Kit*

"The book is so down-to-earth and so easily understood. I especially found the 'hot tips' very informative."
— Irma Serventi, reader, on *The Credit Repair Kit*

"The emphasis on planning a workable course of action will appeal to any who want a concrete application book rather than a philosophy course."
— Reviewer's Bookwatch on *The Small Business Survival Kit*

LAW FOR DUMMIES®

by John Ventura

IDG BOOKS WORLDWIDE

IDG Books Worldwide, Inc.
An International Data Group Company

Foster City, CA ♦ Chicago, IL ♦ Indianapolis, IN ♦ New York, NY

Law For Dummies®

Published by
IDG Books Worldwide, Inc.
An International Data Group Company
919 E. Hillsdale Blvd.
Suite 400
Foster City, CA 94404
www.idgbooks.com (IDG Books Worldwide Web site)
www.dummies.com (Dummies Press Web site)

Library of Congress Catalog Card No.: 96-77268

ISBN: 1-56884-860-9

Printed in the United States of America

10 9 8 7 6

1B/QS/QS/QQ/IN

Distributed in the United States by IDG Books Worldwide, Inc.

Distributed by CDG Books Canada Inc. for Canada; by Transworld Publishers Limited in the United Kingdom; by IDG Norge Books for Norway; by IDG Sweden Books for Sweden; by IDG Books Australia Publishing Corporation Pty. Ltd. for Australia and New Zealand; by TransQuest Publishers Pte Ltd. for Singapore, Malaysia, Thailand, Indonesia, and Hong Kong; by Gotop Information Inc. for Taiwan; by ICG Muse, Inc. for Japan; by Intersoft for South Africa; by Eyrolles for France; by International Thomson Publishing for Germany, Austria and Switzerland; by Distribuidora Cuspide for Argentina; by LR International for Brazil; by Galileo Libros for Chile; by Ediciones ZETA S.C.R. Ltda. for Peru; by WS Computer Publishing Corporation, Inc., for the Philippines; by Contemporanea de Ediciones for Venezuela; by Express Computer Distributors for the Caribbean and West Indies; by Micronesia Media Distributor, Inc. for Micronesia; by Chips Computadoras S.A. de C.V. for Mexico; by Editorial Norma de Panama S.A. for Panama; by American Bookshops for Finland.

For general information on IDG Books Worldwide's books in the U.S., please call our Consumer Customer Service department at 800-762-2974. For reseller information, including discounts and premium sales, please call our Reseller Customer Service department at 800-434-3422.

For information on where to purchase IDG Books Worldwide's books outside the U.S., please contact our International Sales department at 317-596-5530 or fax 317-572-4002.

For consumer information on foreign language translations, please contact our Customer Service department at 1-800-434-3422, fax 317-572-4002, or e-mail rights@idgbooks.com.

For information on licensing foreign or domestic rights, please phone +1-650-653-7098.

For sales inquiries and special prices for bulk quantities, please contact our Sales department at 800-762-2974 or write to the address above.

For information on using IDG Books Worldwide's books in the classroom or for ordering examination copies, please contact our Educational Sales department at 800-434-2086 or fax 317-572-4005.

For press review copies, author interviews, or other publicity information, please contact our Public Relations department at 650-653-7000 or fax 650-653-7500.

For authorization to photocopy items for corporate, personal, or educational use, please contact Copyright Clearance Center, 222 Rosewood Drive, Danvers, MA 01923, or fax 978-750-4470.

is a registered trademark under exclusive license to IDG Books Worldwide, Inc. from International Data Group, Inc.

ABOUT IDG BOOKS WORLDWIDE

Welcome to the world of IDG Books Worldwide.

IDG Books Worldwide, Inc., is a subsidiary of International Data Group, the world's largest publisher of computer-related information and the leading global provider of information services on information technology. IDG was founded more than 30 years ago by Patrick J. McGovern and now employs more than 9,000 people worldwide. IDG publishes more than 290 computer publications in over 75 countries. More than 90 million people read one or more IDG publications each month.

Launched in 1990, IDG Books Worldwide is today the #1 publisher of best-selling computer books in the United States. We are proud to have received eight awards from the Computer Press Association in recognition of editorial excellence and three from Computer Currents' First Annual Readers' Choice Awards. Our best-selling ...*For Dummies*® series has more than 50 million copies in print with translations in 31 languages. IDG Books Worldwide, through a joint venture with IDG's Hi-Tech Beijing, became the first U.S. publisher to publish a computer book in the People's Republic of China. In record time, IDG Books Worldwide has become the first choice for millions of readers around the world who want to learn how to better manage their businesses.

Our mission is simple: Every one of our books is designed to bring extra value and skill-building instructions to the reader. Our books are written by experts who understand and care about our readers. The knowledge base of our editorial staff comes from years of experience in publishing, education, and journalism — experience we use to produce books to carry us into the new millennium. In short, we care about books, so we attract the best people. We devote special attention to details such as audience, interior design, use of icons, and illustrations. And because we use an efficient process of authoring, editing, and desktop publishing our books electronically, we can spend more time ensuring superior content and less time on the technicalities of making books.

You can count on our commitment to deliver high-quality books at competitive prices on topics you want to read about. At IDG Books Worldwide, we continue in the IDG tradition of delivering quality for more than 30 years. You'll find no better book on a subject than one from IDG Books Worldwide.

John Kilcullen
Chairman and CEO
IDG Books Worldwide, Inc.

Steven Berkowitz
President and Publisher
IDG Books Worldwide, Inc.

Eighth Annual Computer Press Awards ≥1992

Ninth Annual Computer Press Awards ≥1993

Tenth Annual Computer Press Awards ≥1994

Eleventh Annual Computer Press Awards ≥1995

About the Author

John Ventura is a small business owner, best-selling author, and attorney. He is also a national authority on consumer and small business financial and legal problems.

John earned an undergraduate degree in journalism and a law degree from the University of Houston. He envisioned providing ordinary people with affordable, caring legal services, and he hoped to educate people on how to use the law to protect their rights.

He and a partner established a law firm in Texas, building it into one of the most successful consumer bankruptcy firms in the state. When the partnership ended, John began a consumer law firm in the Rio Grande Valley of Texas where he now has three busy offices. He also has a fourth office in Laredo, on the Texas/Mexico border. His firm offers legal advice and assistance in the areas of bankruptcy, personal injury, and estate planning. John estimates that during his 18 years as a lawyer, his firm has helped more than 12,000 consumers and small business owners.

Today, John is a frequent guest on radio programs across the country. He has also been interviewed by such publications as *The Wall Street Journal, Newsweek, Inc. Magazine, Kiplinger's Personal Finance Magazine, Money Magazine, The Chicago Tribune, Playboy,* and *The New York Times.*

A regular contributor to *Home Office Computing Magazine*'s legal column, John also writes a regular column on small business and consumer legal issues for a number of Texas publications, and he hosts a local, weekly radio program in Texas called *Legally Speaking.* In addition, he is the author of six books for consumers and small business people.

John lives with his family near the beach on South Padre Island, Texas.

Publisher's Acknowledgments

We're proud of this book; please register your comments through our IDG Books Worldwide Online Registration Form located at http://my2cents.dummies.com.

Some of the people who helped bring this book to market include the following:

Acquisitions, Development, and Editorial

Project Editor: Tim Gallan

Editor: Michael Simsic

Technical Reviewer: Karen Mendenhall

Editorial Manager: Kristin A. Cocks

Editorial Assistants: Constance Carlisle, Chris Collins, Heather Dismore, Ann Miller

Production

Project Coordinator: Cindy L. Phipps

Layout and Graphics: E. Shawn Aylsworth, Brett Black, Linda M. Boyer, Elizabeth Cárdenas-Nelson, Dominique DeFelice, Maridee V. Ennis, Kelly Hardesty, Angela F. Hunckler, Todd Klemme, Jane E. Martin, Anna Rohrer, Brent Savage. Gina Scott

Proofreaders: Michael Bolinger, Kelli Botta, Rachel Garvey, Dwight Ramsey, Nancy L. Reinhardt, Robert Springer, Carrie Voorhis, Karen York

Indexer: Sharon Duffy

General and Administrative

IDG Books Worldwide, Inc.: John Kilcullen, CEO; Steven Berkowitz, President and Publisher

IDG Books Technology Publishing Group: Richard Swadley, Senior Vice President and Publisher; Walter Bruce III, Vice President and Associate Publisher; Joseph Wikert, Associate Publisher; Mary Bednarek, Branded Product Development Director; Mary Corder, Editorial Director; Barry Pruett, Publishing Manager; Michelle Baxter, Publishing Manager

IDG Books Consumer Publishing Group: Roland Elgey, Senior Vice President and Publisher; Kathleen A. Welton, Vice President and Publisher; Kevin Thornton, Acquisitions Manager; Kristin A. Cocks, Editorial Director

IDG Books Internet Publishing Group: Brenda McLaughlin, Senior Vice President and Publisher; Diane Graves Steele, Vice President and Associate Publisher; Sofia Marchant, Online Marketing Manager

IDG Books Production for Dummies Press: Debbie Stailey, Associate Director of Production; Cindy L. Phipps, Manager of Project Coordination, Production Proofreading, and Indexing; Tony Augsburger, Manager of Prepress, Reprints, and Systems; Laura Carpenter, Production Control Manager; Shelley Lea, Supervisor of Graphics and Design; Debbie J. Gates, Production Systems Specialist; Robert Springer, Supervisor of Proofreading; Kathie Schutte, Production Supervisor

Dummies Packaging and Book Design: Patty Page, Manager, Promotions Marketing

♦

The publisher would like to give special thanks to Patrick J. McGovern, without whom this book would not have been possible.

♦

Author's Acknowledgments

Thank you to Mary Reed, whose vision matches my own and whose hard work on our projects far exceeds mine. I also want to thank her for the sound of the wind chimes I often hear when we talk by phone. They remind me that life can be simple and sweet.

I want to thank Heather Stobaugh, Stephen Sharpe, and Carlo DeChiro for their hard work researching such a broad topic as The Law.

Also, a heartfelt thank you to the people I work with every day: my friends and associates at the Law Offices of John Ventura, P.C. They guarded my time when I needed to work on this book, and they share my pleasure in helping people resolve their legal problems.

Thank you to Tim Gallan and Michael Simsic of IDG Books for their invaluable questions and comments during the editing process. Finally, a special thanks to Kathy Welton, my publisher and friend, who helped me get into the wonderful world of book writing! She epitomizes what is best about the publishing industry. I have great respect for her.

Dedication

To my lovely and caring wife Mary Ellen, and to my clients who are a daily reminder that the law is supposed to help, not hurt, people.

Contents at a Glance

Cartoons at a Glance

By Rich Tennant

page 45

page 313

page 269

page 7

page 197

Fax: 978-546-7747
E-mail: richtennant@the5thwave.com
World Wide Web: www.the5thwave.com

Table of Contents

Part IV: Other Legal Stuff 269

Chapter 24: Ten Great Free and Almost-Free Sources of Information and Legal Help 327

Chapter 25: Ventura's Top Ten Law-Related Home Pages on the Internet 333

Appendix: Sample Letters 339

Introduction

● ●

I've been a practicing attorney for 18 years, and over the years, I have counseled many, many consumers and small business owners. Through my work, I have come to realize that most people are woefully ignorant of the laws that affect their lives, and they often pay a steep price for their ignorance.

Some people are denied important loans due to credit bureau errors that they don't know how to correct, or they get into trouble with the IRS because they don't understand their obligations as business owners. Others are victimized by unscrupulous employers, or they end up in needless and expensive lawsuits. Still others are taken advantage of by door-to-door salespeople or by telemarketers, or they can't get their landlords to make much-needed apartment repairs.

As I thought about how little most people know about our laws and the problems that often develop as a result, I began to envision writing a book that would explain the law to everyday people in simple, straightforward language, not in legal mumbo-jumbo. The book would cover many of the laws that affect our lives: workplace and employment laws; laws relating to personal finances, retirement, and health care; laws relating to families and housing, divorce, and even privacy.

My book would help readers "take the law into their own hands," so to speak. I don't mean that they ought to become vigilantes; rather, the book's reliable, easy-to-understand information about legal rights, responsibilities, and obligations would help readers make the laws in their lives work *for* them, not against them. It would help them avoid legal problems and, when problems do develop, resolve them as quickly as possible with a minimum amount of cost and hassle. My book would give readers a better understanding of when to call an attorney and how to find a good one they can afford.

I also envisioned this book as a resource for the multimedia age. Recognizing that an ever-increasing number of today's consumers are going online for their information, my legal handbook would inform readers about the legal information they can access from online services and the Internet.

The book I dreamed of is this book, *Law For Dummies*.

What's the Problem?

If you're like many Americans today, you probably feel overwhelmed by the rules, regulations, and red tape that seem to govern and complicate every aspect of your daily life. Every time you turn around, another law is telling you what to do and how to do it, or what not to do and what will happen if you do! As Anatole France once said about us, "America, where thanks to Congress, there are forty million laws to enforce ten commandments!"

As our laws and our society have become more complicated, many of us have responded by becoming dependent on attorneys to tell us our rights and help us resolve our problems — often by filing lawsuits. In fact, we've become the most litigious country in the world! If you're a consumer, you're paying higher prices because of our nation's litigiousness. If you're a business owner, your bottom line is being hurt.

Knowledge Is Power

So what can we do? I say this: Get smart. Become informed about the law. Understand how to avoid legal problems and how to resolve them yourself when you can. Knowledge is power!

But where do you get the knowledge? You probably didn't get much legal education in high school or college. I know I didn't, and neither did my kids. And most people aren't going to teach themselves about the law unless they want a sure cure for insomnia. Traditionally, the unfortunate reality has been that most of us don't get a legal education until we have a legal problem — an expensive way to learn, both emotionally and financially!

Why You Need This Book

Law For Dummies helps you become more informed about your legal rights, responsibilities, and obligations in a wide range of subject areas. It also improves your understanding of how to use laws without resorting to attorneys. Here are just a few of the legal problems that this book addresses:

- You've been denied an important loan because of incorrect information in your credit report, and you don't know how to get the erroneous information removed.

- Your ex-spouse, who lives in another state, has suddenly stopped making his child support payments. You depend on that income to help meet your children's needs, but you don't know your rights or who can help you.

✔ You run a small business and frequently use independent contractors to help you accomplish your work. Recently, you were talking with another business owner who told you that she is in hot water with the IRS because two workers she had treated as independent contractors were actually employees according to the IRS. She is worried about how she's ever going to come up with the back taxes that the agency claims she owes for the misclassified workers. Now you're concerned that you might also be misclassifying workers, and you're wondering what your options are if you end up in the same situation as your friend.

✔ Your strong-willed, elderly father is in a nursing home and doesn't want to be there. He is also refusing the medical treatment that his doctor has ordered. Is there anything you can do?

✔ Your next-door neighbor is not maintaining his property. Not only has it become an eyesore, but you're also worried that the collecting garbage may be a danger to the children in your neighborhood. What can you do to get your neighbor to clean up his act? Can you get your local government to help, or do you need to take legal action?

How Is This Book Organized?

Law For Dummies starts out with the general in Part I and then goes to the specifics in the remaining parts. The following briefly describes what's in each part:

Part I: Basic Legal Stuff

The first three chapters introduce you to this country's legal system, including its philosophical underpinnings; explain the jurisdictions of the various courts in our country, from small claims to the Supreme Court; discuss alternatives to lawsuits — things you can do yourself to resolve your legal problems. And if an attorney's help is necessary, these early chapters provide practical information about how to find and work with a good one.

Part II: Laws That Affect Your Daily Life

This part covers a whole range of seemingly unrelated topics — everything from family law to home buying to starting your own business. The common thread among these chapters is that they discuss laws that affect the most important aspects of your personal life: your family, your job, and your property.

Part III: Tough Stuff: Being Sick, Getting Older, Dying

Getting sick, growing old, and dying happen to the best of us. Yet, these facts of life can be troubling to deal with, not to mention frightening sometimes. How are we going to pay for the health care we or a loved one may need? How are we ever going to fund our retirement? What can we do to make sure that our loved ones are well cared for after we die? What resources can help us? The chapters in this part will help you understand the laws governing things like medical care, social security, pensions, and estate planning.

Part IV: Other Legal Stuff

In this part, I cover topics for which the laws are very complex, are currently inadequate, or are currently in a lot of flux. Specifically, I deal with immigration, criminal law, juvenile law, and privacy.

Part V: The Part of Tens

Every *Dummies* book ends with some top-ten lists, and this one is no different. In this part, I present the following topics:

- Common mistakes consumers make when hiring an attorney
- The best Web sites for legal information
- Easy ways to avoid legal problems
- Free and almost-free sources of legal information and help

How to Use This Book

You can use *Law For Dummies* in a number of different ways:

- If you have a specific question about the law as it relates to a particular area of your life, just turn to the chapter that talks about that area. (Just peruse the table of contents or look up the topic in the index.) For example, if you are fired from your job and you want to know your rights, refer to Chapter 6. If you and your spouse are buying a home — the single biggest financial transaction you've ever made — and you want to be sure that you do everything right, read Chapter 10. And if you're a small business owner with a home-based business and you want to avoid problems with the IRS, Chapter 7 is the one for you.

✔ You can read the book cover to cover to gain a more comprehensive understanding of the American legal system. That way, if legal problems later develop in your life, you'll already be aware of a law that can help you.

✔ You can use the book as a guide to resources that you can use to help yourself when legal problems develop. You will also find references to low-cost or no-cost sources of legal advice. These resources include government agencies, nonprofit organizations, CD-ROMs, reports, brochures, and even other books.

✔ Last, but certainly not least, those of you who enjoy wandering around the Internet can use this book to find out about online legal information you can access, law-related chat groups you can join, or actual copies of laws you can download. No other book about consumer law offers all this!

I'm almost making the law sound like fun!

Icons Used in This Book

What do those funny little pictures in the margins mean? Read on.

This arrow with dart board targets information that will help you solve problems or simply get things done in an efficient manner.

This icon flags particularly noteworthy information — stuff you shouldn't forget.

You don't have to read the information next to this nerdy guy because it relates to more technical aspects of the law. If, however, you are having a legal problem and want to learn as much as possible about the law involved, the technical stuff can be helpful. And if you want to impress ("bore" might be more appropriate) your friends and family members with your grasp of the law, the technical stuff is just what you need!

This icon flags all kinds of dangers and scams you should avoid. Heed the advice next to this icon to avoid headache, heartache, hair loss, and financial ruin.

This icon highlights reliable resources and organizations that you can turn to for additional information and help after you've read what this book has to say about a subject.

This icon calls your attention to the location of additional information available on the Internet or provided by an online service. For example, if you want to learn more about your constitutional rights, you can access a collection of articles from the Electronic Frontier Foundation at `ftp.uu.net` using this path: `/doc/literary/obi/EFF/*`. And if you want to download a sample living will, take advantage of the resources at the Indiana University School of Law: `http://www.law.indiana.edu/`.

The law can get pretty dry and boring, so occasionally this book uses real-life stories to illustrate legal problems. If you want to read about everyday people and the law, look for this icon.

Part I
Basic Legal Stuff

In this part . . .

Chapter 1 describes how this country's legal system works. It discusses the court system, civil trials, and contracts. Chapter 2 presents ways that you can solve basic legal problems without the help of an attorney. Chapter 3 helps you discern when you need an attorney and then helps you find the right one for you.

Chapter 1

All about Our Legal System

*W*hat do you think of when you hear the words *legal system?* If you're like many Americans, you probably think of a court room where lawyers, using language you can't understand, argue with one another, and where a jury of people you don't know, or a judge in a black robe behind an imposingly high desk, makes decisions about your life using laws you know little or nothing about. Not only is that an intimidating image, but it's only a very small part of the picture! Our legal system is much more than just courtroom action.

This chapter will expand your definition of what our legal system is by providing you with information you probably never got in high school — or don't remember learning, anyway. Maybe you slept through class the day that subject was covered! With a more complete understanding of our legal system, you'll be better able to avoid getting into legal hot water, and you'll feel more confident about exercising your legal rights when you do.

And now for your remedial crash course on our legal system . . .

What Are Laws and Where Do They Come From?

Our laws reflect society's standards, values, and expectations. They establish "the rules of the game" in our personal interactions and in our business dealings, helping to ensure that we are treated fairly and that we treat others fairly. Laws establish our responsibilities and our rights and help us both avoid problems and resolve problems.

The laws that govern our lives come from six basic sources: the U.S. Constitution, the Bill of Rights, statute law, administrative law, common law, and case law.

The Constitution

The Constitution is the granddaddy of all U.S. law, the supreme law of the land and the standard against which all other laws are measured. It established this country as a republic and determined the structure of our Congressional system. The Constitution applies to all Americans.

The Constitution is a "living" document because our lawmakers can amend it to respond to changes in our country's needs, concerns, and values. Presently, the Constitution consists of seven articles, the ten amendments that make up the Bill of Rights, and 16 other amendments that have been adopted over the years.

The Bill of Rights

The Bill of Rights defines the fundamental rights of all Americans. It places limits on how much control the federal government can exercise over our lives by guaranteeing certain freedoms, which include the following:

- The right to free speech
- The right to freedom of religion
- The right to freedom of the press
- The right to a speedy and public trial
- The right to bear arms
- The right to protection against unreasonable searches and seizures

State law

In addition to the U.S. Constitution, each of the 50 states has its own constitution, which provides the basis for the state's own laws. States can make their own laws so long as those laws don't conflict with federal laws and don't violate the tenets of the U.S. Constitution. In fact, state laws frequently expand or enhance federal laws. For example, the federal Fair Credit Reporting Act says that consumers have the right to receive a free copy of their credit report if they apply for credit, employment, or insurance and are denied it due to information in their report. Some states have passed their own laws related to credit bureaus, laws that specify that consumers are entitled to a free copy of their credit report every year, whether or not they are turned down for credit, insurance, or employment.

When a federal law relates to a legal problem you are having, check with your state attorney general's office to find out if your state also has a law that can help you.

Statute law

Another basic kind of law is *statute* law — laws adopted by the U.S. Congress and by state and local elected officials. These laws most affect our daily lives, which is why we should be familiar with them. These laws apply to such things as our credit rights, the rules of the road, the right to leave our property to others, our rights and responsibilities as married couples or parents, and so on. Many of these laws are covered in this book.

Administrative law

Administrative law is perhaps better described as rules and regulations created and enforced by regulatory agencies. For example, the Internal Revenue Service has the power to tell us what we can and can't deduct on our tax returns and can fine us when we violate its rules; the Federal Trade Commission can establish rules governing what telemarketers and debt collectors can and can't do when they contact us, and this agency can take legal action against businesses that ignore those rules; and the Environmental Protection Agency has the power to control the kinds and levels of emissions that businesses may release into the environment, and this agency can impose penalties and other sanctions on companies that endanger our water supply and clean air.

Common law

The next source of our laws is common law. We can trace its origins all the way back to 12th century England when there were no legal precedents to guide the decisions of judges. These early judges used current customs and their own common sense to help them decide how to resolve legal controversies. Their legal decisions created legal precedents that guide our judges even today.

Case law

When a judge interprets and applies the law in a particular case, he or she creates a legal precedent. That precedent is expected to guide judges in that same court and all lower courts within the same jurisdiction when they decide similar cases in the future.

Court TV's Web page (http://courttv.com/) is an invaluable resource for those of you who want to learn more about the law in general and about important cases in particular. It can direct you to summaries of recent Supreme

Court cases as well as civil rights, business, and computer and technology cases. You can also access Court TV's law library and glossary as well as a site where you can review sample legal forms. And its Teen Court site can begin your teenager's education about the various roles that the law plays in society. Every week, it focuses on a different issue, ranging from animal rights to censorship, and it also features discussions of various aspects of the juvenile justice system.

Civil Law versus Criminal Law

We have two major categories of law: civil and criminal law. Each has its court systems and procedures.

The vast majority of legal problems in the United States involve civil law: consumer problems, spats between neighbors, family problems, and so on. In fact, family problems such as divorce, child custody, and support represent the majority of civil law cases.

You can file a civil lawsuit yourself, or your attorney can do it for you. You are the *plaintiff.* You might sue because you want to receive monetary compensation for a perceived wrong or because you want to force someone, the *defendant* in your lawsuit, to do or not do something. By the way, when you try to force someone not to do something, you are seeking *injunctive relief.*

Criminal law deals with crimes against society: murder, theft, assault, embezzlement, abuse, arson, and much more. You cannot initiate a criminal lawsuit yourself; only a federal or state prosecutor can do that. Defendants found guilty in criminal cases face monetary penalties, public service, prison time, or even death, depending on the defendant's past criminal history and the seriousness of the crime.

Because the potential penalty in a criminal case is so much more serious than what a defendant faces in a civil case, the burden of proof in a criminal case is much higher than in a civil case. In criminal court, the prosecuting attorney must prove "beyond a reasonable doubt" that a defendant is guilty. In a civil case, however, a defendant is guilty if the "preponderance of the evidence" points to guilt.

Our Court Systems

Our court system is actually many court systems: a federal system and 50 state systems. Each has its own structures and procedures. All are multi-tiered. Legal cases begin in a lower court and sometimes work their way up to a higher court. Some cases initiated in a state court system ultimately end up in the federal court system.

State courts

Most legal issues are resolved in state trial courts, the courts at the lowest tier in a state's court system. O.J. Simpson's criminal and civil trials were both conducted in a California trial court. Depending on the specific structure of your state's court system, trial courts may be city or municipal courts, justice of the peace or *jp courts,* county or circuit courts, or even regional trial courts.

Most states have two levels of trial courts: trial courts with *limited jurisdiction* and trial courts with *specific jurisdiction.* Jurisdiction simply refers to the types of cases a court can hear. For example, trial courts of limited jurisdiction — which can include municipal courts, magistrate courts, county courts and justice of the peace courts — hear some kinds of civil cases, juvenile cases, minor criminal cases and traffic violations. Most legal problems are resolved in this kind of trial court.

Some trial courts with limited jurisdiction also hold pretrial hearings for more serious criminal cases.

Courts of general jurisdiction include circuit courts, superior courts, district courts, or courts of common pleas, depending on your state. They hear lawsuits that involve greater amounts of money or more serious types of crimes than the cases heard in trial courts of limited jurisdiction.

Many states also have specialized trial courts that hear cases related to a very specific area of the law. These courts can include probate courts, family law courts, juvenile courts, and small claims courts.

Next tier up in the typical state court system are the appellate courts. These courts don't hold trials but instead review the decisions and procedures of the trial courts in their systems and either uphold or reverse their decisions or modify the amount of a monetary reward. Sometimes appellate courts order retrials.

Lower court decisions are not automatically appealed. You must initiate an appeal and provide a legal basis for appealing. Thinking that you "got a raw deal" is not enough.

Every state has a court of last resort, generally called the "supreme court." Although supreme court decisions are final within a state court system, sometimes they can be appealed to the U.S. Supreme Court. Like appellate courts, supreme courts review the decisions and the procedures of lower courts; they don't hold trials.

Federal courts

Most of the federal court system is divided into districts and circuits. There is at least one federal district in every state, but populous states can have multiple districts. Texas has northern, western, southern and eastern districts.

Generally, federal lawsuits start out at the district level in a federal court. Most are civil, not criminal, cases involving legal issues that fall within the jurisdiction of the federal government, not state government. If a lawsuit deals with certain types of federal law, it is heard in a special federal court. Tax court, bankruptcy court, court of federal claims, and court of veteran appeals are all examples of special federal courts.

Each federal circuit includes more than one district and is home to a Federal Court of Appeal. This court plays a role analogous to a state appellate court.

At the very top of the federal court system is the U.S. Supreme Court. Its legal interpretations are The Final Word on the law in this country. The nine justices who sit on the Supreme Court are nominated by the President and approved by the U.S. Senate. They can remain on the court until their death or until they resign.

Only a very small number of cases are ever heard by the U.S. Supreme Court. To get to that level, a case must usually work its way up through the lower tiers of a state court system and/or the federal system. The justices choose the cases they hear every year based on a case's implications for Americans in general or for a certain group within society, not just the impact on the parties actually involved in the lawsuit itself. What follows are some of the Supreme Court cases that meet these criteria:

- *Brown vs. The Board of Education of Topeka.* This ruling was the beginning of the end of racial segregation in America's public schools.
- *Roe vs. Wade.* Gave all American women the right to decide for themselves, in consultation with their doctor, whether or not to have an abortion.
- *Miranda vs. Arizona.* This ruling gave persons who are arrested the right to be informed of their legal rights at the time of their arrest: "You have the right to remain silent. . . ."

The Constitution only allows certain kinds of cases to be heard by the federal courts. In general, these courts are limited to cases that involve the following:

- Issues of Constitutional law
- Certain issues between residents of different states
- Issues between U.S. citizens and foreigners
- Issues that involve both federal and state law

Our legal system is based on the *adversarial process,* which means that fundamental to all court procedures, regardless of the court, is the belief that all parties in a legal dispute must have an equal opportunity to state their case to a neutral jury or judge and to poke holes in what the other side says. Attorneys usually do most of the case-stating and hole-poking.

So that everyone has an equal chance to win in a lawsuit, both sides are required to play by the same set of rules. This requirement helps level the playing field, ensuring that everyone is treated fairly. Attorneys learn these rules in law school.

For a humorously irreverent but fact-filled tour of the legal system and many of the important laws that affect our lives as consumers or businesspeople, check out Inter-Law's 'lectric Law Library at http://www.inter-law.com/. From this location, you can download legal software and sample legal forms, learn about court rules and state and federal laws affecting many of the topics covered in this book, refer to a legal encyclopedia and dictionary, read the transcripts of actual legal cases, and even get a few laughs at the expense of the legal establishment by reading lawyer jokes!

All about Contracts

Written and unwritten contracts are essential parts of our legal system and form the basis of many of our personal and business transactions. To protect yourself, especially when money is involved, and to avoid legal entanglements, a basic understanding of contracts is essential.

Contracts are voluntary, legally-binding agreements between two or more people to do or not do something. Whether you realize it or not, you enter into contracts all the time: when you borrow money from a bank, enroll in a health club, get married or divorced, sign for a home loan, lease office equipment, buy a car, hire a roofer, sign a credit card agreement, and so on.

Legally binding contracts have certain characteristics. At the risk of losing you with too much legalese, here they are:

- ✔ All parties to a contract must be mentally capable of understanding what they're agreeing to. So if your four-year-old son or your senile Uncle Al agrees to a contract, the contract is not legal and won't stand up in court. Although there are exceptions, all parties to a contract must be legal adults — 18 or 21 depending on your state.

- ✔ The contract can't involve doing or selling anything illegal. So for example, if you sign a contract to invest in your friend's marijuana field and don't get the return on investment you were promised, you're out of luck because your contract isn't legal.

- ✔ You must be able to prove that a contract exists. Doing so shouldn't be difficult if it's written and you've kept a copy. If the contract is oral or "understood," however, proving its existence may be a challenge and may require the help of an attorney.

- ✔ The contract must involve an offer, an acceptance, and consideration. Here's where the legalese begins to get tough.

You have an *offer* if you clearly indicate to someone else (the *offeree*) your intention to enter into a contract. Suggesting to someone that you want to talk about a transaction or negotiate something is not an offer. You have to "put an offer on the table" so that someone else can respond by accepting or rejecting it.

If your offer is accepted voluntarily, then you've got an *acceptance*.

And finally, if both you and the other party to a contract voluntarily give, exchange, perform, or promise one another something of value, then you've got *consideration*.

Here's a real life example of what I mean: Over dinner one night, you and a friend casually discuss the possibility of your buying your friend's sailboat, but you don't make an offer. So far, no contract. Later, after talking with your spouse, you decide to make your friend an offer, and after some back and forth negotiating, you and your friend agree on a purchase price and the terms of the purchase because you're going to pay your friend for the boat over a period of six months. So far, you've got an offer and an acceptance. To clinch the deal, you give your friend a check as a deposit on the cost of the boat and make arrangements to pick up the boat the following week. With that, you now have a consideration and a legally binding contract. So if the following week you go out to get the boat only to find that the boat is gone because your friend sold it to someone else for more money, or if you take the boat but after two months stop making payments on it, each of you in your own way has broken your contract, and you have grounds for taking legal action against the other. (By the way, this transaction really needed a written contract, not an oral contract, even if you are dealing with a friend.)

Although legally valid contracts are most often thought of as written, contracts can also be oral or "implied."

By the way, if you behave as though you accept an offer but you don't actually say that you accept, you have legally accepted the offer.

Written contracts

The best contract is always a written one where all the things that have been agreed to — the *terms* of the contract — are spelled out, right there in black and white. Terms usually include the following:

- ✔ Who's obligated to do what and for how much
- ✔ Deadlines
- ✔ Answers to questions such as "What happens if . . . ?"

As important and helpful as written contracts are, they are not necessary for every single agreement or transaction you make in life. But if money is involved, or if you have a lot at stake financially or emotionally, a written contract is essential. That's true even if you're dealing with a close friend or relative.

The story of small business owner Mike S. helps illustrate why written contracts are so important. Mike sold his business to his brother for $20,000 and a handshake — no contract. After all, if he couldn't trust his brother, whom could he trust! During the first couple months of their agreement, Mike's brother had some health problems that prevented him from paying Mike the monthly installments they'd agreed on. Six months came and went and Mike still hadn't seen a red cent. Then his brother sold the business and recouped his investment. Mike felt certain that finally he'd get his money. Yet two months later, he was still unable to collect from his brother, who claimed he needed every dollar he made from the sale. Mike was left with a difficult dilemma: Take his brother to court or forget about his $20,000? If he went to court, it would be his word against his brother's because they had nothing written down. Either way, his relationship with his brother would never be the same.

In some states, certain kinds of contracts must be in writing to be legally enforceable. They usually involve promises to

- ✔ Guarantee someone else's debt. For example, you might sign a contract to help a close relative secure a bank loan.
- ✔ Sell real property.
- ✔ Buy or sell goods worth more than $500 or lease goods worth more than $1,000.
- ✔ Do something that can't be performed in a year.
- ✔ Give someone certain property after your death (which is why you write a will).

Form contracts

Fill-in-the-blanks contracts are appropriate for straightforward agreements; however, they are not going to work if you need to deal with unusual or special situations or concerns.

Implied contracts: How can I be held to something I didn't agree to?

When you do something and an unstated expectation exists that you will follow the initial action with another action, you've entered into a special, legally enforceable contract called an *implied* or *understood* contract. For example, if you go to a grocery store and fill up your cart with chicken and vegetables, you've implied that you'll be paying for your groceries at the cash register. In other words, you and the store have an understood contract. If you break that contract by shoplifting, the store can take legal action against you because this kind of contract is legally enforceable.

For contract basics provided in a question and answer format, go to `http://www.urlink.com/le/library/Cont/1.html`.

What if I want out?

That a legal contract is binding on everyone who signs it provides society with an important benefit. To understand that benefit, stop and think for a moment what life would be like if contracts could be canceled willy-nilly just because someone decided that an agreement was inconvenient or because a better deal came along! Imagine the chaos. Banks might begin changing the terms of our loans whenever they wanted; we could no longer be assured that the price we were quoted for something would be what we'd actually have to pay; marital and divorce agreements "wouldn't be worth the paper they're written on." Talk about lack of trust!

Notwithstanding its binding nature, however, a contract can be broken under certain conditions, which include the following:

✔ You are defrauded by another party to the contract. For example, you signed a contract to buy a majority interest in a Texas oil well with promises that you'd soon be making barrels of money. You, however, were never told one critical detail — that the well hadn't produced in years and that geologists didn't expect it to produce anytime soon.

✔ One party to the contract *breaches* the contract — a fancy phrase for not living up to the terms of the contract. If the company you hired to put a new roof on your house never completes the job, it has breached your contract.

If a contract you sign is breached, you may have the right to sue for monetary damages and/or to sue to compel the other party to meet the terms of the contract.

✔ You signed the contract because you were being threatened. For example, if you signed a contract because someone held a gun to your head, the contract isn't legally binding.

✔ You and the other parties to the contract agree to cancel it.

What to Expect If You're Involved in a Lawsuit

Allegations relating to breaches of contracts are responsible for most of our litigation. No matter whether you sue over a contract problem or you're the defendant in such a lawsuit, knowing what to expect, if nothing more, makes the process less stressful for you.

TIP

Contract dos and don'ts

- If you don't want to agree to something in a contract, before you sign it, cross out what you don't like and initial what you're deleting. If you want to add something, write it in and initial it. Although the other party to the contract may not want to go through with the deal after seeing your changes, at least you aren't agreeing to something you're not comfortable with.

 Whether you're adding or deleting, be sure your changes appear on every copy of the contract before you sign it. The same goes for contract changes made by someone else. Don't trust someone who says, "Just sign here and I'll make those changes later" because the changes may never get made. But if you've signed the contract, you are obligated to meet its terms.

- If you don't feel comfortable negotiating a contract or even discussing the details, ask someone you trust implicitly to do it for you. For contracts that involve a lot of money or that obligate you to do something really important, hiring an attorney to help with the negotiations can be a good idea.

- Don't (that means NEVER, EVER!) sign a contact without reading it completely.

- Don't be pressured into signing a contract. Take the time you need to think about it.

- Never sign a contract you're not happy with or don't understand. If you ask for an explanation of something in a contract and the answer you get is unsatisfactory, don't be embarrassed to say, "You didn't answer my question" or "I still don't understand." Remember, once you've signed on the dotted line, it's usually too late to back out.

Incidentally, because most legal problems are matters of civil, not criminal, law (thank goodness), this chapter focuses on describing a civil lawsuit. If you want to know about criminal lawsuits, just flip ahead to Chapter 20.

In the beginning . . .

To initiate a lawsuit, you must file a *complaint* with the court that has jurisdiction over your particular legal problem — within a certain period of time. That period of time is called the *statute of limitation,* and it's a different length for different kinds of legal problems. If you wait until after the statute of limitation has run out, you're out of luck, no matter how serious the legal problem.

You can file a complaint for yourself as you would if you were using small claims court, or your attorney can file one for you. The complaint explains the reason for your lawsuit, discusses the relevant law, and states what you want the court to do for you.

After you or your attorney file the complaint, the defendant in your lawsuit will receive a *summons,* which is an official notification of the lawsuit. Usually, a summons is *served,* or personally delivered, by a sheriff or marshal, although it may be sent via certified or registered mail.

The plot thickens . . .

The defendant must file an *answer,* or formal response, to the charges in your complaint by a deadline specified in the complaint. If the defendant doesn't meet the deadline or ignores the complaint, the court will enter a default judgment against the defendant, which means that you win your case without anymore time or expense!

Before filing an answer, however, the defendant's attorney may try to end the lawsuit by filing a *motion to dismiss.* If the court denies the motion, the lawsuit will move forward and the defendant must file an *answer.* The defendant can also respond by filing a lawsuit or counterclaim against you. The defendant may take this action in order to pressure you into dropping your lawsuit or settling quickly, knowing that although one lawsuit can be expensive, two can be a bank breaker.

Compromise, compromise!

The court may encourage if not require you and the defendant to try to resolve your differences outside of court through *mediation.* Mediation is an opportunity for you to talk things over with the help of a trained mediator in order to try to identify a solution both of you can accept. (I talk more about mediation in the next chapter.)

If mediation doesn't work, your case moves into the *discovery* phase, a potentially time-consuming and expensive part of a lawsuit. In fact, when your attorney's bills from this phase start coming in, you may think back on your mediation session and regret that you hadn't been more willing to compromise! Take heart, however, because you still have time to settle, as you or the defendant can propose a settlement at any time. Often, such a proposal happens after or during discovery when both sides have begun laying their cards on the table, and it has become obvious to one side or the other that the cards are stacked against them. The judge may also encourage you to settle by scheduling a pretrial conference to talk things over. Ninety percent of all civil lawsuits are settled before going to trial.

Either you or the defendant can also end the lawsuit early by filing a *motion for summary judgment* before or during discovery. This action is appropriate when there is no disagreement over the facts of your case, so there's no need for witnesses to be called or evidence to be introduced. If the court grants the motion, the lawsuit is decided based on the facts of the case and relevant law.

Just the facts! Nothing but the facts!

Discovery is when the lawyers for each side in your lawsuit do much of the formal information gathering that they need in order to develop their case and prepare for trial. They may collect that information by

- ✔ **Taking depositions:** Potential witnesses are asked to answer oral or written questions under oath.
- ✔ **Filing interrogatories:** You and/or the defendant respond under oath to a set of written questions from the other.
- ✔ **Filing motions to produce documents:** Each side asks the other to produce documents related to the case.
- ✔ **Filing *requests to admit*:** Each side asks the other to admit or deny certain facts about the case so that those facts won't have to be proved during the trial. Doing so saves time and money.

It's show time!

If your case has completed the discovery phase and there is still no settlement, a trial date is set. The trial will either be a *bench trial,* heard and decided by a judge, or a *jury trial.* A bench trial is usually cheaper, but your attorney may feel that a jury is more apt to decide in your favor.

Some states prohibit jury trials for certain kinds of cases, such as divorce and probate.

Usually, to have a bench trial, both parties in a lawsuit must waive their constitutional right to a trial by jury.

If you opt for a jury trial, the judge plays an important role in the trial by deciding questions of law, making decisions regarding what is and isn't admissible in court (evidence that an attorney can or cannot introduce for the jury's consideration), advising the jury about the law, and providing the jury with guidelines that they must use to help them arrive at a verdict.

Winning isn't everything

If you're a lawsuit novice, you may be surprised to find out that even if you win your case and you're awarded money by the court, you may never see a dime of it. No, you don't get to leave the court with a check for the amount of your award!

It's up to you and your attorney to make sure that you get paid. If the defendant doesn't write you a check for the full amount, you can try to negotiate an installment payment plan with the defendant. But if the defendant doesn't agree to it or can't pay you anything due to lack of ready cash, your attorney will have to ask the court to help enforce the judgment by allowing you to do the following:

- ✔ Garnish the defendant's wages. A percentage of the defendant's paycheck automatically goes to you. Only some states allow this form of collection.

- ✔ Seize and sell assets that the defendant owns and apply the proceeds toward your award. Or place a lien on the defendant's property so that it can't be sold or used as loan collateral without you being paid.

- ✔ Levy against the defendant's bank accounts. You get access to the money in those accounts up to the amount of your award.

If your attorney feels that the defendant is trying to hide money or assets that might be used to satisfy the judgement against the defendant, your attorney can ask the court to issue a subpoena requiring the defendant to appear in court to answer certain questions under oath. If the subpoena is issued and the defendant fails to show up, your attorney can ask the court to find him or her in contempt of court. If the defendant is found in contempt, the court can either fine the person or send him or her to jail.

Be careful that you don't get so carried away with collecting your judgment that when you do finally collect, you have little to show for your efforts after paying filing fees, attorney fees, and other legal expenses.

If justice wasn't done

If either you or the defendant in your lawsuit are unhappy with its outcome, and if you have sufficient grounds, you can appeal the final verdict. Grounds for appeal must be based on errors in courtroom procedure that caused the trial to be unfair to one party or the other, or based on questions regarding the judge's interpretation of the law. No, you can't appeal just because you don't like a trial's outcome!

You have only a limited period of time to file your appeal, as little as ten days depending on your case and the court you're dealing with.

Chapter 2

Do It Yourself: Solving Your Own Legal Problems

··

In This Chapter

▶ Problem-solving advice

▶ Dispute resolution: mediation and arbitration

▶ Small claims court

··

Some Good News and Some Bad News

First, the bad news: There are no guarantees in life. Even if you follow my basic rules for avoiding legal entanglements in the next section, and no matter how careful you are in your dealings with others, legal problems may still develop.

Now the good news: You can resolve most everyday legal problems yourself. Most of them are not complicated — or at least not at their outset; most are not the result of someone else's deliberate negligence or dishonesty; and most don't happen because someone is "out to get us."

Easy Ways to Solve Legal Problems

More often than not, everyday legal problems are the result of miscommunication and honest mistakes; therefore, whether your problem is with a neighbor, employer, business, friend, ex-spouse, or whomever, save your money, don't hire an attorney right away, and follow my legal problem-solving advice first.

Communicate

Contact the person or business you're having the problem with. If you're dealing with a small business, start with the manager or owner; if the business is medium to large, you probably need to contact a customer relations or consumer affairs representative. If you get nowhere with the first person you contact at a business, talk with his or her superior. This person may be more open to working things out or may have more decision-making authority.

Nip it in the bud

Don't delay in dealing with a problem. Procrastinating usually means that it will grow worse.

Offer a reasonable solution

Before you contact someone about a problem, think about how you'd like it to be resolved. If appropriate, propose a compromise solution that makes everyone a winner.

Be polite

Yelling, accusing, and using insulting language does not encourage anyone to work with you to resolve a problem. In fact, it does just the opposite. A non-accusatory, "I'm sure we can work things out" attitude can work wonders.

Prove it

Pull together any documents or records you have that help explain your problem and that might support the resolution you're seeking. Documentation can include contracts, warranties, repair records, receipts, bills, canceled checks, photos of any damage the problem may have caused, and so on.

Keep records

Every time you communicate about the problem, whether in person or by phone, keep a record of whom you speak with and the date of your conversation, and note any promises or agreements made. If you communicate via letter, keep a copy for your files. And if you send supporting documentation with your letter, send copies, not originals. Good record keeping that documents what you do to resolve your problem can be invaluable if you have to take legal action later.

Get it down in black and white

If you're able to resolve your problem and especially if the resolution involves money, put your agreement in writing and have everyone involved sign it. You may want an attorney to review your agreement or even draft one for you. Keep a copy of the agreement for your files.

I know we're still at the let's-try-to-avoid-an-attorney stage of problem solving, but sometimes, a "better settle or here's what will happen" letter from an attorney can signal to the other party that you mean business and can help resolve a problem quicker than if the letter comes from you.

Dispute Resolution

If my problem solving advice gets you no where, don't despair! You still have options — dispute resolution for example.

Dispute resolution is an increasingly popular means of settling legal disagreements outside of court. In fact, many courts now require or encourage the parties to a lawsuit to try dispute resolution before scheduling a trial. *Mediation* and *arbitration* are two types of dispute resolution. People most often use arbitration to settle business and contractual problems. In fact, many contracts include an arbitration clause that says that arbitration must be used to resolve contract-related problems.

The American Arbitration Association's World Wide Web Service features A Beginner's Guide to Alternative Dispute Resolution, which contains a directory of the Association's regional office closest to you. The site also provides suggested rules and forms for dispute resolution. Check it out at `http://www.adr.org/`.

Mediation

You can use mediation to settle just about any problem that involves civil law, including disagreements between neighbors or employer and employee, marital problems that don't involve abuse (including divorce-related property settlement negotiations), landlord-tenant problems, consumer-business disputes, and even problems between you and your children.

Mediation is all about communication. If you and the others involved in a problem agree to try mediation, during a mediation session, you all have an opportunity to explain your side of the problem, and you are expected to listen to one another with an open mind. A trained mediator, sometimes an attorney, acts as a neutral party, helping everyone stay calm and focused on the issue. The mediator does not decide who is right or wrong and does not resolve the problem. That job is for you and the other session participants to do.

If you're able to resolve your problem, it's best, and may even be required, to formalize your agreement in writing and get it signed by everyone. Sometimes the mediator drafts an agreement, or you may need to hire an attorney to do so. After it's written and signed, you've got a legally binding contract.

Mediation has many advantages. It's a lot cheaper than hiring an attorney (sometimes even free!), and it's quicker than going to court. No waiting months for a court date or spending hours, maybe days, away from work in a stuffy courtroom. Another advantage of mediation is that it's non-confrontational, which means less stress than a lawsuit. Most important, when you participate in a mediation session, you and the other participants are in control: You decide together, not a judge or jury, the solution to your problem. If the session is successful, mediation makes everyone a winner — unlike a trial, where there is a winner and a loser. And if mediation is unsuccessful, you can still hire an attorney.

Arbitration

Arbitration is a more formal method of voluntary dispute resolution and not unlike a trial. Participants in an arbitration session, or the attorneys who represent them, present their sides of the issue, sometimes even bringing witnesses to testify. An arbitrator runs the session and acts much like a judge to decide how a problem will be resolved. Generally, the arbitrator's decision is binding on all participants, like it or not.

Many communities have dispute resolution centers. Contact your local or state bar association to learn about the one closest to you. Also, some Better Business Bureaus offer dispute resolution services.

For more information about the subject, you may want to call one of the following:

Academy of Family Mediators
1500 South Highway 100, Suite 355
Golden Valley, MN 55416
612-525-8670

American Arbitration Association
140 West 51st Street
New York, New York 10020-1203
212-484-4041

American Bar Association
Section of Dispute Resolution
740 15th Street, N.W.
Washington, D.C. 20005
202-662-1000

National Institute for Dispute Resolution
1726 M Street, N.W., Suite 500
Washington, D.C. 20036
202-466-4764

Organizations and agencies you should know about

If your legal problem involves a business, then resources like the media, nonprofit groups, associations, and government agencies may be able to help you. Although none of them can solve your problem for you, they can often pressure a business into settling with you.

Better Business Bureau (BBB)

This nonprofit business organization has local offices throughout the country. Although the BBB in your area cannot resolve problems for you, if it's a local business that you're having trouble with, the BBB may be willing to encourage it to settle with you.

The media

Public exposure by the media can be embarrassing to a business and sometimes can even affect its bottom line. So if your problem is especially poignant or dramatic, you may want to contact your local television stations and newspapers to see if they can give you some attention. You may be amazed by what a little negative publicity can accomplish!

Industry trade associations

In the interest of maintaining a positive image for their members, some trade associations assist consumers having problems with one of their members. Their assistance may include mediation and arbitration. Use the *Encyclopedia of Trade Associations* at your local library to get the name, address, and phone number of the association to contact.

Your state attorney general's office or the consumer protection office of your local, county, or state government

These offices can explain your rights under the law and suggest additional steps you might take to resolve problems, but they do not take legal action on your behalf. If, however, you and other citizens file complaints against a particular business or category of business and establish a pattern of abuse or law breaking, these offices will take action to ensure that other citizens are not victimized in the future.

The Federal Trade Commission

Perhaps no other regulatory body is as important to consumers and businesses than the Federal Trade Commission or FTC. Originally established by Congress to help ensure a competitive marketplace for consumers and businesses, over the years, the FTC's authority has expanded. Today, it has the power to enforce a wide variety of important consumer protection laws enacted by Congress as well as the trade regulations written by the FTC. Here are just a few of the legal areas that the FTC oversees:

✔ **Protecting consumers from deceptive or unsubstantiated advertising:** Among other things, FTC activities in this area focus on tobacco and alcohol advertising and advertising claims for food and over-the-counter drugs.

✔ **Enforcing a wide variety of laws that relate to consumer credit:** the Equal Credit Opportunity Act, the Fair Credit Reporting Act, the Truth in Lending Act, and the Fair Debt Collection Practicies Act.

✔ **Regulating business marketing and warranty practices:** For example, it takes action agains fraudulent telemarkeing schemes; helps enforce the provisions of the Magnuson-Moss Act, which requires that warranty information be available to consumers before they make a purchase; and enforces the Franchise and Business Opportunities Rule, which requires that sellers of franchises and business opportunities provide potential buyers certain information.

✔ **Protecting consumers from consumer frauds and market failures that impose substantial costs on consumers:** The FTC's activities in this area focus on consumer fraud in investments such as art, precious metals, and oil leases, and also certain types of lotteries.

✔ **Enforcing laws and trade regulation rules:** the Mail Order Rule, Care Labeling Rule, Used Car Rule, Cooling-Off Rule, and so on.

This book covers many of the laws and rules enforced by the FTC.

The FTC has ten regional offices throughout the country and a central office in Washington, D.C. The regional offices conduct investigations into alleged violations of the law, provide education and information to consumers and businesses, and coordinate activities with local, state and regional government offices.

Its Office of Consumer and Business Education located in Washington publishes a wide variety of informative materials to educate consumers and businesses about their rights and responsibilities related to the laws administered by the FTC. To learn about those materials, write to Office of Consumer and Business Education, FTC, Washington, D.C. 20580 or call 202-326-3650. Or you can go to its Web site located at http://www.ftc.gov. You can find the text of more than 140 consumer and business publications here.

If you have a consumer problem or complaint, you can inform the FTC by contacting its Correspondence Branch, FTC, Washington, D.C. 20580; 202-326-2222.

If you want to be placed on the FTC's mailing list for regular updates on FTC's rulings and actions that may affect you, write to its Office of Public Affairs, FTC, Washington, D.C. 20580 or call 202-326-2180.

State or federal regulatory agencies

The business practices and activities of many types of businesses (from banks, insurance companies, and brokers to utilities, phone companies, telemarketers, and licensed trades such as plumbers and electricians) are regulated by government regulatory agencies. You can get information from these agencies about your rights if you're having problems with a business they regulate. You can also file a formal complaint with these agencies against a regulated business. Like state and local consumer offices, these regulatory agencies do not act on behalf of a single consumer but only take legal action against a business if the volume of consumer complaints they receive about it establishes a pattern of disregard for the law.

The People's Court

Small claims court is a do-it-yourself court where ordinary people, including businesses, can act as their own attorneys and where paperwork and legal mumbo jumbo are kept to a minimum. The court is a quick and inexpensive way to resolve relatively simple, non-criminal matters. Cases heard in small claims court commonly involve problems relating to car repair, property damage, small business issues, and landlord-tenant disputes. In the vast majority of states, your case is heard by a judge, not a jury.

Contact the small claims court in your area to find out the specifics for bringing a lawsuit in that court. It should have printed information to send you and people you can talk to.

Ordinarily, you can only sue for monetary damages in small claims court. If, therefore, you want to sue someone to force him to do or not do something (live up to the terms of a contract, for example), then small claims court is not the court for you. Also, as its name implies, suits brought in small claims court involve relatively small amounts of money — usually a maximum of $2,000 to as much as $5,000, depending on your state. These maximums are on the rise nationally, however.

You can reduce the amount you sue for so that it meets your state's maximum. Doing so is called "waiving the excess."

Going to trial

All of the things a lawyer might do to initiate a civil lawsuit and prepare for a trial are your responsibilities in small claims court. It's up to you to file the appropriate paperwork, meet deadlines, and arrange to have each of the defendants in your case served with a notice of your lawsuit. You are also responsible for deciding the following:

✔ What evidence is important to your case

✔ Whether or not to call witnesses

✔ Which witnesses might be most convincing

✔ How to present your evidence so that you increase your chance of winning

If you call witnesses, talk with them ahead of time about your lawsuit, about the defendant's position, and about what you need the witness to say. This action is perfectly legal as long as you're not asking a witness to lie. This pretrial preparation can help ensure that you don't lose your case because a witness inadvertently sabotages it.

If the defendant does not appear in court on the date of your trial, you will probably win your lawsuit by default; otherwise, you learn the judge's decision by mail.

A growing number of judges are now announcing their decisions while the plaintiff and defendant are still in the courtroom, which gives the judge an opportunity to explain the decision.

If the court rules in your favor, the judge has the discretion to award you the full amount of money you asked for in your lawsuit or something less. The judge can also order the defendant to pay your award in a single payment or in a series of payments.

Depending on your state, if you're the plaintiff in a small claims case, you may not be able to appeal the judge's verdict. If you're the defendant and lose, you can usually appeal.

Representing yourself in small claims court

✔ Dress neatly.

✔ Be polite.

✔ Be organized. Know what you are going to say and be as specific as possible. To bolster your case, when possible, provide receipts, contracts, warranties, invoices, canceled checks, letters, and so on. When appropriate, illustrate your problem with used car parts, shoddy merchandise, and photos of damage.

✔ Be as brief as possible when presenting your case to the court, and don't get carried away! If you go on too long, introduce too many witnesses, or start acting like you think you're an attorney, you risk alienating the judge and losing your case.

✔ Be certain that before you end your presentation, the judge knows that you want to be reimbursed for your court costs if you win.

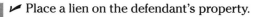

Getting your money

Winning in small claims court is only the beginning: You still have to collect your money. The court won't do it for you, and hiring an attorney is usually not cost-effective given the small amount of money involved.

If the defendant in your case is a good loser and readily pays up, lucky you! But if your lawsuit is like most in small claims court, you have to take the initiative to collect. Start by writing a polite letter that references the lawsuit and the judge's decision and that asks for payment. Send it certified mail. If that doesn't work, another letter might be in order. Or you may want to ask the court's permission to use another collection method:

- ✔ Place a lien on the defendant's property.

    In some situations, you can execute on the judgment. When this happens, the property is seized and sold in a public distress sale, probably at below market value. Depending on the amount of any outstanding loans on the property, and depending on whether any government agency or creditors already have liens on the property, you may see little money from the sale because others get their money first.

- ✔ Levy on the defendant's bank account. You get whatever is in the account at the time of the levy, up to the amount of the judgment. Of course, you need to know where the defendant banks. It's likely that after you levy on the account, the defendant will change banks, so if you don't get the amount of your full judgment with the first levy, a second levy is probably not a real possibility. There are also restrictions placed on bank levies.

- ✔ Garnish the defendant's wages so that you can take a percentage of them up to the amount of the judgment. Obviously, you have to know where the defendant works. Some states prohibit this collection technique.

- ✔ If the defendant is a business, levy on its assets including its available cash.

Other possible options for collecting your money include levying on stocks and bonds and motor vehicles (including boats and recreational vehicles, planes, and any property that is not exempted by your state). Using any of these collection options will cost you money, some of which you can recover from the defendant — assuming you are ever able to get access to funds.

Given the potential collection problems you face when you use small claims court, before filing a lawsuit in that court, be realistic about your chances for collecting if you win and about how much of your time and money the collecting may take. If the defendant has no significant assets — land or real estate, office equipment, or bank accounts — small claims court may not be worth your time or money.

Judgments are only good for a limited number of years — usually from five to ten. If you're unable to collect your money from a defendant within the judgment period set by your state, you can renew it if you do so before the expiration date. Call your small claims court to learn how. You can also renew any existing liens related to your collection efforts.

Chapter 3

Solving Legal Problems with an Attorney

● ●

In This Chapter

▶ Knowing when to hire an attorney

▶ Finding the right attorney

▶ Getting to know an attorney

▶ Paying for your attorney

▶ Developing the right relationship with your attorney

▶ Acting as your own attorney

● ●

*I*n today's litigious society, not using an attorney when you have a legal problem may sound like a wild, radical idea. But in fact, it's really an old-fashioned concept that has withstood the test of time!

Not so long ago, hiring an attorney was a serious step, and most people resolved their legal problems themselves with a friendly letter, a polite phone call, or a calm, face-to-face conversation. Today, these simple, no-cost/low-cost problem-solving tools seem to be going the way of the penny postcard and the rotary phone. "I'll see you in court!" has become an all too familiar refrain, and we've come to view legal problem solving as something only lawyers can do for us. As a result, our hard-earned money is helping many lawyers earn very comfortable livings, something you're not going to hear them complaining about!

At the same time, paradoxically, many of us fail to use attorneys when we should — when they can give us the up-front advice and guidance we need to avoid expensive legal troubles, or when they can help us resolve a problem before it gets really serious. We may not get their help because we don't know how to find a good one, because we don't want to spend the money, or even because we're unaware of when an attorney's help is a good idea.

Obviously, we need to strike a balance between using attorneys too much and not using them enough. This chapter explains when you need an attorney and when you don't (and helps you save an immeasurable amount of money and hassle in the process!). For practical advice and information about how you can resolve everyday legal problems yourself, see Chapter 2.

When You Need an Attorney

Let's start with when and why to hire an attorney. Get an attorney's help if

- ✔ You're faced with complicated or emotionally difficult business or personal decisions that have important financial implications for you or for your loved ones. Up-front legal advice about your legal rights, the legal risks involved, and ways to minimize them can help you avoid costly mistakes, not to mention headaches and heartaches. An ounce of prevention is truly worth a pound of cure when it comes to lawyers and legal help.
- ✔ You've tried unsuccessfully to resolve an important legal problem yourself.
- ✔ You've been sued.

Here are some common, real-life examples of when you need an attorney:

- ✔ You're getting married for the second time and want a prenuptial agreement.
- ✔ Your spouse is battling you for custody of your kids.
- ✔ You're starting a business and want to make sure that you do what you can to protect it from potential legal pitfalls.
- ✔ You want to provide for your spouse and children after you die by writing a will.
- ✔ Your business is failing, and despite your efforts to negotiate with your creditors and slash expenses, you think it's bankruptcy time.
- ✔ You paid a contractor a substantial amount of money to remodel your home, and he refuses to finish the job to your satisfaction.

What to Look for in an Attorney

Now that you understand when to hire an attorney, you're probably thinking, "What should I look for in an attorney, and how do I find a good one?" The answer is this: Define your needs, establish your budget, and comparison shop — just like you would for any other important purchase. This section should help you understand what to look for when you're shopping for an attorney.

The right qualifications and experience

Remember the old adage about "horses for courses"? The same holds true for attorneys. Not all are equally skilled and experienced, and some lawyers are better than others for certain kinds of legal problems. If your problem is relatively simple, an attorney with a general practice will probably fit the bill. This kind of attorney handles a wide variety of relatively simple legal problems, including drawing up a straightforward contract, helping collect on past due bills, and writing a simple will.

But if your problem is legally complicated or involves a very specific area of the law, you probably need a specialist. For example, if you're getting divorced or heading for a child custody battle, look for a family law attorney. If you're contemplating bankruptcy, hire a bankruptcy attorney. If your child is in legal trouble, find an attorney who specializes in juvenile law. If you've been seriously injured in an accident, you need a personal injury lawyer. And so on.

Twenty states permit lawyers to become certified in an area of the law, usually by passing a special exam. Although certification doesn't guarantee an attorney's skills or effectiveness, it does tell you that the attorney has a special interest in a certain area of the law and has pursued advanced education in that area. States that certify lawyers are Alabama, Arkansas, Arizona, California, Connecticut, Florida, Georgia, Idaho, Louisiana, Maine, Minnesota, New Jersy, New Mexico, North Carolina, Ohio, Pennsylvania, South Carolina, Tennessee, Texas, and Utah.

Other important factors

You need to look for an attorney who talks to you in plain English, not in legalese; who answers your questions without acting like they're an imposition; and who returns your phone calls within a reasonable period of time. These are not unrealistic expectations! After all, you're paying the bill!

You want an attorney who demonstrates interest in your case and who provides you with the information you need to make good decisions regarding your legal problem.

You'll feel more comfortable if you have an attorney you can trust. You may have to share highly personal and even embarrassing information about your life with this person.

Last but certainly not least, you need an attorney you can afford. More about this subject later in the chapter.

Things you should know when you hire an attorney

- Before paying any money, be sure that you and the attorney sign a fee agreement. This binding contract spells out the work the attorney will perform and the costs involved

- Unless the fee agreement says otherwise, attorneys are free to change their fee arrangement with you at any time if the scope of the work that they're doing for you changes.

- If you're being charged by the hour, your lawyer's clock is usually ticking every time you meet or whenever you talk by phone, even if it's just to talk about the status of your case. So know what you're going to ask before you call, and be as concise as possible.

- Retainers may not be refundable. For example, if you fire your attorney, you may lose the retainer. So before paying one, find out whether you can get it back and under what circumstances. This information should be spelled out in the fee agreement. See "It's Time Now to Talk Dollars and Cents" later in the chapter for more on retainers.

- You have the right to detailed, itemized, monthly invoices if you request them. They are a good idea if you're paying your attorney on an hourly basis or if you are liable for all or a portion of the expenses that your attorney runs up related to your legal problem.

- If you ignore your attorney's invoice and your case is still active, your attorney can ask the court's permission to stop representing you. If your case is over, you can be sued for nonpayment.

Where to Find an Attorney

With 896,140 lawyers practicing in the U.S. and about two-thirds of them in private practice, the kind of lawyer I've just described does exist. Use the following resources to find a good attorney:

- Trusted friends, family members, or business associates who have had legal problems like yours and were satisfied with the help they received.

- Your local or state bar association. They usually maintain a list of attorneys, organized by specialty, although just being on the list is not a bar association endorsement.

- Lawyer ads. They won't give you any information about an attorney's abilities, but they can help you identify lawyers with a specific specialty.

- Court personnel. The people who work in the courts on a daily basis know who the good lawyers are. Although officially, they are not supposed to refer you to a specific attorney, the truth is, many will do so if you ask.

If money is tight

If you're unable to afford the expense of an attorney, don't despair. You may find resources in your community that you can use:

- The Legal Services Corporation is a federal organization that helps sponsor Legal Aid offices across the country. Presently, there are more than 300 Legal Aid offices. These offices provide a limited variety of free or low-cost legal services to people who qualify on the basis of income. Although each office decides on the kinds of cases it handles, Legal Aid tends to focus on legal issues such as landlord-tenant problems, credit, utilities, family issues (divorce, adoption, and so on), foreclosure, and unemployment. To find a Legal Aid office near you, look in your local phone book, call your local or state bar association, or contact the Legal Services Corporation at 750 First Street N.E.,

11th Floor, Washington, D.C. 20002-4256; 202-336-8800.

- Some law schools run low-cost/no-cost legal clinics for consumer. Often they are associated with Legal Aid. Many local bar associations also sponsor legal clinics.

- Low-cost/no-cost legal clinics can help with relatively simple, routine legal problems like traffic violations, uncomplicated divorces, simple wills, and more.

- If you're accused of a crime and can't afford an attorney, the U.S. Constitution guarantees you the right to a lawyer who will defend you. If you request legal help, the court either appoints a public defender or a private attorney to work with you. In either case, the legal help is free.

Getting to Know You; Getting to Know All About You . . .

To find the best lawyer for you, schedule a "get-acquainted" meeting with a couple attorneys. You may be charged a reduced fee or perhaps nothing for an initial meeting. The following are good questions to take to such a meeting. Don't hesitate to bring a pen and paper so that you can make notes about each lawyer's answers.

- How many years have you been practicing law?
- What kind of cases do you handle most often?
- Approximately what percentage of the cases you've handled have been like mine? Of these, what percentage did you win?
- Based on what information you have, what do you see as the strengths and weaknesses of my case? How strong is it?
- How do you charge for your services? Will you put that in writing?

✔ How much should I be prepared to pay from start to finish if you take my case?

✔ Will I be consulted before you make any important decisions regarding my case? (You should be.)

✔ How long do you think it will take to resolve my legal problem? (If it's going to take longer than a month, ask if the attorney will provide you with a monthly written progress report.)

✔ Can I get an itemized bill? (You have the right to specify exactly what details you want included on your bill.)

✔ Who is actually going to be working on my case — you, another attorney, a paralegal? (If another attorney or a paralegal will be doing most of the work, find out about that person's experience and successes in handling cases like yours.)

Expect straightforward answers, as the preceding are not tough questions! Don't consider an attorney who seems irritated by the questions or reluctant to answer them.

It's Time Now to Talk Dollars and Cents

Exactly how much you have to pay for an attorney's help depends on any number of factors:

✔ Whether an attorney practices in an urban or rural area. Urban attorneys tend to charge more than rural lawyers.

✔ The size and reputation of the law firm an attorney practices with. An attorney with a big firm is apt to cost more than one with a small firm or a solo practitioner.

✔ The number of years an attorney has been practicing and the attorney's reputation. Experienced, well-regarded attorneys tend to cost more than ones who are relatively new to law.

On average, an attorney's hourly rate can range from about $100 per hour in a smaller community to as much as $500 per hour in a large, metropolitan area.

How much you pay for legal help is also affected by these factors:

✔ The complexity of your legal problem.

✔ The amount of work your case will require and how much time the lawyer will have to spend in the courtroom rather than in the law library. Courtroom time is more expensive than research.

✔ Your relationship with the attorney. If you have an on-going business relationship with an attorney or law firm, you may be charged less than a one-time or infrequent client.

✔ The method used to calculate your legal fee.

✔ How much of the expenses associated with your case you have to pay.

Most lawyers charge by the hour; however, an attorney may charge you a flat fee if your legal need is straightforward, with a clear beginning and end. For example, you want a lawyer to draft a simple will or contract for you.

Most attorneys will expect you to pay them a *retainer,* especially if your legal problem is going to take months to resolve and will cost a lot of money. A retainer is an amount of money paid to an attorney to begin work on a case. It's a down payment on the total cost of the attorney's services.

If your legal problem involves a lawsuit for money, an attorney may take your case *on contingency,* which means the attorney gets a percentage of the winnings, usually a third, if he or she wins your lawsuit. And if the attorney loses, you may have to pay nothing but the expenses associated with your case. Personal injury and medical malpractice lawsuits are commonly billed this way. Criminal cases are never handled on contingency, and many states forbid lawyers from taking domestic cases on a contingency basis.

It's to your advantage if your attorney's share of the winnings is based on the net, not the gross award. If the attorney is adamant about using the gross monetary award as the basis, ask the attorney to take a smaller percentage.

Some attorneys may not want to take your case on a 100-percent contingency basis and instead may want to receive some guaranteed money with the balance paid on contingency. Attorneys who charge this way should be willing to take a smaller than usual percentage of the winnings.

Some states limit the amount of expenses a client has to pay in a contingency fee case.

A lawyer's fees are rarely etched in stone. So during a get-acquainted meeting with an attorney, don't hesitate to ask whether he or she is willing to accept something less than what's proposed. You may also be able to negotiate the amount of legal expenses you have to pay. The worst an attorney can say is "no."

Some attorneys may be open to letting you pay for their services on an installment basis, and some are open to allowing you to do some of the work on your case yourself — research, phone calls, and errands, for example.

Don't propose to help work on your case unless you're certain you have the time to help; otherwise, you could slow the progress of your case and possibly run up its costs.

Prepaid legal plans

Prepaid legal plans are a source of legal help that many people don't know about. Some employers, unions, and credit unions offer membership in these plans as a benefit to their employees or members, but you can also find plans that individuals can join. A good idea if you have many ongoing legal needs, prepaid legal plans operate much like prepaid health organizations: In exchange for paying a monthly fee, you get legal advice or representation from one of the plan's member attorneys.

Know exactly what you are or aren't getting for your money before enrolling in a prepaid legal plan because the quality and type of lawyers and the types and costs of services offered can vary from plan to plan. All plans, however, usually entitle you to a limited number of services and/or a limited number of hours of legal assistance each month. Anything over the limit costs extra.

For additional information about prepaid legal plans, try one of these resources:

American Prepaid Legal Services Institute
531 North Fairbanks Court
Chicago, IL 60611-3314
312-988-5751

National Resource Center for Consumers
of Legal Services
P.O. Box 340
Gloucester, VA 23061
804-693-9330

The Attorney-Client Relationship

Attorneys are expected to act in accordance with various codes of ethics. These codes control how they treat their clients, the quality of their work, their fees, and what they can tell others about a case. If they violate an ethical standard, they can be fined, censured or even lose their license to practice law. For example, your attorney may not share with anyone information about your case that you've shared with him or her (unless you reveal that you are going to commit a crime or fraud). That's *privileged* information, which not even a court can force your attorney to reveal. Information that your attorney may learn from others about your case is considered *confidential,* however. With some exceptions, your lawyer may only share confidential information with others if doing so will help you. Some exceptions include the following: The court issues an order to share the information with it, or confidential information causes your attorney to believe that you may be going to commit a criminal act, especially a violent one.

If you file a formal grievance against your attorney for misconduct, or if you sue your attorney for malpractice, the attorney can use both confidential and privileged information related to your case in his or her defense. The same holds true if you and your attorney become involved in a fee dispute.

Legal-related expenses you may have to pay

Although every legal case is different and may involve different legal expenses, here are some of the more common expenses:

- Photocopying
- Long-distance calls
- Postage
- Overnight delivery and courier services
- Court fees
- Facsimiles
- Travel

Some attorneys mark up expenses, which means you're billed for more than the actual amount of an expense. Ask the attorneys you talk to if this is their policy. If it is, view it as negotiable.

It takes two to tango, and that applies to working with an attorney. Being a cooperative client can help resolve your legal problem more quickly, save you money, and help ensure that your attorney achieves the results you want. Here are some suggestions for how you can be a good client:

- Be honest with your attorney and forthcoming with the facts. No attorney wants to be blindsided by a client.
- Return phone calls.
- Meet any deadlines your attorney sets for you.
- Obey court orders.
- Show up for all appointments related to your case.
- Let your attorney know about any changes that might affect your case.
- Follow your attorney's advice regarding who and who not to talk with regarding your case.
- Be open to your attorney's suggestions for ways to settle your legal problem short of going to trial.
- Be on time with your payments.

If You're Unhappy with Your Attorney

Your attorney works for you. So if you have a question about an invoice or about something your attorney does or doesn't do, or if you're not satisfied with the quality of your attorney's work, don't stay silent and stew. Ask for an explanation and express your concerns. You can even fire your attorney and hire a new one. What follows are some common client-attorney problems and how to deal with them.

You get what you think is an excessive invoice

Ask for an explanation and for an adjustment if necessary. If you're unhappy with the explanation, or if your attorney refuses to adjust the bill, contact your local or state bar association to find out what you can do. Arbitration or mediation may be a possibility.

You're unhappy with the quality of your attorney's work

Talk with your attorney about your concerns. If you don't get a satisfactory explanation or if things don't improve, you can fire the attorney. Fire an attorney in writing, and when you do, request that your case file be returned to you. Be prepared to lose any retainer you may have already paid. Also, you may have to pay the attorney for work already performed before you can get your case file.

If your case is in active litigation, or if there are important deadlines associated with your case, find another lawyer to handle your case before firing your current attorney; otherwise, you may jeopardize your case.

Don't discuss the details of your case with your new attorney or ask him or her to do anything for you until you've fired your old one. It's a violation of an attorney's code of ethics to work on a case while another attorney is still officially handling it.

If you feel that your attorney failed to do what was promised or failed to act in a professionally responsible manner

File a formal complaint against the attorney. Every jurisdiction has its own set of ethical standards for lawyers and a disciplinary review process for those accused of violating them. Call your state's bar association to learn about the complaint process in your state. Suing your attorney for malpractice may be another option depending on the circumstances.

Why Didn't I Think of That First?

Now that you understand when you should hire an attorney, how to find one, and what to expect when you work with one, it's time to discover what you can do to avoid attorneys. Although it should be clear to you by now that there are times when an attorney's help is advisable if not downright essential, in truth, most legal problems can be prevented, and when they do develop, most can be resolved without an attorney's help. Some simple rules of thumb:

- Know the laws that affect your life and understand your legal rights. You can learn about many in this book.

- Approach your business and personal transactions with a spirit of fairness and honesty. That means "Do unto others as you would have them do to you." It may be trite, but living by this Golden Rule can help keep you out of legal hot water.

- Bring a healthy dose of skepticism to any opportunities you may be offered, especially if they involve money. If something sounds too good to be true, it probably is!

- Get things down in black and white before you pay any money or agree to pay any money. I'm talking contracts (which are discussed in Chapter 1).

- Thoroughly read any contract you're asked to sign and get all your questions answered before signing.

For more info on solving everyday legal problems without an attorney, see Chapter 2.

Can't I Act as My Own Attorney?

Sure you can; no law says that you can't. But if you're in the middle of a legal crisis — you've been sued; you're in jeopardy of losing your business; you're in a messy divorce — acting as your own attorney is not a good idea, especially if the other party has one. You are immediately at a serious disadvantage: You don't know the nuances of the laws involved; you don't know how to make the law work for you; and you aren't familiar with legal processes and procedures. Are you convinced yet?

Bottom line: If you want a fair shot at resolving a legal problem, and especially if the other side has an attorney, get a lawyer. In the end, hiring one can be a lot cheaper than not hiring one.

Part II
Laws That Affect Your Daily Life

The 5th Wave   By Rich Tennant

"I always assumed elves just naturally dressed like this. I never imagined it was a condition of employment."

In this part . . .

This part covers several different but important legal topics. I start out with a couple of chapters on family law. I then discuss legal issues that relate to being on the job and starting your own business, followed by chapters that address credit and personal finance issues. Next, I provide a chapter on buying and selling a home and a chapter on the responsibilities of home ownership, and I end this part with a chapter on driving and the law.

Chapter 4

Relationships, Marriage, and Divorce

*I*n this day and age, we can no longer even pretend that families on TV shows like *Leave it to Beaver* and *Father Knows Best* represent the American norm. More couples are living together without being married; a growing number of gay and lesbian couples are becoming more open about their relationships and beginning to demand legal rights as couples. According to the 1990 U.S. Census, unmarried couples, heterosexual and same sex, now represent more than 3 million households!

Although family law — the kind of law that deals with marriage, divorce, and parent-children relationships — is still largely based on a traditional definition of family, the changes we are experiencing are forcing our legal system at all levels to rethink its assumptions about the rights and obligations that come with certain personal relationships. For example, our legal system is having to answer hard questions like what's fair when it comes to divorce; should unmarried heterosexual couples have the same rights and responsibilities as married couples; and what about gay and lesbian couples? Because of these and many other issues, family law is in great flux.

As many of us know from personal experience, you can never guarantee that our close personal relationships will be trouble free, or that if there is "trouble in paradise," we'll be able to resolve our differences with a minimum amount of angst and damage to our pocket book. If, however, you understand how family law affects your legal rights and responsibilities before you get married, file for divorce, start a family, take a live-in lover, and so on, you will have a greater appreciation for the legal implications of what you're about to do and a better understanding of the steps you can take to minimize the potential for legal and financial problems down the road.

Love No Longer Equals Marriage

Remember the old, popular song about love and marriage going together like a horse and carriage? That's not necessarily true anymore. Although couples who are in love and who want to be together are still most likely to get formally married, many opt just to live together. Others become informally married in states where common law marriages are legally recognized.

How you structure your relationship affects your legal and financial obligations both while you are together and (heaven forbid) after you split up. Given that marriage is a time-honored tradition that the law continues to view as a relationship that should be promoted and supported, the rights and responsibilities that married couples have to one another during and after marriage are very well defined. The law is much *less* clear when it comes to other kinds of live-in relationships; therefore, when you're madly in love with someone and are certain that you'll live "happily ever after," it's important that you understand the potential implications of getting married versus just living together. Unfortunately, many of us don't gain a true appreciation for the legal pros and cons of each option until our relationship falls apart.

Living Together

Although some changes are beginning to occur, in most states, if you live in an unmarried relationship with someone, neither of you has any automatic legal rights or responsibilities to the other while you're together or after you split up.

You and your partner can, however, voluntarily give yourselves rights and responsibilities, including many of the ones that automatically come with marriage, in a legally binding cohabitation agreement. For example, your agreement can spell out how you share your living expenses and any property that you may acquire as well as the terms of your "divorce" if you split up. Get an attorney's help if you want to be sure that your agreement is legally binding.

If you have children with a live-in partner, both of you may not automatically assume the legal obligations and rights of parents. It depends on your state's laws and the specifics of your relationship. See Chapter 5 for information on parental responsibility.

Cohabitation agreements are good ideas for gay and lesbian couples who consider themselves married and who want to provide themselves with some of the same rights and obligations that heterosexual couples automatically get through marriage. Presently, no state legally recognizes same-sex marriages.

Although formalizing your relationship in a cohabitation agreement can help eliminate some of the important drawbacks to living together, legally, your relationship still has some important drawbacks or limitations that you should know about. Here are some examples:

🖙 You may not be able to add your partner to your health insurance plan.

🖙 You aren't entitled to visit your partner in intensive care.

🖙 You do not have automatic rights to inherit from your partner.

Presently, about 35 cities and counties as well as the state of Vermont recognize domestic partnerships between couples of the same sex and between unmarried heterosexuals, which usually means (at a minimum) that one partner can put the other on his or her health insurance policy.

To address some of these drawbacks and limitations, gay and straight couples should consider taking some additional steps to provide their partners with some of the other rights and benefits associated with heterosexual married couples.

🖙 Make your bank accounts and other important property joint property. That way you're both equal owners.

🖙 Make your partner the beneficiary of your life insurance policy, employee benefit plan, retirement account, and so on.

🖙 Remember your partner in your will.

🖙 Give your partner a durable power of attorney to make business and financial decisions and transactions on your behalf should you become mentally or physically incapacitated. (This subject is covered near the end of Chapter 16.)

🖙 Give your partner a durable power of attorney for health care. This document helps ensure that if you become critically ill and unable to make medical decisions for yourself, your partner has the legal right to be consulted about your medical care and treatment. (For more on this topic, see Chapter 17.)

Purchasing key assets as *joint owners with the right of survivorship* legally guarantees that when one partner dies, the other assumes 100 percent control of the property, and the assets do not have to go through probate.

We're married because we say we are

Some states allow heterosexual couples to enter into informal marriages simply by living together and acting as if they're married. This arrangement is called a *common law marriage.* These couples are legally married with all of the same rights and responsibilities as couples who are formally married. In fact, to end a common law marriage, you have to get legally divorced, just like any other married couple.

If you have a common law marriage and move to a state that doesn't allow common law marriages, your new state will recognize your marriage as legal.

The following states recognize common law marriages:

Alabama	Ohio
Colorado	Oklahoma
The District of Columbia	Pennsylvania
Georgia	Rhode Island
Idaho	South Carolina
Iowa	Texas
Kansas	Utah
Montana	

Prenuptial Agreements

Some couples negotiate prenuptial agreements before they get married. In these agreements, couples establish their own rules for their marriage and for their divorce, rather than leave it up to a third party, such as a judge, to determine who gets what if the marriage ends. Usually, prenuptial agreements relate to money and other property.

Couples most often use prenuptial agreements when one spouse-to-be owns significantly more property than the other or has the ability to make significantly more income during the marriage. Business owners also are making increased use of prenuptials as a way to help protect their businesses from the repercussions of a possible divorce. Frequently, couples who have prenuptial agreements have been married before, understand that marriage doesn't always mean living happily ever after, and want to avoid another expensive, protracted, and messy fight over property if divorce happens again.

Although the concept of a prenuptial agreement certainly has its practical merits, broaching the subject with your intended can be awkward, not to mention unromantic. After all, who wants to talk about finances and legal agreements and the possibility of divorce when you're madly in love and everything is hearts and roses. Talk about putting a damper on your romance!

Given that an estimated 50 percent of all American marriages end in divorce, and considering the emotional, not to mention financial, toll a divorce can take on everyone involved, spelling out the terms of your divorce before your marriage falls apart is really not a bad idea!

You can't negotiate child support and custody in a prenuptial agreement.

If you decide to prepare a prenuptial agreement, get an attorney's help so that you can be assured that it is legally enforceable in your state. Each of you should have your own attorney who can look out for your best interest and make certain that what you're agreeing to is fair to you. In fact, some states *require* separate attorneys. To save on costs, you and your future spouse may want to work out the general details before you meet with your attorneys.

You Need to Be Licensed

Before you can become legally married in a formal ceremony, you have to apply to your state for a marriage license; you can usually do this at your county courthouse. To get the license, you have to meet certain basic requirements. Although they vary somewhat from state to state, here are the most typical requirements:

- ✔ **Age matters.** You can't marry unless you're at least 18 years old or unless you have the permission of your parents or guardian.

- ✔ **Health counts.** You may have to prove that both of you have been vaccinated for certain diseases or that you've each had a recent physical exam, and you may also have to get a blood test for venereal disease. If either you or your partner tests positive, your state may not issue you a marriage license, or it may only do so if both of you are aware of the test results. Presently, only Illinois requires that couples be tested for AIDS, but more states are likely to begin requiring that test.

- ✔ **No close relatives.** You can't marry your parent, grandparent, sibling, aunt, or uncle. Some states also prohibit marriages between step parents and step children, and you may not be able to marry a first cousin either.

- ✔ **Only one spouse at a time.** If you're already married, you can't get married again, even if your religion recognizes multiple marriages. In fact, bigamy is a crime in most states.

- ✔ **You must understand the significance of marriage.** Your state won't grant you a marriage license if the state has reason to believe that you can't or don't understand the significance of marriage due to mental illness, mental incapacitation, or drug or alcohol abuse.

Most marriage licenses are valid only for a few months at most. So if you wait too long to tie the knot, you may have to obtain another license.

What makes a prenuptial agreement legally valid?

States have different requirements for what makes a prenuptial agreement legally enforceable. Here are the more common ones:

✔ Both of you must participate in preparing the agreement, and you both must sign it.

✔ Both of you must fully disclose your assets and liabilities to the other, including anything you know that you will be inheriting or any significant gifts you know you will be receiving in the future. Sharing this information ensures that each of you knows before signing the agreement what you're giving up and what you're getting.

✔ The agreement must be fair to both of you at the time the agreement is negotiated.

✔ Both of you must be entering into the agreement because you want to, not because you are feeling coerced. Also, there can be no fraud involved.

A prenuptial agreement does not have to be forever. If things change in your lives and you decide you want to amend the agreement or even void it, you can. But be sure to do it in writing and get the changes or the revocation witnessed and notarized.

Getting Married

If you're like most married couples, you tied the knot in a formal civil or religious ceremony and were married by a justice of the peace, a judge, a minister, a priest, or a rabbi — someone legally authorized to perform the ceremony. When you recited your marriage vows, you probably promised to love, honor, and cherish one another — the romantic side of marriage. But when you married, you also entered into a legally binding contract with your spouse. The contract gives both of you legal obligations and rights that are defined, recognized, regulated, and enforced by your state. For example, your marriage contract obligates each of you to support the other, although the law leaves it up to you to decide how you will provide that support. Both of you can work outside the home, or your marriage can be more traditional with one spouse earning the income and the other caring for your home and any children you may have.

Unless you both signed a prenuptial agreement to the contrary, you also agreed to share the property you acquire and the income you earn while you're together, as well as many of your debts. Exactly how you share depends on the property laws of your state, and usually, this issue isn't a concern unless you decide to get divorced. I get into property law and divorce later in this chapter.

Marriage also entitles each of you to a share of your spouse's estate when your spouse dies, regardless of whether you spouse has a will or not. Among other things, marriage also gives you the right to file joint tax returns and the right to visit your spouse in intensive care.

The name game

It used to be that, as a matter of course, when a woman married, she took her husband's name. Things are different now, and if you're a woman, it's perfectly acceptable to keep your own name, take your husband's, or combine the two. In fact, the law allows women — and men as well — to use any name they want to.

Let the Social Security Administration know of any name change so that your Social Security number will be transferred to your new name and you won't jeopardize your benefits. Also, get a new driver's license, tell your creditors about your name change so that you don't have problems with your credit record, and change your name on important documents like bank accounts, brokerage accounts, and your passport.

Breaking Up Can Be Hard to Do

If it's become obvious that you're not going to live "happily ever after," you have three ways to end your relationship:

- ✔ **Annulment:** Pretty much a thing of the past.
- ✔ **Separation:** Living apart is usually an interim measure before a divorce, but some couples separate and never divorce.
- ✔ **Divorce:** Divorce legally ends your marriage and leaves both people free to remarry.

Pretend it didn't happen: Get an annulment

A legal annulment is a court action that voids a marriage and frees both partners to remarry. Annulments can involve agreements about spousal support as well as child custody and support.

In the not-so-distant past, when divorces were more difficult to obtain than they are now, annulments were much more commonplace. Now they are most often sought by couples whose religion prevents them from divorcing.

A legal annulment is not the same as a religious annulment. If your church annuls your marriage, you are still legally married.

To get an annulment, you have to tell the court why you want one. Your reasons are your *grounds* for the annulment. Grounds may include fraud (your spouse lied to you prior to your marriage, and if you had known the truth, you would not have married that person), duress, bigamy, impotence, or mental incompetence.

If you've been married for a "long time," you will find it difficult to get an annulment. "Long time" can range from a couple of months to a couple of years, depending on your state.

Separation

If your marriage is in trouble but you want to try to work things out, you may decide to give yourself some breathing room by separating. Maybe being apart will help each of you assess your relationship and work on the problems that are contributing to your marital difficulties. Sometimes, distance does make the heart grow fonder.

Separating can also be a deliberate prelude to a divorce. You and your partner may be unable to get along with one another, and it may be clear that your marriage is over. Or your partner may simply leave without consulting you or despite your objections. That action can instigate a divorce.

While you're separated, you're still married, and therefore, you still have all of the legal rights and responsibilities that come with marriage. Usually, separating is a private matter between you and your spouse, so ordinarily, the court does not get involved in it. Some states, however, recognize *judicial separations* that do involve the court. This sort of thing is another option for couples whose religion prevents them from getting divorced. In a judicial separation, the court approves or decides the terms of a couple's separation, almost as if they were getting a divorce.

Some people separate with no intention of divorcing so that one spouse can remain covered by the other's health insurance policy.

If minor children are involved, or if one of you depends on the financial support of the other, and even if your separation is amicable, it's best to formalize your separation with a legal agreement that details its financial terms, spells out how you're going to share responsibility for your children, and sets out other important duties that each of you may have to the other. That way, if either spouse fails to live up to the agreement and legal action becomes necessary, you have a written contract that provides tangible evidence of what was agreed to. If you draft the agreement yourselves, each of you should hire your own attorney to review it for fairness and thoroughness as well as spot any potential legal problems. Get it witnessed and notarized to be extra sure that it stands up in court.

If you're the family's primary breadwinner, and if you and your spouse have children together, not having a written separation agreement can put you at risk for being accused of abandonment after your divorce proceedings begin. Such an accusation can not only affect the outcome of your divorce settlement but can also affect your custodial rights to your children. It can even result in a court awarding your spouse retroactive child support for the period of your separation, plus interest.

Divorce

Not all that long ago, society frowned on divorce and actively discouraged it by making divorce a difficult and expensive legal process. Couples were expected to stay together, for better or worse, and to divorce only if things became absolutely intolerable. Furthermore, state laws required that the spouse who filed for divorce had to provide grounds for the divorce by accusing the other of adultery, desertion, mental cruelty, abuse, and other such failings. If the other spouse contested the divorce, the spouse who filed would have to prove the grounds, and sometimes, the other spouse would counter-file and make his or her own allegations. Divorce could get really messy and expensive, too.

Society's attitudes toward divorce started shifting in the 1960s. People began to recognize that sometimes marriage just didn't work out and that the mud slinging and emotional upheaval associated with fault divorces wasn't good for anyone, except lawyers. So a growing number of states began recognizing *no-fault divorces.* To get a no-fault divorce, all a spouse usually has to do is claim "irreconcilable differences," "irretrievable breakdown," or separation. Today, although fault divorces are still available in some states, the majority of U.S. divorces are granted as no-fault.

Interestingly, some states are considering ending no-fault divorces as a way to reduce the divorce rate. At the time this book was researched, however, no state had actually taken this action.

Divorce Online (`http://www.divorce-online.com`) is a valuable resource for people in the process of divorcing or thinking about divorcing. You can find articles and information related to the legal, psychological, and financial aspects of divorce. You can access a professional referral service to locate attorneys, therapists, and financial planners who may be able to help you, and you can browse a location called "He Said . . . She Said" where you can post messages and talk to people dealing with the same issues as you.

For a look at divorce-related issues and concerns from the male perspective, go to The World Wide Web Virtual Library: Men's Issue Page at `http://www.maricopa.gov/support/ssc/sscinfo/divorce/divorce.html`.

The divorce process

When you file for divorce, you actually initiate a civil lawsuit against your spouse. To settle it, you have to come to an agreement that addresses how you divide up your marital property, whether either of you get spousal support (for how long and how much), and if you have minor children from your marriage, how you deal with their custody and support. Before your divorce is final and your agreement legally binding on both of you, the court must approve it.

Like most lawsuits, your divorce may never go to trial. But if you, your spouse, and your attorneys are unable to negotiate all aspects of your divorce agreement outside of court, a trial is scheduled and the judge decides things for you.

If I'm getting a divorce, do I need an attorney?

If your divorce is a no-fault and you and your spouse are comfortable working out its terms together, you probably don't need much legal help. But both of you should hire attorneys before you begin working out the details of your divorce so that each of you has a clear understanding of your individual rights and obligations, is aware of anything you should do or shouldn't do before divorcing, and understands any special issues you may need to consider. For example, if all of your credit is in your spouse's name, you will probably have trouble borrowing money or getting a credit card in your own name once you're divorced. So if possible, you may want to delay your divorce until you've time to build credit in your own name. Also, your attorneys may be able to suggest ways to divide up your marital property and debts that you might not otherwise think of.

Consider using mediation to help you work out the terms of your divorce.

Your attorneys should review the divorce agreement you work out before it's final to make certain that you have not inadvertently created potential problems for either of you and so that each of you can be assured that it's fair.

There are times when getting legal help is absolutely essential. These times include the following: if you and your spouse are too estranged to work together; if your marital property is substantial or especially complex (so that dividing it between you may be problematic); or if taxes are an issue. If your divorce negotiations also involve decisions about spousal support and/or child custody and support, legal help is often a good idea.

If you have a hard time asserting yourself with your spouse or if you feel especially guilty about the divorce, getting an attorney's help can ensure that you're not shortchanged in your settlement.

Who gets what?

Unless you've signed a prenuptial agreement and waived your property rights, your state's property laws entitle each of you to a share of your marital property. Most states are *separate property* states, but nine are *community property* states: Arizona, California, Idaho, Louisiana, Nevada, New Mexico, Texas, Washington and Wisconsin.

Community property states

If you live in a community property state, the property that you acquire during your marriage and the income you earn belong to *both* of you. It generally doesn't matter whether only one of you paid for something or whether you earned more than your spouse. You are each joint owners of your property — and your debts too. The philosophy behind community property law is that it takes two to make a marriage and that as a team, one way or another, you both helped create the wealth that you built during your marriage as well as any debts you may have racked up. Divorcing spouses in community property states are usually expected to divide up equally both their marital property and the debt from their marriage; however, judges in community property states do have latitude to order other arrangements.

Separate property states

Separate property states use the concept of *equitable distribution* — that is, what is fair — to decide how a couple's property and debt are divided up when they divorce. "What's fair" is determined on a case by case basis according to specific criteria your state has established. Fairness can mean that you and your spouse split the value of your property and debt 50/50, 75/25, 90/10, whatever. Examples of the typical criteria that a separate property state uses to determine an equitable split include the following:

- How much each of you earn and could earn in the future.
- Your current standard of living as a couple.
- How much separate property each of you owns.
- The contribution each of you has made to your marriage. Homemaking is considered a job and therefore is taken into account.
- The employee benefits either of you are entitled to.
- The length of your marriage.
- Your age and health.
- Whether or not there are minor children involved and who will have custody of them.
- The degree to which each of you contributed to the end of your marriage. This is a factor in only some states.

Obviously, property settlement negotiations in separate property states can be much more complicated than in community property states.

Both community and separate property laws say that if you receive an inheritance or gift while you're married, it's yours alone and is not treated as marital property when you divorce. Also, both kinds of laws view property that you bring to your marriage as yours alone, unless you later commingle it with marital property.

Who gets the house?

It's not a hard and fast rule, but usually, if you have custody of the kids, you get the house unless you and your spouse agree to something different. Sometimes, a property agreement stipulates that the spouse can stay in the house until the children all reach the age of 18, at which time the house must be sold and the sale proceeds split between both former spouses according to the terms of their agreement.

What about pensions and other retirement benefits?

In community property states, pensions and other retirement benefits earned during a marriage are viewed as belonging equally to both spouses. In separate property states, how you divide up these assets is something to be negotiated.

When a couple gets divorced, regardless of what kind of property law their state recognizes, if they have included one another in their wills, their divorce automatically voids that part of their wills.

Spousal support

When traditional marriages were more commonplace and a couple divorced, the husband was usually expected to provide his former wife with enough income throughout her life so that she could live in the same style she enjoyed when she was married. That obligation only ended if she remarried, or in some states, if she began living with another man.

Today, however, with more women working outside the home, it's no longer a given that a divorced woman receives alimony or spousal support from her husband; and in most states, men as well as women can now receive it. In addition, the traditional "for the rest of your life" support is being replaced by temporary alimony that is provided long enough to help a spouse get an education or build a post-divorce career so that he or she can be financially independent.

If your spouse can't earn a living or if there is a significant disparity between what you earn and what your spouse earns, and if that disparity is expected to continue, the court may require that you make long-term support payments to your ex.

Like other aspects of your divorce negotiations, you and your spouse can work out your own agreement about whether or not either of you receives spousal support, and if so, how much and when. If you can't, or if the court doesn't feel that your agreement is fair, it makes this decision for you. Some states require that support payments be based on a percentage of how much the bigger earner makes, while others leave the size of payments to the discretion of the court.

If your unmarried live-in relationship ends, one partner may sue the other for *palimony* — a share of the property you acquired while you were together and/or financial support. If there are minor children from the relationship, the parent with custody may also sue for child support. Palimony is not recognized by all states, and even when it is, the right to palimony is usually difficult to prove.

Other facts about spousal support

- ✔ If you're concerned that your ex-spouse may not live up to the terms of your support agreement, you can ask your spouse to post a bond guaranteeing the payments.

- ✔ If your former spouse doesn't pay up, you can ask the court to get the payments reinstated and to collect the payments that you didn't receive. The court can collect payments through one of the following ways: ordering your ex-spouse's employer to garnish his or her wages; placing liens on property that your former spouse may own; and tapping into your ex's bank accounts. Remember, however, that bureaucracies work slowly, so it may take a long time before you see any money.

✔ You can ask the court for an increase in the amount of spousal support you're receiving if you have a legitimate reason for needing more money. The court will probably not consider wanting a bigger wardrobe or wanting to take an expensive vacation adequate reasons! Here are some reasons the court may swallow, however: Your alimony agreement doesn't provide for automatic adjustments to keep pace with inflation, so you need an increase just to keep your financial head above water; you've become too ill to work; you've been injured and can't work temporarily.

✔ If you're paying support and want to reduce your payments, the court may give you the okay if you provide it with a good reason.

✔ If your former spouse believes that you no longer need the amount of support you've been receiving, he or she can petition the court for a downward adjustment.

✔ If you're making spousal support payments, they are tax deductible. If you're receiving them, you must include them in your gross income when doing your taxes.

What about the kids?

If you and your spouse have minor children, your divorce negotiations also involve decisions about how to handle their care and support after you're divorced. Discussions about their care has to address two basic issues: Who will have physical custody and who will have legal custody? If you have physical custody, the children spend most of their time with you. If you have legal custody, you have the right to make all final decisions about how your children are raised — their education, religion, health care, and so on. But depending on your post-divorce relationship, you're free to allow your former spouse to have input into your decisions. If you have physical custody of your kids, most likely, you have legal custody too.

If you have physical custody of your children, your spouse probably has visitation rights, which means that he or she is able to spend time with them. The specifics of those visitation rights, including the exact days of the week, holidays, and other special times, are spelled out in your custody agreement.

The attitude of the law toward child custody has changed over the years, just as every other aspect of divorce has changed. In the nineteenth century, children were viewed as their father's property, so they tended to go with Dad when their parents split. Starting in the twentieth century, most states began to view both parents as having an equal right to the physical and legal custody of their children, and therefore, custody decisions were supposed to be based on what was in the "best interest of the children." In reality however, the courts tended to favor mothers over fathers. Now that bias is changing as more mothers work outside the home, parents share the care of their children more equally, and as more fathers begin to assert their right to raise their children. *Joint custody,* or sharing the physical and/or the legal custody of children, has therefore become an increasingly popular option not only for divorcing parents, but also for a growing number of states, assuming there is reason to believe that the parents can cooperatively raise their children after their divorce.

Many joint custody agreements include a provision that requires ex-spouses to use mediation when they're unable to settle issues related to their children.

Before deciding on joint custody, be sure to consider the arrangement's potential pros and cons.

Joint custody pros

- You and your former spouse both have the chance to remain actively involved in your children's day-to-day lives.
- Your children have an easier time maintaining an ongoing relationship with each of you.

Joint custody cons

- The arrangement is more expensive because you both have to maintain separate homes for the kids.
- Shuttling back and forth between your two homes may be stressful for your children.
- You and your spouse are required to interact and cooperate.

More considerations

However you decide to handle custody of your kids, your agreement should be written. To avoid confusion and to minimize the potential for conflict, the agreement should be as specific as possible about your individual rights and responsibilities as parents without being so rigid that the rules can't be bent occasionally if necessary.

If you and your spouse can't work out a custody agreement, the court does it for you after a custody hearing or trial. During the hearing, friends and family may be called to testify about your characters and about your individual relationships with your children. Also, experts such as social workers and psychiatrists may testify about your lifestyles, personalities, and so on. These hearings can be emotionally grueling.

The judge's custody decision is based on what he or she believes is in your children's best interest. That decision, however, is guided by state-established criteria:

- The age and physical health of each parent
- The mental health of each parent
- The age and sex of the children
- Which parent has been the primary care provider for the children
- The quality of home and community each parent can offer the children

✔ The work and travel schedules of each parent

✔ Whether either parent has a history of drug or alcohol abuse

✔ The emotional bond the children have established with each parent

If your children are old enough to have a preference, the judge may find out their opinions by talking with them.

Increasingly, the courts are beginning to recognize the rights of gay parents in their custody decisions.

Although rare, if the court decides that neither you nor your spouse can do a good job of raising your children, it will award custody to someone else, a relative when possible.

After a custody agreement has been approved by the court and is final, you and your ex-spouse are legally bound to abide by all of its terms, which means that if you have custody of your child and your husband has visitation rights, you can't deny him those rights because you're angry with him or don't like his new girlfriend. If, however, you feel that the arrangement you agreed upon is not working out and is detrimental to your child, you can petition the court to modify your agreement.

If you have reason to believe that your ex may be harming your child or may be considering child-napping, inform the court immediately. It may suspend or cancel your ex-spouse's visitation rights, or the court may allow them to continue but only in a supervised setting with a third party present.

The Parental Kidnapping Prevention Act makes child-napping by a non-custodial parent a federal offense. If you believe that your ex-spouse has kidnapped your child, call the office of the U.S. Attorney General, your local police, and your state attorney general's office.

According to The Uniform Child Custody Jurisdiction Act, all states are required to enforce a child custody agreement made in another state.

Decisions about child support

Child support payments are supposed to help provide a young child with the same standard of living after a divorce as he or she enjoyed prior to when the child's parents divorced. Up until recently, the father was almost always responsible for child support payments, but now that two-paycheck families have become commonplace, that is no longer the rule. Generally, the parent with physical custody of the kids receives financial support payments from the other parent.

All states are required by the federal government to use a standard formula when determining the minimum amount of child support a parent should pay. What the formula should be is up to each state to decide. State formulas tend to take into account the following criteria:

  ✔ The amount that each parent earns

  ✔ The number of minor children the couple has

  ✔ The needs of each minor child, including basic needs like food, clothing and shelter, routine medical care, lessons, and educational opportunities

If a child has special needs such as medical problems not covered by insurance, the court may order payments that are higher than what the formula indicates. If you and your spouse are able to work out your own agreement regarding child support, the court uses its formula to make sure that your agreement is fair.

If the amount you are receiving in child support is not adequate to meet your child's needs, you can ask the court for an increase. To keep pace with the change in cost of living, many agreements include an automatic annual cost-of-living increase. Another option is to peg automatic increases in child support to stages in a child's life. The theory here is that as a child grows older, the cost of raising that child increases.

If you are making child support payments and changes in your life — a pay cut or prolonged illness, for example — are making it difficult if not impossible to continue paying the amount of child support you agreed on, ask the court to let you make smaller payments. It may grant your request for a limited amount of time or indefinitely, deny your request, or possibly order you to use your savings, liquidate assets, or find a better-paying job so that you can continue the same level of payments.

Theoretically, child support payments must be spent on the care of the children, not on other things.

Other things you should know about making child support payments

  ✔ Child support payments are not viewed as taxable income.

  ✔ You can't claim child support payments as tax deductions.

  ✔ You can't claim your minor children as tax deductions unless they live with you more than half of the year or unless your former spouse gives you the deductions by completing an IRS Form 8332.

  ✔ If you're obligated to make child support payments, federal law requires that you provide your minor children with medical insurance unless equal or better insurance coverage is available for a comparable or better price, or you and your former spouse agree on a different arrangement that the court approves.

  ✔ Unless your child support agreement says otherwise, your obligation to pay child support continues until your child turns 18, even if your ex-spouse gets married to a millionaire!

  ✔ Dying is not necessarily an acceptable reason for not supporting a minor child! You are expected to make adequate provisions for that possibility by including your child in your will, setting up a trust for your child, naming your child as a beneficiary of your life insurance policy, and so on. If you die without having provided for the support of your minor child, your child can sue your estate for support!

✔ If your ex-spouse is paying child support and files for personal bankruptcy, that obligation is unaffected. Also, your ex-spouse cannot use bankruptcy to wipe out any delinquent child support payments that he or she may owe to you. If your ex-spouse files for bankruptcy, contact your family law attorney as soon as possible to find out if there is anything you should do to ensure that the payments continue.

Deadbeat dads . . . and moms

A *USA Today* study of 1992 U.S. census data revealed that only about half of the 5.3 million parents who were supposed to receive child support payments were actually receiving the full amount! Also, census data shows that of the 8 to 9 million women caring for children with no father present, only about half have legally-binding support agreements. We can assume that many of these women were not married to the fathers of their children.

As the problem of deadbeat dads and moms reaches crisis proportions, placing children in jeopardy, the federal and state governments are looking for new ways to enforce existing child support agreements and to establish support orders where no agreement exists. For example, the federal Family Support Act says that all states must have laws mandating that all new and modified child support orders include a provision for automatic wage deductions. That way, if a parent falls behind on his or her child support payments, the parent's employer can be required to begin deducting money from the parent's paycheck, which goes to the custodial parent.

Federal law also requires that all states use proven methods of collection to ensure that parents get the support they are due. These proven actions include the following:

✔ Placing liens on the delinquent parent's real or personal property — real estate, vehicles, boats, and so on. Although a lien does not necessarily mean that the other parent will see any money right away, it does mean that the delinquent parent is unable to transfer, borrow against, or sell the property until he or she has taken care of the past due child support.

(Usually, you cannot place a lien on the primary residence of a former spouse nor on any property that he or she may need to earn a living.)

✔ Taking any state or federal tax refunds that the non-paying spouse is entitled to.

✔ Fining or jailing a former spouse for contempt of court.

✔ Tapping into any unemployment compensation payments, veteran's benefits, or other state and federal benefits that the delinquent parent may be receiving.

✔ Garnishing the delinquent parent's wages.

Some states are also trying new, more innovative collection techniques, including revoking the professional and drivers' licenses of parents who fall behind on their child support payments and posting their names and photos on the Internet.

If you are having trouble collecting child support from an ex-spouse, or if you are not getting any child support from a child's father because you do not have a legally-binding support agreement, get in contact with the Child Support Enforcement (CSE) program immediately by calling your state or local human services department. The CSE program is designed to collect support payments from parents who are legally obligated to pay child support. It can help you even if you do not have a legal support agreement with the child's father or if you and the father were never married. The program is a joint effort of the federal government together with state and local governments. Although the specifics of the program vary from state to state, no matter where you live, the program offers four basic services: It helps you establish the paternity of your child; it locates the child's father; it establishes a child support order where no such agreement exists; and it helps enforce existing agreements. CSE offices must also make child support debts over $1,000 available to credit bureaus when they request the information. In some states, this is information that credit bureaus request regularly.

The CSE personnel in your area also know how to use other federal laws that may be helpful to you, or they can refer you to someone else who can tell you about them. These laws include the following:

- ✔ The 1992 Child Support Recovery Act, which makes it a federal crime for a parent to willfully avoid making child support payments to a child living in another state if the amount owed in back child support is more than $5,000 and if that amount has been past due for more than a year. Those found guilty of violating this law face imprisonment and fines.

- ✔ The Uniform Interstate Family Support Act (UIFSA), which makes an order of support in one state enforceable in all others. UIFSA spells out specific processes for initiating interstate enforcement actions. The enforcement process can be initiated in your own state or in the state where the father of your child now lives.

Unmarried women and child support

If you're unmarried and have a child, most states expect the father to assume all of the legal responsibilities that come with paternity, whether you're living together or not. If the child's father denies paternity, you can sue him, and he has to prove that he's not the father either by submitting the results of blood tests or DNA tests or by proving that he's sterile or impotent and could never have fathered a child. After paternity is established, the CSE program can help you obtain and enforce a legal support order.

The Uniform Parentage Act has been adopted by more than a third of all states. It allows any interested party, not just the mother, to file a paternity suit on behalf of a child.

Chapter 5

Parenting and Child Care

● ●

In This Chapter

▶ Rights and responsibilities of parenting

▶ Abuse and neglect

▶ Adoption

▶ Surrogates

▶ Child care

● ●

*G*one are the days when most children lived in two-parent households and moms stayed home. Today, kids are as likely to live with one parent as two, and nearly half of all employees come from dual-worker households, which means that moms as well as dads are working outside the home; women are less dependent on their husbands for financial support; and quality child care is becoming an issue for a greater number of parents.

Here's another important development: Although the majority of couples who want children use the "old-fashioned way" to begin their families (or they adopt children), a growing number of couples are using science to help them become parents.

Regardless of how you start your family, and regardless of whether or not you're a single parent or you share parenting with a partner, you should be aware of your parental rights and responsibilities. This information is particularly important given the following:

✔ State and federal lawmakers are working to expand parental rights and better enforce existing parental responsibility laws.

✔ Local governments are beginning to pass their own parental responsibility laws.

To Be or Not to Be a Parent

For some couples, starting a family is the logical next step after marriage while others may not want children at all. Whatever your decision, it's one you are free to make for yourself.

The U.S. Supreme Court has ruled that the decision to have or not have a child is a private, personal one. If you're a woman, no one can force you to have a baby, not even your husband, and you have the right to use contraceptives to prevent getting pregnant. If you do become pregnant, no one can force you to have an abortion either.

Disagreeing about whether or not to have children can be grounds for divorce in some states.

In 1973, the Supreme Court ruled in the landmark decision, *Roe vs. Wade*, that all women have a constitutional right to a safe, legal abortion. Specifically, it ruled that during the first trimester of a pregnancy, the state may not limit or regulate this right other than to insist that an abortion be performed by a licensed physician. Beginning in the second trimester, however, the court ruled that states may place limits on that right, but only to protect a woman's health. It also ruled that to protect a fetus, beginning in the third trimester — the point at which a fetus can survive outside a woman's body — the state can limit a woman's access to an abortion or even prevent her from having one, unless an abortion is necessary to preserve the woman's health or life.

In 1992, the Supreme Court reaffirmed its decision in *Roe vs. Wade* but ruled that states may place restrictions on abortions as long as they do not impose "an undue burden" on pregnant women. As a result, some states now require women who consent to an abortion to wait 24 hours before having one, and some states require minors who want an abortion to either notify a parent or guardian of their intention or get permission from a parent or guardian to have the medical procedure.

Being a Parent Is Serious Stuff

When we think about having a baby, we're often more apt to romanticize the idea of a child than we are to consider the serious implications of what we're about to do — that we're not only increasing the size of our family but also assuming new legal responsibilities and obligations. In fact, starting a family is one of the most significant steps any of us will ever take.

Although you can divorce your spouse and rid yourself of many of the legal obligations that come with marriage, you can't divorce your kids! They're for keeps, or at least until they become legal adults — 18 or 21, depending on your state.

Legal obligations

As a parent you have a Constitutional right to make basic decisions about how your minor children are raised, including where they are educated, how they are disciplined, where they live, the values you impart to them, and so on. But you also have a legal obligation to provide for their basic needs while they are minors or until they turn 18 or 21, depending on your state. There are times when this obligation can last even after your child becomes a adult (if your child is seriously disabled and unable to support him or herself, or if your child would be on welfare without your support, for example). And there are times when your parental obligations end early — if your child is legally married before 18 or becomes an *emancipated* minor. An emancipated minor is a child whose parents have voluntarily surrendered their legal rights and responsibilities in regard to the care, custody, and support of the child. The child is free to make his or her own decisions and provide for his or her own financial support.

Education

Your child must attend school for a minimum number of years. In most states, your child must begin school at age 5 or 6 and stay in school until age 14 or 16.

If you want to home school your child, be sure it's legal in your state, and know what your state requires of home schoolers.

In response to what some parents, policymakers, and politicians view as the negative influence of certain kinds of educational and health information in schools, state and national lawmakers are introducing parental rights bills. These bills attempt to expand the rights of parents in regard to a school's curriculum, counseling, and health programs.

Medical care

Generally, it's your responsibility to make sure that your child receives necessary medical care. This responsibility doesn't mean that just because a doctor recommends something, you're obligated to provide it. For example, if your doctor suggests that regular allergy shots will make your daughter sneeze less or that your son's teeth can be straightened with braces, it's up to you to decide whether or not you want to provide them with the care.

In most instances, you have the right to consent to any medical care your child receives. Your consent is not necessary, however, if:

- ✔ Your child needs emergency care and you're not immediately available.

- ✔ Your child is pregnant and needs prenatal care or wants treatment for a sexually-transmitted disease or alcoholism.

- ✔ Your child needs lifesaving medical treatment and you refuse to give your consent. A court can intervene and mandate the treatment.

Your state can require that your child receive certain immunizations. Usually, if you don't provide them, your child won't be able to attend school, and that puts you in violation of your state's education requirements for minor children.

Some states will exempt a child from having to receive certain immunizations if such immunizations are dangerous to the child's health or if your religion prohibits them.

If physical, emotional, or financial problems are preventing you from meeting your parental obligations, you have the right to ask the state to care for your child. Usually, your child is placed in foster care. But before making such a request, consult with an attorney because if you're not careful, your parental rights may be terminated, and after you lose them, they can be tough to get back.

Discipline and liability

As a parent, you have the right to use "appropriate" discipline with your minor child. But if your discipline, or your failure to discipline, threatens the life or the physical well-being of your child, your state can take your child away from you and even prosecute you. I talk more about "appropriate discipline" shortly.

If you're unable to control your child, you have the right to ask the court for help. It won't step in if you're having trouble getting your son to keep his room clean — the problem must be much more serious than that. If your young child is endangering him or herself or others, however, and if your child has a history of problems, the court may declare your child "in need of services" and begin actively supervising him or her.

Parents can be held liable for the consequences of a minor child's actions — vandalizing property or intentionally harming someone, for example — especially if the state can prove that the parents were aware of what their child was doing and did little or nothing to stop the child.

A Michigan couple learned this lesson the hard way recently when a jury convicted them of violating a city ordinance that requires parents to "exercise reasonable parental control" over children under 18 years of age. The court fined each of them and ordered them to pay more than $1,000 in court costs because their son repeatedly smoked marijuana and stole several thousand dollars from his family's church, among other things.

In most states, though, a parent's legal liability is usually significantly less than the actual dollar value of any damages that their child may cause.

Foster parents

Foster parents care for children when their parents are unable or unwilling to care for them or because the children are being abused or neglected. Children may live with foster parents until they can return to their biological parents or until adoptive parents can be found for them.

Foster parents have most of the duties and rights of a child's birth parents. They receive a stipend from the state to help pay for the cost of caring for a foster child.

Legal guardians

If you are unable to meet your parental responsibilities and don't want to put your child in foster care, another option is to appoint a legal guardian, a close friend or relative perhaps, to care for your child. The guardian has all of your legal rights as a parent. Legal guardians must be approved by a court.

To help ensure that the guardian cares for your child according to your wishes, and to make sure that you will have no trouble reassuming your role as parent when you are ready, it's best to hire an attorney who can help you draw up a contract defining the terms of the guardianship, including its duration and any specific instructions you have for the guardian.

Abuse and Neglect

All states have parental child abuse and neglect laws. Neglect is generally considered to be failure to provide a child with adequate shelter, clothing, food, "reasonably necessary" medical attention, and supervision. For example, if you leave your minor child home alone while you go to work or to a party, don't keep your child clean, or deny your child food for a period of time, you may be charged with neglect. Whether or not it's "neglect" depends somewhat on the age of your child. For example, you're more apt to be charged with neglect if you leave your 3-year-old child home alone than if you leave your 16-year-old alone.

Abuse most commonly refers to situations where you, or another adult responsible for your child, intentionally harm the child physically. Abuse can also include sexual abuse and extreme verbal abuse, especially in public. Although all of us are aware of situations where adults so physically mistreated a child that there was no doubt in our minds that the child had been abused, in other instances, things may not be so clear-cut. In fact, what may seem like abuse to one person may be viewed as "appropriate discipline" by someone else.

If you kick a child out of your home, you may be charged with abuse and neglect, depending on your state's laws.

If you suspect that a child is being abused or neglected, no matter what your state, you have a legal responsibility to report your suspicions to your police department or to your local, county, or state child protection agency or welfare agency. Some states have specific reporting requirements for professionals such as doctors, nurses, teachers, and social workers — people most apt to come into contact with a child who is being mistreated.

Some states have passed laws to protect you from the possibility of being sued for libel or slander if you report a case of suspected abuse, and after an investigation, the accused is found not guilty.

If a court finds that a child is being abused or neglected, the child is usually placed in temporary foster care with the goal of reuniting child and parents after the problems contributing to the neglect or abuse are addressed. When, however, the abuse or neglect is particularly bad, or if it's an ongoing problem, the state may terminate the parents' rights, and the child is put up for adoption.

Adoption

Many couples who are unable to have biological children decide to adopt instead. When they do, they assume all of the legal rights and responsibilities that come with being a parent.

Although adoptive parents are most often married, as society's definition of a family changes, state laws regarding who can adopt are changing too. Single people can adopt in many states, and in a growing number of states, unmarried couples, both heterosexual and homosexual, are also becoming adoptive parents.

Each state has its own set of criteria for what makes an adoption legal. Individuals who participate in an illegal adoptions face prosecution. Legal adoptions usually have the following characteristics:

- The adoption must have followed state laws.
- Usually, if the child's biological parents are married, they must have consented to the adoption. If they are unmarried, the mother must have provided her consent; whether or not the father must have consented varies from state to state.

- ✔ If a court determined that the adoptive child's biological parents were "unfit" to raise the child, their parental rights must have been terminated.

- ✔ The adoptive parents cannot have paid excessive fees to an intermediary or to the adoptive child's biological parents.

- ✔ The adoption must have been approved by a court.

- ✔ The family court approving the adoption believes that it is "in the best interest of the child."

Most states have a waiting period for a mother who puts her child up for adoption so that she can be sure that she wants to take that step.

The highest courts in three states — New York, Vermont, and Massachusetts — have ruled that unmarried couples, including homosexual couples, can adopt, assuming a family court decides that an adoption is in the best interest of the child. Lower courts in 11 other states have issued similar decisions.

The Adoption Network (http://www.infi.net/adopt/indexnf.html) is a one-stop resource for adoptive parents and prospective adoptive parents. Among other things, it includes the answers to frequently asked questions, the text of publications that address adoption-related issues, legal resources by state (including summaries of state adoption laws, attorney referrals, and organizations that can be of help), and detailed information about other adoption resources on the Internet.

Fathers and adoptions

Most states require that if you decide to put your child up for adoption and you know who the child's father is, you must let the man know about your plans. You may or may not need his consent. Usually however, if you and the child's father are not married, and if he has helped support the child and maintained regular, ongoing contact with the child, he probably has the right to withhold his approval. In addition, if he asks the court to give him the right to raise the child by himself, the court will probably grant his request.

Types of adoptions

There are three basic types of legal adoption: agency adoptions, related adoptions, and private adoptions.

Agency adoptions are arranged by public and private agencies. Private adoption agencies are licensed by the state. Agency adoptions are legal in all states. If you work with an agency, you will have to go through a formal process designed to help the agency ensure that you will be good parents.

Agency adoptions typically provide adoptive parents with more legal safe-guards than private adoptions. Agencies are also more apt to place restrictions on whom they will help adopt, however. For example, they may not work with individuals over a certain age.

Some states regulate the fees that an agency can charge an adopting couple. But no matter what the state, if the adoptive parents are adopting a child who isn't born yet, they are expected to pay the costs of the birth mother's pregnancy and any adoption-related expenses she may incur.

Private adoptions are not legal in all states. Usually, a doctor, lawyer, or someone else in contact with the biological parents of a child arranges for the adoption. Private adoptions typically allow the biological parents to play a greater role in deciding who will adopt their child than if they worked through an agency.

Through a private adoption, you can adopt a child who lives in your state, in another state, or even in another country. But because they tend to be more complicated, out-of-state and especially foreign adoptions cost more than the typical in-state, private adoption.

If you're considering a foreign adoption, find an agency who specializes in them. It will know how to locate a baby and how to deal with the inevitable bureau-cratic red tape.

Related adoptions take place when a child is adopted by relatives. The parents of the child may have died or may be unable to care for their child due to illness, drug use, or other problems. Adoptive relatives, like any adoptive parents, must go through a process to make the adoption legal.

If you're adopted

If you're adopted, at some point in your life, you may become curious about your birth parents and may even want to meet them. The ease with which you'll be able to do so depends on whether your adoption was traditional or *open*. In an open adoption, although the birth mother gives up all her parental rights and responsibilities in regard to her child, she retains the right to contact or visit her child. In some states, adopted children who are at least 18 years old may learn the identity of their birth parents if everyone agrees to it.

Traditionally, adoptions have always been highly confidential so that the privacy of everyone involved is protected. So if your adoption was a traditional one, learning about your birth parents may be more difficult although not necessarily impossible. You have to work through a court, and you may need the help of an attorney who knows how to cut through the bureaucratic red tape.

Using a Surrogate

Scientific advances have given many men and women, who in the past were unable to start a family, the chance to become parents. Although these advances are offering new hope to would-be parents, the laws regarding how these advances should be used and the rights of those who use them are still being defined.

If you're unable to conceive a child or cannot carry one to term, you may decide to use the services of a female surrogate. Depending on your particular problem, the surrogate will be artificially inseminated by your husband's sperm and will then give birth to the baby for you, or an egg you donate will be fertilized by your husband *in vitro* and then implanted in the surrogate who will later give birth. If the problem lies with your husband, you may want to use a male surrogate or a sperm bank to help you start a family.

If surrogate parenting is legal in your state, find out if there are any laws governing the relationship between you and the surrogate. For example, you may be prohibited from paying a surrogate because the exchange of money is viewed as equivalent to baby selling.

Be careful about using a broker to help you with the surrogate process. If the broker's only service is locating possible surrogates, in the eyes of the law, the broker may be selling babies. In such a situation, you and the broker can be prosecuted.

Always hire an attorney who is familiar with the applicable laws of your state to prepare an airtight contract for you that will help protect your legal right to the child. Don't rely on any paperwork that a broker, doctor, sperm bank, or surrogate may provide.

An airtight contract is especially important if you work with a female surrogate. In the contract, you want the surrogate to waive all of her rights to the child after it's born; otherwise, she may have a change of heart after the baby is born, and you may find yourself in court battling for the baby. If the surrogate provided the egg, she is the baby's biological mother and your husband is the father; therefore, before you can adopt the baby and become its legal parent, she must waive her parental rights. If you end up in a court battle with a surrogate, she may get visitation rights, custody, and even child support, depending on the nature of her role in bringing the baby into the world, whether or not there was a surrogate contract, and exactly what the contract said.

Generally, the same potential for legal problems doesn't exist when you work with a sperm donor or a sperm bank. If you work directly with a sperm donor, it's unlikely that he will assert his parental rights to any child he may father because doing so means that he will also have to assume all of the legal obligations that go with being a parent. If you work through a sperm bank, sperm bank donors usually don't have any parental legal rights or obligations. Many states give sperm donors no parental rights. And in fact, if your husband consents to your being artificially inseminated with donor sperm, most states view your husband as the child's legal father.

Child Care

Good child care is a concern for many parents today. You may find it reassuring to know that to help ensure a basic level of safety and care at day care centers, most states and many local governments require that day care centers be licensed and meet certain minimum standards for child-to-caregiver ratios, nutrition, sanitation, and safety. To find out about the rules for child care providers in your area, look in the government listings section of your phone book under "Child Care Providers" or "Family or Social Services."

In many states, day care centers operated by a religious entity do not have to be licensed.

If you're lucky enough to be able to afford in-home child care, don't learn the hard way, as some top-level government nominees did during the early days of the Clinton presidency, that you need to comply with many federal reporting and taxing requirements. In addition, your state may have its own requirements.

Federal law requires that if you pay your child's at-home caregiver more than $1,000 in a given year, you must pay half of that person's Social Security and Medicare taxes when you file your annual federal tax return. (This law is retroactive to 1994 and applies not just to child care providers but to any home help, including housekeepers, gardeners, cooks, and so on.) But if the caregiver is under age 18 and classifies his or her primary occupation as student, not household help, you do not have to pay these taxes. Also, if you pay the caregiver $1,000 or more over a three-month period, you must also pay his or her federal unemployment taxes.

To find out if your state requires you to pay taxes, liability insurance, and so on for at-home caregivers, call your insurance agent or your state's department of labor.

Don't ignore your tax obligations to the IRS. If you do and the IRS finds out, you may find yourself owing that agency a lot of money. You will be liable for all of the taxes you didn't pay plus interest — at a high rate — and you will also have to pay substantial penalties on the back taxes. Contact the IRS at 800-829-1040 to find out the terms and conditions of your reporting and tax obligations.

It's a good idea to draw up a written contract between you and your home-based child care provider that stipulates the employee's responsibilities, hours of work, compensation, and benefits.

Au pairs

Hiring an *au pair* to live at your home and help care for your children is an option that many couples use to resolve the issue of quality child care. Au pairs are usually young European women, although there are male au pairs, between the ages of 18 and 25. They come to the U.S. for a maximum of 13 months on exchange visitor visas to live with a family and provide it with child care and possibly light household work in exchange for free room and board, a weekly stipend, and health insurance. Because an au pair is not considered a foreign worker but rather a participant in a cultural exchange (theoretically, by living together, you and the au pair are teaching one another about your cultures), you do not have to pay his or her social security or other taxes.

The United States Information Agency (USIA) works with a number of nonprofit organizations in this country who help match families with au pairs. The job responsibilities, number of hours an au pair must work, and an au pair's living conditions are all strictly defined.

Chapter 6

The Law and Your Job

· ·

· ·

Unless you've won the lottery or your proverbial rich uncle has left you a small fortune, you probably spend most of your waking hours working at a job. Even Snow White's seven dwarfs went to work!

Whether you're gainfully employed or looking to be employed, you should be aware that the federal government has passed many laws to protect your rights in the workplace. These laws cover everything from being hired and fired, to your rights on the job, to the minimum you are paid, to safety at work. Your state has also passed laws that affect you and the workplace. Many of these laws reinforce or expand the rights provided by the federal laws.

Although the Employee Relations Web Picks site (`http://www.webcom.com./~garnet/labor/welcome.html`) appears to have been developed for human resource professionals, what better way to know your rights on the job than to read what they're reading! You can find links to a wide variety of information resources on subjects relating to employee benefits and employment law.

The U.S. Department of Labor maintains a Web page at `http://www.dol.gov/`. Among other things, it offers comprehensive, detailed information about the federal laws and regulations that affect you as an employee.

Applying for a Job

To explain how employment laws may affect you, I'll start where all employees start — with the job application process.

The interview or job application

Generally, you cannot be asked questions that have nothing to do with your job qualifications, including questions about your age, ethnic origin, sexual preference, race, religion, political affiliations, marital status, whether or not you have any children or intend to have them, your medical history, and whether you have any disabilities.

Employers can ask you personal questions if they relate to a job's *bona fide occupational qualifications* and if the employers ask the same questions of all applicants for the same job.

References

State laws limit the kinds of information that a past employer can provide to a prospective employer. Generally, a past employer can provide only information about the following: the position you held, the salary you received, the dates that you worked for the former employer, the reason you left the job, and the circumstances surrounding your departure (you were doing a great job but wanted more challenges; you couldn't get along with anyone, and so on). In other words, a past employer can provide essentially just enough to verify what's on your résumé or job application and comment on your past job performance, as long as those comments are verifiable.

Background checks

A prospective employer can conduct a background check on you if the information sought is strictly job related. Also, according to the federal Fair Credit Reporting Act, a prospective employer can review a copy of your credit history if knowing about your finances is job related. For example, a prospective employer may review your credit history if the job you're applying for requires you to handle large sums of money. But the law says that the employer must notify you if you're denied the job because of your credit history. A limited number of states say that you must be notified at the time your credit history is checked.

Testing and Job Applications

Depending on the job you're applying for and the state you live in, certain types of pre-employment tests are legal, including job-related intelligence or skills tests and drug tests, so long as all applicants are required to take the same tests. This section of the chapter describes the rules regarding other kinds of tests.

Affirmative action

An affirmative action plan (AAP) is a plan that outlines how a business recruits, hires, and promotes minorities and women in order to improve workplace disparities that are the result of discrimination or to make amends for past discrimination. Most private employers are free to decide for themselves whether or not to have an AAP. Government agencies are required to have them, and employers with government contracts — local, state, or federal — may be required to have them too. If, however, an employer that is not required to have an AAP is sued for discrimination and found guilty, the employer may be required to implement one.

The Americans with Disabilities Act (ADA) says that you cannot be required to take a medical or psychological test as part of the application process. But you can be required to take one after you've been offered a job, assuming that the employer meets certain conditions. If the tests show that you have a problem that may interfere with your ability to do the job you've been offered and that hiring you will create an "undue hardship" on the business, the employer has the right to rescind the offer. The employer must hire you, however, if "reasonable accommodations" can be made that will allow you to perform the job satisfactorily.

What follows is the legal low-down on some tests and requirements you may encounter:

✔ **Drug testing:** Drug screening tests are permitted under federal law; however, some states have laws that restrict drug testing or have established guidelines for such testing.

✔ **AIDS testing:** You can be required to be tested for AIDS, but only after you've been offered a job. If you test positive, the employer cannot take back the offer unless it can prove that there is a job-based reason why someone who is HIV-positive should not be hired.

✔ **Fingerprinting and photographs:** Some states allow employers to require fingerprinting and photographs when they're hiring for certain kinds of positions, including police officers and child care workers, but usually only after the employer has made a job offer.

✔ **Lie detector tests:** The Federal Employee Polygraph Protection Act (FEPPA) says that private sector employers cannot require you to take a lie detector test unless you're applying for certain kinds of positions, including jobs in the security industry or jobs with companies that manufacture, dispense, or distribute controlled substances. This law does not apply to public sector employers. Most states have their own laws governing the use of polygraph tests.

Some states require employers to obtain written permission from a job applicant before certain medical tests are conducted.

Job Offers That Come with Conditions

If you're a white-collar professional and are offered a new job, as a condition of employment, your prospective employer may want you to sign an agreement called a *covenant not to compete.* This agreement restricts your ability to work for one of the employer's competitors or to begin a business that competes directly with your employer if you voluntarily leave your new job or are fired from it. Most of such agreements apply to a limited geographic area and are good for only a limited period of time.

Obviously, a covenant not to compete benefits your new employer and not you because it limits your options should you and the employer part company. So avoid signing one if you can. If you can't avoid it and you really want the job, it's a good idea to hire an attorney to review the agreement before you sign it. The attorney can suggest changes you should try to negotiate, or he or she can negotiate them for you.

If you do sign a covenant not to compete and later violate it, your former employer has the right to sue you and possibly your new employer as well. But if the court determines that the terms of the agreement were overly stringent or restrictive, it may let you off of the hook or order you to comply with new, less onerous restrictions.

 You may also be asked to sign a confidentiality agreement as a condition of your employment. Such an agreement might require you to not divulge certain proprietary information like special formulas, business plans, product details, or copyrights. Be sure you understand exactly what you're agreeing not to do before signing.

On the Job

After you're hired, it's important that you understand your rights in the workplace. And where better to start than with your first paycheck!

Getting paid

The federal Fair Labor Standards Act (FLSA) establishes the minimum wage that employees must be paid and establishes the rules for overtime. The current federal minimum hourly wage is $4.25. At the time this book was written, Congress was considering an increase in the minimum wage, phased in over a two-year period, of $.90. Many states have their own minimum wage and overtime laws for businesses that operate within their borders. Most states match the federal minimum, but some have established lower or higher minimums.

Overtime and comp time

Although you may put in 60 hours per week to get your job done, you can receive overtime pay only if you're classified as a *nonexempt* worker — someone who is paid by the hour. People in professional, administrative, or executive positions are typically classified as *exempt* workers because they are usually paid a salary. They therefore don't receive overtime pay; independent contractors, trainees, and apprentices don't either.

If you're eligible for overtime pay, federal law says that whenever you work more than 40 hours in a given work week, you must be paid one and a half times your regular hourly rate for the extra time you work. Overtime for certain categories of workers such as police officers, firefighters, hospital workers, nursing home employees, and so on is calculated differently because their work "weeks" are often longer than those of other professions. For example, police officers who work a seven-day week receive overtime after 43 hours, while those who work a 28-day period get overtime after 171 hours. Firefighters who work more than 53 hours in a seven-day period are eligible for overtime, and those with a 28-day work period are eligible for overtime after 212 hours.

If you work for a public sector employer, in most cases, when you're eligible for overtime, your employer can offer you *comp time* — time away from your job that is equivalent to the extra amount you would receive in your check. Usually, you have the right to choose whether you want overtime pay or comp time. If, however, you work in the private sector or for a nonprofit organization, your employer must pay you when you're eligible for overtime; there is no comp time.

Generally, if you believe that you're not being paid according to the requirements of the Fair Labor Standards Act, you can file a complaint with the federal Department of Labor's Wage and Hour Division, which will investigate your complaint. Although regional offices are in all states, you can contact the main office at Room S302, 200 Constitution Avenue, Washington, D.C. 20210; 202-219-8305. You can also sue your employer in state or federal court for twice the amount of the back wages and overtime you are owed.

When do I get my paycheck and why did you take out so much?

All states have laws regulating how and when you must be paid. Most require that you be paid at least twice per month.

When you get your paycheck, you may be surprised to discover that it's not for the amount you had expected. That's probably because you forgot about paycheck deductions. For example, the federal government requires your employer to withhold federal income and Social Security taxes from your paycheck. Your state may make similar requirements of your employer.

Depending on your state, your employer may be allowed to deduct certain expenses from your paycheck, such as pay advances and the cost of job-related tools, equipment, and uniforms, so long as the deductions do not cut into your minimum wage or overtime pay. The same rule applies to instances when an employee working at a retail outlet is held responsible for cash shortages. And if you give your okay, your employee can deduct things like charitable donations, union dues, insurance premiums, and contributions to retirement accounts, even if these deductions do bring your pay below the minimum wage.

Most states prohibit employers from docking an employee's pay for disciplinary reasons; however, some states allow employers to deduct money from an employee's paycheck to compensate for monetary losses that the business may have suffered due to the employee's dishonesty or negligence. These deductions must be spread out over a series of paychecks so that the amount the employee receives during a given pay period does not fall below the minimum wage.

If you work for tips, federal law says that your employer can pay you less than the minimum wage — half the minimum wage if you make at least $20 per month in tips. But depending on your state, your employer may have to pay you more than half.

The benefits of a job

Being able to pay your bills because you're getting a regular paycheck is certainly the most important benefit of being employed. Depending on the company you work for, however, your job may provide other benefits as well, including a paid vacation, insurance, and a retirement plan. Although most additional job benefits are optional for employers, if they do decide to offer them, employers are usually expected to make the same benefit or benefit package available to all employees within a particular category. An employer may therefore be able to offer different benefit packages to employees in different categories. For example, an employer may offer one set of benefits to all exempt employees and a different benefit package to all executives paid over $150,000 per year.

Some states require employers to offer their employees health insurance.

No federal law requires employers to provide their pregnant workers with paid maternity leave. But because pregnancy and childbirth are technically considered disabilities, you can use paid disability leave during your pregnancy or childbirth if your employer offers paid disability leave. Some states require employers to provide up to 16 weeks of unpaid maternity leave.

An extra job benefit that is required

Under the Family and Medical Leave Act (FMLA), the federal government requires all employers with at least fifty workers as well as most public agencies to allow qualified employees — employees who have worked for them for at least 12 months and for at least 1,250 hours — to take off up to 12 work weeks per year without pay for such things as

- ✔ The birth of a child

- ✔ The adoption of a child

- ✔ The care of a spouse, child, or parent with a serious health condition

- ✔ A serious health problem such as an illness or injury that prevents an employee from working

If you take advantage of the FMLA, your employer must maintain your health insurance. You may be asked to reimburse your employer for the cost of the insurance if, at the end of your leave, you decide not to return to work. If you do return, you must be allowed to come back to your old job or to an equivalent one with the same pay and benefits.

While you're on leave, your seniority and other benefits do not accrue, and you cannot collect unemployment insurance. Also, your employer can count your accrued vacation, sick leave, and personal days toward your requested leave of absence.

Some states have laws similar to the FMLA. Many of these laws are more generous than the FMLA. For example, a few states, as well as Puerto Rico, require that employers provide temporary disability insurance to their workers during their leave of absence.

 You may not be eligible to take advantage of the FMLA if your salary is within your employer's top ten percent pay bracket. If you and your spouse work for the same company and you both want to use the FMLA, you must divide the 12 weeks of leave between you.

Organizations you should know about

If you have questions about the Family and Medical Leave Act, here are some organizations that you may want to contact:

- ✔ For a fact sheet on the FMLA, write to the Women's Legal Defense Fund, 1875 Connecticut Avenue, NW, Suite 710, Washington, D.C. 20009.

- ✔ To get information and advice on the FMLA and other employment-related issues, call the job hot line of 9 to 5, the National Association of Working Women, at 800-522-0925.

If You Think You're the Victim of Employment-Related Discrimination

At some point in your working career, you may believe that you have been the victim of employment-related discrimination. In most cases, your first response should be an informal one — call the problem to the attention of the person you believe discriminated against you or to that person's supervisor. What happened may have been an innocent mistake on his or her part, or you may have misconstrued the situation. Give everyone the benefit of the doubt and an opportunity to clear the air and/or rectify the situation. If the problem remains, you can continue to try to resolve it informally by "working your way up the ladder."

If you suspect discrimination, it's important that you get advice as soon as possible from your state's anti-discrimination agency or an attorney because of the following reasons:

- There are time limits for filing a complaint or lawsuit.
- Some states require that you file a complaint with them before filing with the EEOC, while others require exactly the opposite.
- You have to find out what you need to prove your claim.

You can also contact the Equal Employment Opportunity Commission (EEOC). The EEOC can help you understand if you have the basis for filing a formal complaint against the employer, inform you of your rights, and tell you about your options.

If you file a complaint against your employer with the EEOC, you cannot be fired, demoted, or discriminated against for doing so.

If you do file a formal complaint, the EEOC interviews you, prepares a charge against the employer based on your complaint, notifies the employer of the charge, and asks the employer to provide it with certain documents. It may also interview witnesses. If the EEOC finds no *reasonable cause* that discrimination did occur, it issues you a *right to sue* letter, and you are free to hire an attorney and file a lawsuit in federal court if you wish. You have to do so within 90 days of receiving the letter. The attorney may be willing to take your case on contingency.

To help find an employment attorney who can help you pursue your claim, contact the National Employment Lawyers Association at 415-227-4655.

If you file a complaint with the EEOC and 180 days later, the EEOC has not acted on your complaint, you can request that it issue you a *right to sue* letter.

The Equal Employment Opportunity Commission

Federal anti-discrimination laws are enforced by the Federal Equal Employment Opportunity Commission (EEOC). Contact its main office in Washington, D.C. or the regional office closest to you if you have a question about any of the laws that help protect you from being discriminated against when you apply for a job or after you're hired, or if you want to file a formal complaint against an employer.

EEOC
1801 L Street, N.W.
Washington, D.C. 20507
800-669-4000
800-800-3302 (Toll-free TDD)
800-669-3362 (Toll-free publications request number)

If the EEOC does find reasonable cause, it will contact the employer and attempt to work out a settlement. If the EEOC is unable to resolve the issue out of court, it may file a lawsuit on your behalf; however, the EEOC files very few lawsuits. Assuming the EEOC wins on your behalf, and depending on the basis of the lawsuit, the employer may be ordered to hire you, reinstate you, promote you with a raise that's paid retroactively, reimburse you for the missed salary, and pay your legal fees. The employer can also be fined or penalized in some other way.

If you lose your case, depending on your state, the court can order you to pay the legal fees your employer accrued defending itself against your lawsuit. This penalty is rarely handed down, and the lawsuit must be clearly frivolous; that is, have no basis in law or fact.

Sexual Harassment

Sexual harassment in the workplace is nothing new. We've begun hearing more about it in part because the large number of women who are now in the workforce have compelled federal and state governments as well as employers to acknowledge that sexual harassment happens. Furthermore, with the law on their side, women (and men too) are now less reluctant to be silent when they are harassed.

Sexual harassment is against the law. Title VII of the Civil Rights Act of 1964 views it as a form of employment discrimination, and the Civil Rights Act of 1991 provides victims of sexual harassment with the legal grounds to sue for damages. Also, many states have their own laws outlawing sexual harassment while the laws of others define sexual harassment as a form of sexual discrimination.

If you believe that you are being sexually harassed, you should follow the advice outlined in the previous section on employment-related discrimination. If your state has laws regarding sexual harassment, you should contact the appropriate agency as well as the EEOC.

Sexual harassment is not always obvious. Although the stereotypical case involves a lascivious boss chasing his secretary around the desk, sexual harassment doesn't have to include physical contact or overt verbal advances. According to the EEOC, sexual harassment includes the following:

✔ Leading you to believe that if you don't respond positively to a sexual advance — whether physical or verbal — you'll lose your job, be passed up for a promotion, or receive less desirable work assignments. This kind of harassment is considered *quid pro quo* sexual harassment (that's Latin for something given or done in exchange for something else — an even trade). Only someone who is in a supervisory or managerial position over you — someone who has a certain degree of power over you — can commit this form of harassment.

✔ Creating an intimidating, hostile, or offensive work environment that makes it difficult for you to perform your job. Sexually lewd comments, sexually explicit materials, or unwanted physical touching are all examples of things that can create this kind of environment.

Generally, something must happen more than once — a pattern must be established — before it can be considered sexual harassment. And because reasonable people can disagree about what is sexually offensive, the law also considers the intention of the person accused of sexual harassment. So if you believe that you are being harassed, keep a record of each incident and include who did it, where, when, and what happened. If there were any witnesses to the incident, be sure to note who they were.

Employers are legally obligated to address instances of sexual harassment that they know about. Generally, they're considered legally liable for instances of *quid pro quo* sexual harassment. Also, because they are expected to create an environment for their workers that is not hostile, when a hostile or offensive work environment exists, employers may also be legally liable for any harassment even if the employers are not aware of the particular instances of harassment.

You can be a victim of sexual harassment even if the harassment is not directed at you. For example, you may be the victim of sexual harassment if a coworker is promoted or given better work assignments at your expense in exchange for sexual favors.

If the sexual advances of your manager or supervisor are unwelcome but you comply with them, the law may still view the advances as sexual harassment.

Safety on the Job

Federal law says that you have the right to "safe and healthful working conditions." These conditions are established and protected by the federal Occupational Safety and Health Act, which is enforced by the Occupational Safety and Health Administration (OSHA). Nearly every private sector employer is required to maintain a reasonably safe workplace for their employees and to meet OSHA's health and safety requirements.

If you believe an unsafe or unhealthy situation exists at your place of work — employees are not being adequately protected from certain toxic or carcinogenic chemicals, or equipment is not being regularly inspected and maintained, for example — you can bring the matter to the attention of your employer, or you can become a whistle blower by contacting OSHA at 202-219-5000. (A whistle blower is someone who brings their employer's illegal or unsafe activities to the attention of the government agency or office with enforcement powers.) If you contact OSHA, OSHA will evaluate your information and either contact your employer to tell it that someone has complained and to tell it what it should do to clear up the problem, or OSHA will schedule an on-site inspection.

Your state may have its own work place health and safety agency and laws.

As long as you are not acting out of maliciousness, your employer cannot fire you or harass you in any way for blowing the whistle.

When accidents happen

Despite an employer's efforts to provide a healthy and safe workplace for its employees, on-the-job accidents and health problems do happen. And if you're the victim, you probably have the right to receive workers compensation payments.

At the very least, workers compensation reimburses you for any medical expenses you rack up as a result of your problem. And depending on the severity and permanence of your problem, your compensation may also include temporary or permanent disability. In addition, you may be eligible to receive vocational rehabilitation if you can return to work but just not at your old job.

You have up to one year to notify your employer about any job-related injury or illness; however, it's always best to do it soon after it happens.

Some states exempt very small employers from having to provide workers compensation. Others exempt certain types of workers, including independent contractors, domestic workers, and farm workers. If you fall into one of these exempt categories and are injured on the job or become sick with a work-related illness, you may have to sue the employer to get any financial help.

Other Employee Rights You Should Know About

If you're a member of the United States military, the Veterans Re-Employment Rights Act says that you cannot lose your job because your military obligation takes you away from your work. Your employer must give you an unpaid leave of absence, and you must be allowed to return to your old job with the same salary when you return to work. In addition, all benefits must continue to accrue while you're gone.

If your religion requires that you adjust your work schedule so that you can observe certain religious rites, your employer must make the necessary accommodations unless doing so creates an "undue hardship" for the business.

Generally, your employer does not have the legal right to reprimand or dismiss you for your behavior off the job. But if your behavior jeopardizes your employer's "legitimate business interests," you can be terminated. The following are some examples of when you might be risking dismissal:

- ✔ You work as a CPA for an accounting firm. A client of the firm appproaches you about doing some work for it on the side. The project that it asks you to take on is one that your employer would do for $150 per hour. The client asks you to do it for $75 per hour and promises that if you agree to its proposal, it will send more work your way. You agree.

- ✔ You're a salesperson for a computer products firm. To augment your income, you begin selling products that are in direct competition with your employer's via a direct marketing effort that you work on during the evenings and on weekends.

In some states, if alcohol or drug use affects your ability to carry out your job, your employer must give you a chance to get help with your substance abuse problem before you can be fired.

Your employer has the right to establish an employee dress code as long as it's not discriminatory or excessively costly to employees. If an employer establishes different dress codes for men and women, there must be a "legitimate business reason" for doing so.

Your employer can legally bar employees from dating one another. All employees must be told of the policy, and the employer must give any employee a warning before it can discipline him or her for any infraction.

Most states prohibit employers from firing an employee who takes off work to serve on a jury in a state court. In addition, federal law guarantees employees the right to serve on a jury within the federal court system without reprisals from their employers.

In most states, employees have the right to take paid time off, with some restrictions, to vote in any public election.

Federal law gives you the right to work in a smoke-free environment; however, employers can allow smoking in specific offices or areas unless prohibited by state law or city ordinances.

A growing number of employers are establishing written policies giving them the right to read their employees' e-mail to ensure that it is being used for company purposes only and to make certain that e-mail is not being used in a manner that can harm the company. On the other hand, companies such as Apple Computer have adopted explicit policies that prohibit its employees' e-mail correspondence from being monitored in any way.

You may or may not have the right to view what's in your personnel file. That right depends on your state's law and on your employer's policy, among other things. The laws in states that give employees access to their files vary widely in regard to what can be included or excluded from an employee's file, whether or not an employee has a right to dispute or question certain information, whether an employee can copy the contents of his or her personnel file, and so on.

What Your Employer Has the Right to Know about You

With the advent of technology that makes it easier and easier for government, private marketers, and even employers to peek and pry into our lives, our individual privacy is being increasingly jeopardized. But laws do exist that can help us preserve some of our privacy in the workplace. For example, many states limit the rights of employers to use video and audio surveillance techniques to monitor our activities at work. State laws also exist that limit the ability of employers to read their employees' electronic mail as well as the personal mail of an employee that may be delivered to the work place. Generally, at a minimum, these laws require employers to tell their employees that they will be doing these things.

Also, the federal Omnibus Crime Control and Safe Streets Act prohibits employers from tapping or listening to their employees' phone calls. But employers can listen on another extension or monitor their employees' phone conversations if their employees know that their phone calls may be monitored. Some states have their own laws restricting employers' ability to listen to their employees' phone calls.

Employers may also do the following to check up on you:

- Depending on your state, your employer can search you or your property at work if the search is work related. But to avoid accusations of invasion of privacy, assault, intentional infliction of emotional harm, and the like, employers should let their employees know that they may be searched before they conduct a search, conduct their searches in an unintrusive manner, and should not injure an employee during a search. In other words, searches should be conducted with discretion and good judgment.

- Ask that you take a lie detector or polygraph test but only if the employer has evidence that you were involved in a work-related situation that harmed your employer economically or in some other way. The federal Employment Polygraph Protection Act restricts the use of this kind of test. Many states also regulate or prohibit employers' use of polygraph tests.

- Conduct random drug testing, depending on the type of job you have. For example, federal law says that airline pilots and transit workers can be required to submit to random drug tests without notice and can be fired if they refuse. Also, depending on where you live and whether or not safety is a factor in your job, your employer may have the right to test you for drug use without notice if it has reason to suspect that drug use is interfering with your ability to carry out your job. In all other situations, your employer must notify you before the test and must have a written policy for conducting and using the results of such tests.

The Federal Drug-Free Work Place Act says that all companies with federal contracts worth more than $25,000 must establish a drug-free education program for their employees and communicate with them about the program.

Calling It Quits

You can leave your job in several ways. Some are pleasant, like moving on to a bigger and better job, starting your own business, or retiring. Others are a lot less pleasant, like being fired or being laid off due to corporate downsizing or outsourcing.

If you're like most employees, you're considered an *at-will* employee, which means that you can be fired at any time for just about any job-related reason without any notice or severance pay. So much for job security, huh!

You can also be fired because your employer is downsizing or restructuring jobs or because your job has become obsolete. In fact, these reasons for job loss are becoming all too familiar to a growing number of workers no matter what their salary and education.

Access to your personnel file

The Federal Privacy Act gives federal government workers the right to review the contents of their personnel files, to copy whatever they want, and to challenge the information they may find in their files. Other federal laws give private sector employees in particular work situations access to certain information in their personnel files. Also, a number of states have laws giving employees the right to review all of the information in their personnel files and to challenge the information.

There are exceptions to at-will employment and firing. For example, depending on your state, your employer may have to provide *just cause* or *good reason* for firing you. Also, you cannot be fired at-will if you have a contract with your employer that makes other provisions for your firing or if your employer has an employment policy that prohibits such firings.

If you're a government worker, civil service laws protect you from at-will firings. Also, most labor unions have contracts with employers that prohibit at-will firings of their members.

Don't forget, if you feel that your firing is the result of discrimination, you can attempt to get redress by contacting the EEOC following the advice presented earlier in this chapter.

If you feel that your firing was unfair but not necessarily discriminatory, you should contact an employment attorney to discuss whether you have any basis for filing a lawsuit only after discussing the matter with your employer first.

I've got some good news and some bad news about what you're entitled to if you lose your job. Let's get the bad news out of the way first.

Severance pay

You don't automatically receive severance pay. It's up to your boss to decide if you do and how much — unless your employer made a verbal promise to you or has a written policy that provides for severance pay. If you're fired for misconduct, you probably won't get anything.

And now for the good news.

Unemployment insurance

Unless you're fired for gross misconduct, you are probably eligible to receive unemployment insurance if you've been working at your current job long enough. How long is long enough varies from state to state. After applying for unemployment insurance, you can probably collect your benefits for at least 26 weeks.

If you leave your job voluntarily, you may be eligible to collect unemployment if you can prove that your employer made your work situation so intolerable that you had to leave.

Health insurance

Because of the Consolidated Omnibus Budget Reconciliation Act, better known as COBRA, you can remain on your employer's health insurance plan for up to 18 months after you leave your job, whether you were fired or quit, assuming that your employer has at least 20 employees. You do, however, have to pay the full cost of your insurance premium. It's better than nothing!

You can be denied COBRA benefits if you were dismissed for gross misconduct.

Federal Employment-Related Laws You Should Know About

Over the past fifty years, the federal government has passed a myriad of important laws that help ensure that job applicants and employees are treated fairly. Some apply to all employers — private and public sector. Others apply to private sector employers only, and still others apply to all private sector employers but the smallest — usually those with fewer than 15 employees. I can't include all the federal laws in this chapter, but here's the low-down on some of the most important:

Age Discrimination in Employment Act (ADEA)

This law applies to public and private employers with 20 or more employees, employment agencies, and unions. The ADEA says that employers cannot do the following:

- Discriminate against employees who are 40 years old or older because of their age.

- Establish a mandatory retirement age for their employees.

- Legally discharge or demote an employee, with a few exceptions, because the employer thinks the worker is too old; however, the employer can use incentives to encourage employees to retire voluntarily.

Americans with Disabilities Act (ADA)

This law applies to public and private employers with at least 15 employees, employment agencies, and unions. Among other things, the ADA prohibits employers from discriminating against employees or potential employees who

- Have a physical or mental disability that substantially affects their ability to perform a critical life activity such as seeing, walking, talking, or hearing

- Used to have such a physical or mental disability — for example, in the past, they were successfully treated for cancer or alcoholism

Temporary physical or mental disabilities are not covered by the ADA.

To help make employment opportunities available to employees who are seriously disabled but fully qualified to do a job, the ADA requires employers to make "reasonable accommodations" as long as they don't place an "undue hardship" on their businesses. These accommodations can include making their facilities readily accessible to those with disabilities, modifying equipment or training materials, and making readers or interpreters available.

The union-sponsored Web site at `http://www.igc.apc.org/cwatx/ada.html` offers a straightforward and graphically-attractive discussion of the Americans with Disabilities Act.

Title VII of the Civil Rights Act of 1964

This law applies to public and private sector employers with at least 15 employees, employment agencies, and unions. Title VII prohibits discrimination in hiring, firing, paying salaries or benefits, promoting, and other aspects of employment on the basis of race, color, religion, sex, or national origin.

Pregnancy Discrimination Act (PDA)

The PDA prohibits employers from refusing to hire or from firing a woman simply because she is pregnant. Employers are also barred from reassigning a pregnant woman to other duties because she is pregnant or from forcing her to take pregnancy leave.

Equal Pay Act (EPA)

The EPA prohibits employers from paying women and men differently if they are performing essentially the same jobs under similar working conditions. Their pay can differ if the difference is based on seniority, merit, or other criteria related to job performance such as the quality or the quantity of an employee's work.

Chapter 7

So You Want to Be an Entrepreneur!

In This Chapter

▶ Business structures

▶ Taxes

▶ Employees and taxes

▶ Patents, copyrights, and trademarks

▶ Bankruptcy

*A*side from falling in love, perhaps no other experience in life can be as intoxicating and as exciting as starting your own business. You dream of your possibilities! You count the money you'll make! You can almost taste your success! Donald Trump, watch out!

Despite your optimism, it's important for you to know that although thousands of businesses are started every year, more than 50 percent of them fail within four years, and 63 percent go bust in six years. Although some of the reasons for this high rate of failure are not within the scope of this book, one important reason is that new business owners do not spend enough time planning to be in business and learning the laws that affect them. Such oversights can be costly, if not financially fatal, for the typical small business owner.

If you're looking for a business opportunity, be alert for scams. Usually sold by aggressive telemarketers or through classified advertising or television infomericals, the income potential of these "opportunities" is often wildly exaggerated, and you'll typically get little or nothing for your up-front cash payment. The Federal Trade Commission has made targeting these business flimflam artists a priority.

This chapter doesn't tell you how to finance or manage your business in order to maximize your chances for success. But it does explain some of the key legal issues that the typical small business owner should be aware of. To get a more complete picture of your legal obligations and rights, you should also read Chapter 6, which discusses employee rights in the workplace and also covers the things that employers are required to do and are barred from doing in regard to employees as well as potential employees.

Illustrated with colorful, lively graphics, The Small Business Channel's Business Directory (located in the Idea Cafe) can get you to a literal plethora of business-related Web sites on such diverse subjects as accounting and taxes, human resources and personnel, and marketing and home offices. The directory features detailed descriptions of each Web site and "the inside scoop" on how to locate the very best information each site has to offer. Check it out at `http://www.ideacafe.com./html/BC.html`.

Getting Off to the Right Start

One of the first and most fundamental decisions you have to make when you're planning to begin a business is deciding what legal structure your business should have: sole proprietorship, partnership, corporation, or some variation. Don't downplay the importance of this decision. It affects any or all of the following:

- The cost of starting and running your business
- How much direct control you have over your business
- The degree to which you are personally liable for any debts your business takes on
- Whether or not you are personally liable for any lawsuits filed against your business
- The ease with which you are able to get loans or investment capital to help finance your business
- The taxes you have to pay

Your business's legal structure even affects the kind of bankruptcy you can file! Although I realize that bankruptcy isn't something most aspiring entrepreneurs want to be thinking about when they're focused on getting a business started, given the high rate of business failure, it would be naïve not to acknowledge the possibility.

Before making a final decision on the best legal structure for your business, it's a good idea to schedule an appointment with an attorney or a CPA. At this meeting, you can not only get detailed information about the pros and cons of each structure in light of your particular business, but you can also find out about other issues and concerns that you should be aware of. To prepare you for that meeting, what follows is a quick rundown of your business structure options.

Sole proprietorships

Sole proprietorships are easy and inexpensive to start, making them far and away the most popular way to organize a business. To begin a sole proprietorship, all you really need to do is start acting like a business. You don't have to fill out any official paperwork to or pay any fees; you have a few extra IRS forms to file each April. Come tax time, all you need to do is complete a Schedule C showing your business revenues and expenses and your net income or loss.

Depending on the kind of business you have, your local government may require you to obtain special licenses, even if your business is a sole proprietorship.

If you take a business name that is different from your own — Accurate Accounting or Caring Child Care, for example — you may have to file that name with your county or with your Secretary of State. This assumed name is your *DBA,* which stands for "doing business as." Filing a DBA helps ensure that you don't use someone else's business name and that another business doesn't take yours. It also lets people who do business with your company know exactly who they're dealing with.

When you run a business as a sole proprietorship, you're its chief cook and bottle washer and everything in-between. You have 100 percent control. In fact, in the eyes of the law, you are your business; there is no distinction. Your business debts are your personal debts. And if your business is sued, it's really you who's sued. In other words, if you structure your business as a sole proprietorship, you are *personally* liable for all of your business debts and legal problems because your personal and business assets are one and the same. This fact is the single most significant drawback to a sole proprietorship.

Obtaining adequate financing for your business is a related problem. Because your business doesn't have a credit history separate from your personal credit history, if you already have a lot of credit or if your credit history is damaged, you will have a tough time borrowing money to help pay for your business's operations and fund its growth.

Things to check out before you start a business

- What permits and licenses do you need to apply for?
- What zoning laws you need to comply with?
- What tax requirements do you have to meet?
- What insurance do you need?
- If your business is a sole proprietorship or partnership, do you need a DBA?
- If your business is a corporation, what are your state and federal requirements?

It's legal but not wise to run your sole proprietorship out of your personal checkbook. If you get audited by the IRS, it can be difficult to prove which expenses were business-related and which were personal.

Partnerships

If you are in a business with one or more persons, you can structure it in two basic ways: as a partnership or a corporation. If you chose to establish a partnership, you are opting for a legal structure that is much like a sole proprietorship. For example, you and your partners are each personally liable for all of your business's financial and legal liabilities. Also, as with a sole proprietorship, your share of your business's income or loss needs to be reported on your personal tax return.

A partnership must file an annual report with the IRS indicating how much it earned or lost in a tax year as well as each partner's share of that profit or loss.

Liability issues

Having partners can be advantageous because they can bring to a business expertise, contacts, and money that a single owner may not have. Partners also share liability for a business's debts and legal problems. Being in a partnership can be problematic, however, as the actions of one partner legally obligate all partners as business owners, and each partner can also be held personally liable. If your partnership incurs a debt that it is unable to pay, or if it is sued and cannot pay the judgment, it doesn't matter whether the debt or lawsuit is the consequence of one partner's action in the eyes of the law. Each of you is personally liable.

Here's an example of what I'm talking about and how it can affect you: Suppose your partner uses the company credit card to wine and dine potential clients while he is at a week-long, out-of-town conference. To impress them, he eats only at the best restaurants and buys expensive bottles of wine.

When you open the credit card bill a month after your partner has returned, you're both astounded at your partner's profligate spending and concerned about how your business will ever come up with the money necessary to pay off the bill in the time required because you've only been in business for six months and money is very tight. You're also worried because you know that if your business can't pay the bill in full, the credit card company has a legal right to collect directly from either you or your partner — from whoever has the money.

A partnership is very much like a marriage: The actions of one partner can have a profound effect on the other. So be sure when choosing a partner that you select someone who shares your business philosophy, is willing to communicate honestly and openly with you, and whose judgment and honesty you trust implicitly.

Formal partnerships

Your partner may be a business associate, a friend, or even a spouse. Regardless, to help ensure that your relationship is a happy one, it's advisable, but not legally required, to negotiate a written partnership agreement. A formal partnership agreement can provide you a number of important benefits:

- ✔ Negotiating the terms of your agreement forces you to define your working relationship and address issues you might otherwise overlook.

- ✔ If partnership problems do develop (and what close relationship doesn't have them?), a written agreement can help you resolve them before your relationship deteriorates in bitterness and acrimony, or even in court.

- ✔ If you decide to end your partnership, a written agreement can help you do it in a matter that is fair to both of you.

If you don't have a written agreement, the general terms of your relationship are defined by the Uniform Partnership Act. Its guidelines, however, may not meet the particular needs of your partnership. The Act has been adopted in some form by all states except Louisiana.

Partnerships can be established to accomplish a very specific business project — a real estate deal, for example. After the project has been completed, the partnership is dissolved.

After you and your partners have talked through the general terms of your business relationship, it's best to hire an attorney to prepare your formal, written agreement. The attorney knows what to include and how to avoid typical partnership pitfalls. Spending money on an attorney at this stage of your business relationship is money well spent because it's a lot cheaper to get legal help to prevent problems from developing than it is to hire an attorney to resolve them.

At a minimum, your agreement should address the following:

- ✔ The rights and responsibilities of each partner

- ✔ What each partner is contributing to the business and the value of the contributions

- ✔ How decisions will be made

- ✔ How business income, debts, as well as profits and losses will be shared

- ✔ How business property will be owned

- ✔ How the books and other records will be kept

- ✔ How disputes should be resolved

- ✔ Provisions for dissolving the partnership, expanding it, buying out a partner, and bringing in a new partner

Unless you make other provisions in your partnership agreement, your partnership will automatically be dissolved if a partner leaves or dies or if a new partner is added.

Limited partners contribute investment capital to a partnership but don't have the right to become involved in the management of the business. Their liability is limited to the amount of their investment.

Corporations

Unlike either a sole proprietorship or a partnership, a corporation has a legal identity apart from its owners. This business structure therefore minimizes or avoids many of the legal and financial risks and headaches associated with sole proprietorships and partnerships. Owners of a corporation have limited liability for the actions of the business, and corporations typically have an easier time obtaining the funds they need to operate and expand.

Setup and paperwork

The advantages of incorporating come at a cost: It takes time and money to set up and maintain a corporation. At a minimum, to begin a corporation, you have to prepare and file articles of incorporation with your Secretary of State's office, pay a filing fee, and write a set of corporate bylaws. Once your business has been established, you must maintain proper corporate records (including minutes of shareholder meetings), file annual reports with your Secretary of State, and file the necessary state and federal taxes for your business. You must keep your personal finances totally separate from your business's finances. No running your business through your personal checking account or "loaning" yourself money from the till.

If a shareholder (owner of a corporation) dies or leaves (sells his or her share of the business), or if another shareholder is brought in (new or existing shares are sold), the corporation continues to exist, unlike what happens in similar situations when a business is a partnership.

A corporation is owned by its shareholders. In most states, a corporation can have just one shareholder, you. Or it can have more shareholders. In fact, selling shares can be a good way to raise funds for your business and represents a business financing technique unique to corporations.

Liability and drawbacks

As I've already indicated, one reason for structuring your business as a corporation is that your personal liability for your business's actions are limited. If your business defaults on a loan or is sued for example, you won't lose any more than your investment in the company. In reality however, especially if your corporation has few shareholders, or if it's new and has no financial track record, or if it's track record isn't strong, you will probably have to personally guarantee any debt that your business takes on, which means that you are liable just as if your business was a sole proprietorship or partnership.

The corporate vocabulary

If you incorporate, you'll be exposed to a whole new business vocabulary. Here are some of the most important terms you need to become familiar with:

The Players:

- ✔ **The Board of Directors** set corporate policy and make long-term decisions for the corporation.

- ✔ **The Officers** manage the day-to-day operations of the business and implement policies set by the Board.

- ✔ **The Shareholders** own the corporate stock. As owners, they elect the directors, amend bylaws, amend articles of incorporation, remove directors, and vote on other basic corporate issues.

The Paperwork:

- ✔ **Articles of Incorporation:** Filing this paperwork formally establishes a corporation. This document usually reflects the corporation's name and purpose, the names and addresses of the persons filing the articles (the incorporators and the name of the *registered agent,* the person to receive official notices related to the corporation), and the number of authorized shares. In some states, you can obtain a standard, fill-in-the-blanks articles of incorporation form from your Secretary of State; in others, you have to write your own based on your state's requirements.

- ✔ **Corporate by-laws:** Written by the Board of Directors, this document spells out basic rules for the corporation. It can be amended as necessary.

- ✔ **Stock certificates or shares of stock:** The written indication of ownership in a corporation.

If you fail to run your corporation as a legal entity that is totally separate from you (for example, you commingle your business and personal assets in one bank account), you may be held personally liable for your business.

Double taxation represents the key drawback to incorporating. A corporation pays federal taxes on its earnings (and possibly state income tax too). After paying its taxes, the corporation may decide to distribute some of its earnings as dividends to its shareholders. If it does, the shareholders also pay taxes on that income. So if you organize your business as a corporation, you may pay taxes twice: first a corporate tax and then an individual tax.

You should know about a special kind of corporation: the Subchapter S corporation. If your business is relatively small (no more than 35 shareholders) and meets a number of other federal criteria, you may want to structure it as a Subchapter S corporation because doing so allows you to get around the double taxation problem.

A Subchapter S corporation does not pay federal corporate income taxes. Instead, rather than pay taxes on the dividends they receive from the corporation, its shareholders pay federal taxes on their share of the corporate profits — at their personal rate.

The limited liability company is a new business structure that is legal in nearly every state. For legal purposes, it's a corporation; for tax purposes, it's a partnership. This legal structure is also free of the disadvantages of both S corporations and limited partnerships. But it has drawbacks too. Talk to your CPA or lawyer about it.

The federal Small Business Administration has established a Web site — U.S. Business Advisor — to assist business owners. According to Vice President Al Gore, it provides "one-stop access to federal agencies that regulate and assist businesses." In short, it tells you about the myriad federal rules and regulations you may need to comply with, and it allows you to download government forms and get information about government-backed loans and other federal assistance that you may be eligible for. Check it out at http://www.business.gov.

Franchises

Some aspiring entrepreneurs opt for getting into business by purchasing the rights to a proven concept rather than starting from scratch with their own ideas. Buying a franchise with an established and respected reputation can put you somewhat ahead in the game of money making, and given that there are franchise opportunities for just about every kind of business you can think of, you can probably find one that interests you.

Legally, when you buy a franchise, the franchisor is selling you a license to begin and run the type of business it is franchising. Typically, your purchase includes the right to the franchise's trademark, trade names, products, and so on. You also purchase certain benefits and rights, which can include training, start-up assistance, discounts on supplies and merchandise, advertising support, ongoing management assistance, and sometimes even a building and land.

In essence, when you buy a franchise, you're buying a valuable business partner with a financial stake in helping you become a success. Because you are usually expected to pay the franchisor a percentage of your profits, the more successful you are, the more money the franchisor makes.

In exchange for selling you certain rights and benefits, you are expected to meet certain requirements. They generally include the following: maintaining a certain level of business quality, spending a certain percentage of sales on business marketing, buying certain products or supplies from the franchisor, and using certain signage.

There are good franchises and not so good franchises, so before you buy one, check it out carefully and make certain that it's actually a good deal for you. Review the information a franchisor sends you as well as the franchise agreement and any other contracts you will be expected to sign. Pay special attention to the franchisor's disclosure statement, or Uniform Franchise Offering Circular (UFOC). The Federal Trade Commission requires a franchisor to provide a potential buyer with a copy of its disclosure statement at their first meeting — at least ten days before a franchise agreement is signed or before any money changes hands.

Always review a franchise contract with an attorney before you sign it. The contract should clearly spell out all purchase details, including the rights and responsibilities of both you and the franchisor. Depending on the amount of money involved, you may even want the attorney to negotiate the contract for you.

A disclosure statement provides a wealth of information, so read it carefully. Among other things, it tells you the history of the franchisor, the track record of its franchises, the names of the franchisor's corporate officers, and their business backgrounds as well as any criminal convictions, bankruptcies, and civil judgments that may be in their background.

The disclosure statement also spells out all relevant costs you will be expected to pay, the kinds of assistance the franchisor will provide you, under what conditions you can sell or lose the franchise, and so on. This statement must also include a copy of the company's latest audited income statement and balance sheet so that you can use the information to help you evaluate the franchisor's financial stability.

Your state may place special requirements and restrictions on a franchisor. Call your state attorney general's office to find out about them.

Go to the federal Small Business Administration's Home Page (http://www.sbaonline.sba.gov/)to get the complete scoop on its small business services and loan programs. You can also download software and the text of many helpful SBA publications. This home page also has links to other Web sites that are useful to business owners. If you're a female business owner, visit the SBA's Women's Business Ownership Home Page, where you can find information on programs and resources for female entrepreneurs. Check it out at http://www.sbaonline.sba.gov/womeninbusiness/.

Organizations that can help you

If you're interested in exploring franchise opportunities, here are a couple of helpful resources:

International Franchise Association
1350 New York Avenue
Washington, D.C. 20005
202-628-8000

Frandata
1155 Connecticut Avenue, N.W. Suite 275
Washington, D.C. 20036
202-659-8640

Call or write this organization to find out about purchasing a franchisor's UFOC.

Working out of Your Home

Technological advances like personal computers, online services, fax machines, and so on have made it easy for many entrepreneurs to run successful businesses out of their homes. In fact, in 1995, an estimated 46 million people worked out of their homes either full time or part time, an increase of about 6.5 percent over the previous year.

These lucky people get to work in their bathrobes, tan while they take phone calls, listen to the sound of wind chimes, and weed their gardens during lunch. Yeah, right! But they do get to avoid commuting to and from an office, and they are spared the pressure and politics of the corporate world.

 Steer clear of home business opportunity scams. Like other business scams, they make promises like "Make BIG BUCKS with OTHER PEOPLE'S MONEY using your answering machine." If you fall for that line, I've got a bridge I'd like to sell you.

Planning ahead

If you decide to begin a home-based business, you should do all of the up-front planning and research recommended for any entrepreneur starting a business. But to avoid getting into legal hot water, you need to check out some special things:

✔ Does your community or housing development prohibit home-based businesses or certain types of home-based businesses?

✔ Does your business have to comply with local zoning ordinances, regulations, licensing requirements, or codes? If your business is in violation of one of these codes and it comes to the attention of your local government, you can be fined or even have your business shut down.

Some condominiums and planned communities have special rules regarding home-based businesses. They can be more restrictive than your state or local government's rules and regulations.

If you're lucky, you live in a community that is "home-based business friendly." These communities recognize that most home-based businesses are non-polluting financial assets that generate little if any neighborhood traffic or noise. Such communities place few if any restrictions on home-based businesses. Other, less enlightened communities may only allow you to operate a home-based business under certain conditions, or their zoning ordinances may effectively prevent you from running certain kinds of businesses out of a home. For example, these ordinances may limit traffic in a neighborhood, restrict or prohibit business signage in a residential neighborhood, impose on-street parking requirements for a business, and more.

If your community has laws that affect your ability to operate a home-based business, consider asking your local government to grant you a *variance* from those laws. A variance exempts your business from having to obey such laws.

Dealing with taxes and insurance

Taxes and insurance are two other issues that you may need to make special provisions for if your business is home-based. Although your basic business insurance needs are no different than if you operated out of a more traditional office space, don't assume that your home owner's insurance policy covers your business property if it's stolen, damaged, or destroyed in your home office, and don't expect that your policy can help you if someone visiting your business or making a delivery is injured while on your premises. So ask your insurance agent or broker if you need another policy.

Although you are liable for the same kind of taxes that any other business with a legal structure like yours owes, when you use a part of your home exclusively and regularly as a business, you can claim it as a tax deduction along with associated expenses, such as a portion of your home's utilities. To get the most up-to-date IRS information regarding taxes and home offices, call the IRS at 800-829-1040 and ask for Publication 587, *Business Use of Home*.

You can download IRS tax forms and information by going to http://www.ustreas.gov.

Death and Taxes

As the saying goes, there is nothing certain in life but death and taxes. You can't escape the grim reaper or the IRS!

Ignorance is not bliss when it comes to taxes. It's your responsibility to understand what kinds of taxes your business must pay, and then you must make sure to get them paid on time and in full. Not doing so can be an expensive and even fatal mistake for a business. That's because the IRS has the power to impose hefty penalties on businesses that don't pay their taxes and high rates of interest on the unpaid tax debt. In addition, the agency has many powerful collection tools at its disposal, including the right to seize your property, levy against your bank accounts, and even shut you down.

Order IRS Publication 583, *Taxpayers Starting a Business,* to get an overview of your tax obligations according to the IRS.

There are three basic types of federal business taxes: income taxes, self-employment taxes, and employment taxes. Your state may impose its own taxes too. The exact kind of taxes you have to pay depends on the structure of your business and on whether or not you have any employees, among other things.

 ✔ **Income taxes:** No matter what legal form your business takes, you have to pay taxes on your business income. The specific income tax obligations of each type of business are reviewed earlier in this chapter.

 If you're a sole proprietor or in a partnership, it's a good idea to make quarterly estimated tax payments instead of having to come up with a lot of money every April 15th. (These payments are essentially down payments on the income taxes that you may owe and are based on your income from the previous year.

 ✔ **Self-employment taxes:** Sole proprietors and partners pay their Social Security taxes once per year by making an annual lump sum payment when they file their tax returns.

 ✔ **Employment or payroll taxes:** If you have employees, you must deduct federal income taxes, Social Security taxes, and Medicare taxes from your employees' paychecks, and you also have to match the Social Security portion.

The IRS requires employers to withhold payroll taxes from their employees' wages and then deposit the total amount in an account at a depository bank. In turn, the bank sends your tax payments to the IRS on a periodic basis.

Getting behind on payroll taxes is one of the major reasons why small businesses fail. If you develop payroll tax problems, consult a tax attorney immediately! If the IRS is threatening to seize your property or shut you down, call a bankruptcy attorney instead.

Payroll taxes represent a potential problem area for many businesses. Some neglect to deduct the taxes from their employees' wages or don't deduct enough; others make the deduction but deposit the tax money in their own bank accounts rather than with a depository bank, using the money to fund their operations and growth. Usually these businesses view their use of the money as nothing more than a loan and fully intend to deposit the money with the depository bank by the time the taxes are due to be paid. In reality however, as many a small and not so small business has learned the hard way, coming up with the money may be easier said than done. Many businesses therefore find it impossible to catch up once they fall behind on their payroll taxes, and when the IRS notices that they've not been paying, it does whatever it can to collect, including holding all "responsible persons" 100-percent personally responsible for the debt and all related penalties and interest. "Responsible persons" can include the business's owners, officers, and bookkeeper — anyone who signs the checks.

To help you meet your payroll tax obligations, consider hiring a payroll tax service to help you. This kind of company handles all tax calculations, completes the paperwork, pays your employees, and lets you know when it's time to pay the IRS.

Know Your Employees

Employers can also get themselves in hot water with the IRS by treating employees as independent contractors for tax purposes. An independent contractor is a self-employed person who provides a service to your business, usually on an hourly or project basis, but who is not controlled, supervised, or directed by you. If you use the services of an independent contractor, you don't have to worry about collecting and paying that person's payroll taxes, but you have to complete and file an IRS 1099 form on any independent contractor to whom you pay at least $600 in any tax year.

Although the IRS has established 20 separate criteria to help employers distinguish between independent contractors and employees, the distinctions between one type of worker and another can still be a puzzle. In fact, delegates to the White House Conference on Small Business in the summer of 1995 voted the employee/independent contractor conundrum the number one issue in greatest need of reform.

Get a copy of IRS Publication 937, *Employment Taxes and Information Returns,* to learn how the IRS distinguishes between employees and independent contractors.

If the IRS decides that someone you've been treating as an independent contractor is really an employee, you are expected to pay the payroll taxes you should have been withholding, plus interest and penalties. If you have misclassified many workers, and if the IRS decides to go back in history and discovers that you've been misclassifying employees as independent contractors for a long time, your tax debt can be substantial. Furthermore, because certain federal laws only apply to businesses who employ a certain number of employees — for example, the Family Medical Leave Act (must have at least 50 employees) and the Americans With Disabilities Act (must have at least 15 employees), to name two — you may also find that after the IRS has begun reclassifying your workers, your business has to begin complying with laws that can cost you even more money.

For two helpful publications on classifying employees, call 800-835-5224 to order *The Independent Contractor Employee Dilemma: Are You At Risk?* ($5) and *Employee or Independent Contractor?* ($6.50).

Hiring foreign workers

When you're hiring new workers, no matter what their nationality, the federal Immigration Reform and Control Act (IRCA) requires that you verify the workers' identities and right to work. (This requirement holds true if you employ workers at your home as domestic or gardening help or to perform some other kind of work.) This provision of the law is intended to help reduce the number of illegal workers in this country and does not apply to independent contractors or to people who may work for you on a very occasional basis because they're not considered employees.

According to the Immigration and Naturalization Service (INS), which enforces this law, you can use many different types of documents to verify both identity and eligibility to work. These documents include a U.S. passport, a certificate of naturalization, a certificate of U.S. citizenship,

and a green card. Identity alone can be verified with a U.S. driver's license or other photo ID, voter registration card, or school ID. The INS also has a separate list of documents that can prove employment eligibility only.

Both you and the new employee must also complete an INS 1-9 form, which confirms that the person has the right work in the U.S. To obtain a small number of these forms, you can contact the INS office closest to you or call the main INS office in Washington, D.C. at 202-514-4330. If you want to buy the forms in bulk, write to the Superintendent of Documents, U.S. Government Printing Office, Washington, D.C. 20402. The INS also allows you to photocopy extra 1-9 forms.

Failure to meet the IRCA's provisions can result in stiff monetary fines and even imprisonment.

If your misclassifications are significant, you may not be able to recover from your mistakes. Bankruptcy may be your best option if there is no way that you can come up with the payroll tax dollars you should have been paying plus the interest and penalties.

Patents, Copyrights, and Trademarks

Depending on the nature of your business, patents, copyrights, and trademarks (or intellectual property rights) may be important to you. Why? Read on.

Patents

Patents provide inventors, and society in general, a number of important benefits. For example, they encourage people to invent. Without patents, we might never have had the telephone, the computer, the airplane, and other innovations that have helped transform society.

Patents also make it easier for inventors to attract the money they need to transform their invention into something that they can market and sell or license.

Patents can only be granted for new and useful inventions and discoveries related to the following:

- ✔ Processes
- ✔ Machines
- ✔ Manufactured articles
- ✔ Compositions of matter, which means chemical compositions and compounds as well as some mixtures of ingredients — medicines, for example
- ✔ Improvements in any of the above

If you invent something new — how about a better mouse trap? — and if you want to "exclude others from making, using, or selling" your invention, you must complete a patent application and file it with the Federal Patent and Trademark Office in Washington.

In the application, you have to describe your invention in considerable detail, including how to make and use it. You may also have to provide a prototype. After you file your application and pay the fee, a lengthy review process begins, and it can take at least a year to complete. If you're granted a patent, you have to pay other fees as well. Your patent is good throughout the U.S. and in all of its territories and possessions.

You can prepare the application yourself, but you're probably better off hiring a registered patent attorney or patent agent to help you. Although they don't come cheap, their knowledge of federal patent law and of the inner workings of the Patent Office itself can be a time-saver and can give you a better shot at getting your invention patented.

According to law, only attorneys and agents recognized by the U.S. Patent Office can represent inventors before the Office. The Patent Office maintains a registry of these attorneys and agents, which can be purchased for a small fee through the Superintendent of Documents, Government Printing Office (GPO), Washington, D.C. 20402.

If you're approached by a company claiming to be an invention marketing business, check it out carefully. To get your money, these businesses exaggerate the potential of your invention, do a haphazard patent search, get you a worthless patent, and do little if any marketing.

When you get a patent, what you're actually getting is time — 20 years after your application is filed — to develop your idea into something you can make money from and the right to exclude others from doing the same. Meanwhile, your application information is available to the general public so that others can use the information to try and develop new inventions of their own, which they in turn can try to patent. And so it goes. . . .

If someone violates your patent, the federal government will not help you enforce it or bring legal action against the violator. You have to file a lawsuit in federal district court to collect damages and/or to prevent further infringements on your patent.

Ideas cannot be patented, but an idea can help create something that can be patented.

Copyrights

The Federal Copyright Act of 1976 allows original created works, including books, software, CD-ROMs, films, artwork, music, and so on to be copyrighted in order to prevent others from copying them without your permission and/or without paying you a fee. For example, I have the copyright on this book! When you copyright something, it means that the entire time your copyright is in effect, you have exclusive right to copy, perform, or display the copyrighted work. A business copyright lasts for 100 years from the time the work was created or for 75 years after the date of publication, whichever is longer. If an individual has a copyright, it lasts for as long as that person is alive plus an additional 50 years.

Copyright law allows for *fair use* of copyrighted material and establishes criteria for determining fair use.

An idea cannot be copyrighted, but the expression of an idea in a work can be. Nor can works whose value is totally utilitarian and not expressive in any way be copyrighted. So if you build a functional table in your workshop at home out of scrap wood with unique utilitarian features, you can't copyright the table; but you may want to patent it. On the other hand, if you create a table out of an old tree, carving the table base into the shape of a tree trunk and carving branches to hold up the table's glass top, that table can have a copyright by virtue of its creative design. On the other hand, a uniquely-designed table whose unique-ness is not in its artistic qualities but in its utility may qualify for a patent.

Getting a copyright is significantly easier than getting a patent. In fact, there is no application process. As soon as your create a work that can be copyrighted, it's copyrighted! It's as easy as that.

To be able to sue someone for infringing your copyright, you must register it with the Library of Congress in Washington. Call 202-707-3000 for a copyright application.

In most cases, if one of your employees creates an original work as part of his or her job, the copyright belongs to you, the employer, not to your employee. So if you create packaging for CD-ROMs, you have the copyright on the designs that your employees create while they're on the job. You are also free, however, to work out another arrangement with an employee by drawing up a written agreement to that effect, signed by both of you.

If you sue someone for violating your copyright, your lawsuit will be heard in federal court. To win your case, you have to prove the infringement, not that you suffered actual damages, and your monetary reward can be as much as $500,000.

Trademarks

A trademark is something that you can use to identify your business's product and distinguish it from others. A trademark can be a name, symbol, shape, device, or even a word. Service marks are similar but apply to a business service. Well-known trademarks include Apple, Häagen-Dazs, and Kodak. McDonald's is a highly visible service mark.

Make sure that no one else is using the trademark you want.

Although you don't have to go through an application process to get a trademark (you get one simply by being the first to use it, and you keep it as long as you continue using it), it's a good idea to register your trademark with the U.S. Patent Office. Being federally registered gives you the right to sue in federal court and recover treble damages for unlawful use of your trademark. Registration involves completing an application, providing samples of your trademark, and paying a fee.

You can get a state trademark, but a federal trademark provides more protection and is good in all states. A state trademark is good only in the state that grants it.

Bankruptcy

I hate to close this chapter with a discussion of an unhappy subject such as bankruptcy. But in fact, it's a fitting last subject because every year, thousands of small businesses end up in bankruptcy.

Businesses have a legal right to file bankruptcy as a way of protecting themselves from the collection actions of their creditors. Some businesses exercise this right because their financial problems are so severe that they can't remain in business. Others use bankruptcy as a way to stay in business.

The federal Bankruptcy Code recognizes many types of bankruptcy. The four most common are Chapters 11, 12, and 13, which are all reorganization bankruptcies, and Chapter 7, which is a liquidation bankruptcy.

Reorganization bankruptcies

Reorganization bankruptcies allow businesses to remain in business by working with the court and their creditors to develop a debt payment plan that enables them to repay much of their debt in a manner that they can afford over a three to five year period. (If you file Chapter 11, you may get more time to pay off your debt.) While a business is in a reorganization bankruptcy, the court protects it from the collection actions of its creditors. If you file a reorganization bankruptcy, you are allowed to run your business without the court's interference while your bankruptcy is ongoing.

Chapter 13 reorganization is only available to sole proprietorships that have no more than $250,000 in unsecured debt and $750,000 in secured debt. Partnerships and corporations cannot use Chapter 13. Chapter 12 reorganization is available to family farmers. Partnerships and corporations must use Chapter 11 to reorganize.

Because Chapter 11 reorganization is significantly more time-consuming and costly than Chapter 13, a significant proportion of the businesses that file Chapter 11 are ultimately forced into Chapter 7 and out of business.

Often, when a partnership files for bankruptcy, its partners end up filing too. As individuals, though, they are eligible for Chapter 13, depending on the amount of their debt. Chapter 13 deals with their personal debt obligations; it cannot be used to reorganize their business.

Chapter 7 bankruptcy

Any kind of business can file a liquidation bankruptcy, which wipes out most of its debts. This action is usually your best option when your business is so debt-ridden and your income so inadequate that there is little chance of you being able to repay your debts and stay in business. Certain kinds of debts, such as taxes, remain, however, and you still have to pay them. Also, you may lose business property when you file Chapter 7, depending on whether your business is a sole proprietorship, partnership, or corporation.

If your financial situation is bad enough, your creditors have the right to force you into bankruptcy by filing an involuntary Chapter 7 bankruptcy.

As soon as serious financial trouble begins, consult with a bankruptcy attorney. The sooner the better. If you have this meeting soon enough, the attorney may actually be able to suggest things you can do to address your financial woes and avoid bankruptcy. Also, the attorney can tell you the things you shouldn't do if you're thinking about filing because certain actions can diminish the potential benefits of bankruptcy. For example, if within 60 days of filing, you run up with a single creditor more than $1,000 worth of debt on luxury goods and services, or if you get a cash advance for that amount, bankruptcy does not wipe out those debts. Also, if you pay one of your unsecured creditors but don't pay any of the others within 90 days of filing, the court can void that payment and get your money back.

Although filing bankruptcy has less of a stigma attached to it than it used to, bankruptcy damages your personal and/or your business's credit record and makes it tough to get new credit at competitive terms for at least seven to ten years — the length of time a bankruptcy stays on a credit record. It's tough enough to build a successful business without having to overcome a bankruptcy.

Bankruptcy is your best response when . . .

✔ You owe back taxes and the IRS is breathing down your neck, threatening to get its money by seizing your business or personal property, by taking money from your bank accounts, or by shutting your business down and liquidating its assets.

✔ Your business owes more to creditors than it can pay, and your creditors are unwilling to negotiate new debt payment plans that you can afford.

✔ Your secured creditors are threatening to take their collateral.

✔ Your business's landlord is threatening to evict you.

Chapter 8

Credit: Getting It, Using It, Losing It

● ●

In This Chapter

▶ Applying for credit

▶ Dealing with credit records and credit bureaus

▶ Protecting yourself from debt collectors

▶ Filing for bankruptcy

● ●

*U*sing credit is the American way. In fact, not having access to it can limit your choices and opportunities in life — it's a necessary evil! For example, without credit, it would probably be close to impossible for you to purchase something as expensive as a new home or car or to pay for your child's college education unless you won the lottery or your rich uncle left you a pile of money. Also, not having credit makes even relatively minor financial transactions like renting a car, reserving a hotel room, or ordering something through the mail more difficult.

As helpful as credit may be, it can also be dangerous. A wallet full of credit cards or a checking account with overdraft protection can get you in a lot of trouble. They can make it all too easy to spend more than you earn. And if you don't make your debt payments on time, you not only end up paying late fees, penalties, and high rates of interest, but you can also damage your credit record, possibly lose your right to use credit, and worst-case scenario, end up in bankruptcy.

Considering the benefits and the dangers of using credit, if you're going to have it, you should know about the federal laws that relate to getting, using, and losing credit. Some of these laws protect you from being discriminated against when you're applying for credit or ensure that you have the information you need to evaluate and compare credit offers. Other laws give you certain rights when you use credit or when you have trouble paying your bills. Still other laws regulate the powers of credit bureaus — powerful, data-rich companies that collect and sell vast amounts of information on virtually every American consumer — and give you the right to file bankruptcy as a means of gaining protection from your creditors when your debts exceed your ability to pay them.

Call your attorney general or state consumer protection office to find out about your state's consumer credit laws. They may give you more rights and protections than the federal laws do.

Getting Credit

Two federal laws protect you when you're applying for credit: the Equal Credit Opportunity Act (ECOA) and the Truth in Lending Act (TLA).

The Equal Credit Opportunity Act

This law says that when you apply for credit, you must be evaluated on the basis of your credit-worthiness only, not on factors that have nothing to do with your ability to repay your debt. The law applies to any creditor who regularly extends credit to consumers, including banks, retailers, bankcard companies, finance companies, and credit unions.

The ECOA and creditors

Among other things, the ECOA says that it's illegal for these creditors to

- Discriminate against you because of your race, sex, age, national origin, or marital status, or because you receive public assistance.

- Ask about your marital status if you're applying for separate, unsecured credit, with one exception: You can be asked about your marital status if you live in a community property state. No matter what state you live in, however, you can be asked about your marital status when you apply for joint credit (credit you and your spouse share) or when the credit is secured or collateralized with property you own.

- Ask whether you have children or plan to have them.

- Consider your age, with certain exceptions.

- Disallow regular sources of income, such as reliable Veteran's benefits, welfare payments, Social Security payments, alimony, child support, and so on. Nor may they refuse to consider or discount any income you earn from a part-time job, pension, annuity, or retirement benefits program.

The ECOA also says that creditors must do the following:

- Let you know whether you've been denied or granted credit within 30 days of receiving your completed application.

✔ Give you a specific reason (or tell you how to get the reason) why you're denied credit or granted less credit than what you applied for. This same rule applies if a creditor closes your account, refuses to increase your line of credit, makes a negative change in the terms of your credit and doesn't make the same change for other consumers, or refuses to give you credit at the same, or approximately the same, terms as were offered when you initially applied for the credit.

Special help for women

When the ECOA was written, it was common for women not to work outside the home and to have little or no credit in their own names. If they became divorced or widowed, they found it very difficult to build a life for themselves on their own because they had no credit history, even though they may have managed their families' finances. They were credit nonentities in the eyes of banks, credit card companies, and other sources of credit. The ECOA therefore included provisions specifically written to help women build credit histories in their own names, separate from their husbands'. The ECOA is an equal opportunity law, though, which means that if necessary, men can use the law to help them build credit identities apart from their wives as well.

To help each spouse build his or her own credit history, the law says that you have the right to the following:

✔ Get credit in your birth name, your first name, and your spouse's last name, or in your first name and a combined last name, such as a hyphenated last name.

✔ Get credit without a cosigner, assuming you meet the creditor's standards.

✔ Have a cosigner other than your spouse if you need one.

✔ Keep your own accounts if your marital status changes or if you change your name, assuming you will be able to continue making payments on those accounts.

A creditor can ask you to update your credit application or reapply for credit after your marital status changes, and on the basis of the new information, the creditor can take your credit away or change its terms.

✔ Have information on accounts you share with your spouse (joint accounts) reported in both of your names.

The law also requires all creditors to provide credit record information to the credit bureaus that they report to in the names of both the spouses when a husband and wife share an account.

To be sure that information on all of your credit accounts is being reported in your name, request a copy of your credit record from the three major credit bureaus, TRW, Trans Union, and Equifax. Instructions for doing so appear later in this chapter.

Help! My credit card is missing!

If your credit card turns up missing, and no matter whether it's been stolen or lost, the TLA says that once you notify — call, don't write — the company that issued it, you do not have to pay any more than the first $50 in unauthorized charges. Obviously, the sooner you report the missing credit card, the better.

To help ensure that you don't encounter any delays in notifying companies about your missing credit cards, make a list of the phone numbers to call and keep it in a safe, accessible place. The numbers should be indicated on the back of your cards.

The Truth in Lending Act (TLA)

This law says that before you sign a credit installment agreement (a contract to pay back what you borrow by making monthly payments), the creditor must give you certain information to help you understand the cost and terms of the credit so that you can compare it to alternative credit sources. The TLA applies to banks, retailers, bankcard companies, credit unions, and others.

The TLA says that you must be given written information that states the amount you're financing, the number of payments you're obligating yourself to make, the dollar amount of your monthly payments, the rate of interest you'll pay on the credit, and most important, the credit's annual percentage rate or APR — its annualized cost.

Another important provision of the TLA helps protect you when you apply for financing and use your home as collateral. (It does not apply to a home mortgage loan.) It says that you have three days, not including Saturdays, Sundays, and legal public holidays, after signing an agreement to notify the lender *in writing* that you've changed your mind and want to cancel the loan. This is the *right of rescission.* For this right to apply, however, you must have signed the agreement in your home or at another location other than at the lender's office. For example, a contractor agrees to help finance the home improvements he is going to perform for you, and you sign the paperwork in your living room.

Using Credit

After you have credit, it's your responsibility to use it wisely, which means making your payments on time and in full and resolving billing and other credit-related problems as quickly as possible so that they don't damage your credit record.

Wise use of credit also means not having too much of it. If you do, and you start being late with your payments or stop making them entirely, your credit record can be damaged, you may begin getting calls from debt collectors, you may lose some of your property, and you may even end up in bankruptcy. In short, your life can become full of stress and worry.

Every time you apply for new credit or for an increase in your credit limit, the creditor reviews your credit record. Each review shows up on your credit record as an "inquiry." Creditors do not like to see a lot of inquiries and are less apt to extend new or additional credit to those who have "too many."

And now, a few words about credit records and credit bureaus

If you have credit, information about who you owe money to, how much you owe, whether or not you pay your bills on time, and a lot more is being collected about you by at least one of the "Big Three" national credit reporting agencies: TRW, Equifax, and Trans Union. In addition, one or more of the nearly 1,000 smaller credit bureaus, most of which are owned or affiliated by one of the Big Three, may also be collecting and storing information about you.

The Fair Credit Reporting Act (FCRA) is the federal law that regulates the activities of the credit bureaus that comprise the powerful, billion-dollar credit reporting industry.

The FCRA was written in the 1970s before computerization changed the face of the credit and credit reporting industry. Although amendments to the FCRA have been introduced in Congress to curb credit bureau powers and to strengthen the ability of the Federal Trade Commission to enforce the FCRA, none have been adopted, and consumers remain inadequately protected.

Where credit record information comes from

Credit bureaus get their information from three main sources:

- ✔ Their subscribers, the creditors who provide information to credit bureaus on how well the consumers to whom they've extended credit are meeting the terms of their credit agreements. Subscribers include banks, credit card companies, large retailers, and so on.

- ✔ Public records. These records tell credit bureaus if you have any tax liens on your property or any judgments against you, or if you've filed for bankruptcy.

- ✔ You. When you complete a credit application, you provide basic information about yourself, such as your Social Security number, age, home address, employer, and so on.

An overview of your FCRA rights

Given the power and influence that credit reporting agencies can have in your life, it's important to be familiar with your rights when you're dealing with them. For example, the law says that you have the right to

✔ Know what's in your credit record.

✔ A free copy of your credit report if you're denied credit, insurance, or employment due to information in your record. By law, you must request your free copy within 30 days of being notified of your denial; however, the Big Three and other credit reporting agencies affiliated with them have voluntarily extended this deadline to 60 days.

✔ Request a copy of your credit report even if you've not been denied credit.

✔ Have a credit bureau investigate information in your credit record that you believe is wrong.

✔ Have information that you contend is wrong or outdated deleted from your credit record if the credit bureau can confirm its inaccuracy or can't verify it.

✔ Have a written statement included in your credit record explaining any negative information it may contain. For example, you may want potential creditors to know that you were late on your debt payments in 1994 because your spouse was hospitalized and the costs of medical care took every penny you had.

✔ Have most negative information automatically deleted from your credit record after seven years although Chapter 7 bankruptcies remain for ten years. (The Big Three and many other credit reporting agencies report Chapter 13 bankruptcies for seven, not ten, years.)

How credit record information is used

Credit bureaus sell their information to creditors, employers, insurers and to anyone with "a legitimate business need" to know what you owe, how you manage your credit, and other information in your credit record.

When you apply for credit, the creditor orders a copy of your credit record and reviews it as part of its credit-granting process. If your credit record includes enough negative information, you may be denied the credit you applied for. Also, insurance companies may check your credit record to decide whether to insure you, and an employer may review it as part of its hiring or promotion decision-making process.

Getting in touch with the Big Three credit reporting agencies

It's a good idea to request a copy of your credit report at least once per year to make sure that it's accurate and so that you can correct any problems in it. Also, if you're denied a job, insurance, or credit due to credit record information, you should review your credit report to make sure that the denial wasn't due to inaccurate or outdated information.

Before applying for a mortgage loan or any other really important credit, request a copy of your report from whichever credit reporting agency the creditor reports to so that you can be sure that it doesn't include inaccurate information that can hurt your chances of getting the credit you want.

If you don't understand something in your credit report, call the credit reporting agency that sent you the report and ask for help. The agency is legally required to have staff available to help you understand the information in your report.

To obtain a copy of your credit record, you need to provide the credit bureau with the following information: your full name (including Jr., Sr., the II, the III, and so on if you use any of these regularly); your date of birth; your current address and your previous address if you've not been at your present residence for at least five years; your Social Security number; your spouse's name and Social Security number if you're married; your daytime and evening phone numbers; and proof of your name and current address — a copy of your driver's license and a utility bill, for example.

TRW's home page (http://www.trw.com/iss) not only provides basic information about its credit reporting services but also offers helpful answers to many questions that consumers have concerning credit-related issues.

What follows are some guidelines for requesting your credit report:

If you want to check the report for accuracy, contact . . .

TRW
National Consumer Assistance Center
P.O. Box 2104
Allen, Texas 75013
800-682-7654

Trans Union
National Consumer Disclosure Center
P.O. Box 390
Springfield, PA 19064-0390
610-690-4904

Equifax
Office of Consumer Affairs
P.O. Box 105873
Atlanta, GA 30348
800-685-1111

In most states, at the time this book was written, the price of your credit record is $8.00 plus state sales tax. Some states have set a lower price. Call your state attorney general's office or state consumer protection office for the exact cost in your state.

Also, TRW offers consumers one free copy of their credit report every year, and some states have laws that require all credit bureaus to make this offer.

If you want to request TRW's free annual credit report, contact . . .

TRW
P.O. Box 8030
Layton, UT 84041-8030
800-682-7654

*If you've been denied credit, employment, or insurance
and want to request your credit report, contact . . .*

TRW
National Consumer Assistance Center
P.O. Box 949
Allen, Texas 75002-0949
800-682-7654

Trans Union
National Consumer Disclosure Center
P. O. Box 309
Springfield, PA 19064-0390
610-690-4940

Equifax
P.O. Box 105873
Atlanta, GA 30348
800-685-1111

Correcting credit record problems

If you discover a problem in your credit report, immediately write a letter to the credit reporting agency that sent you the report explaining what you think is wrong; attach copies of any documentation you may have that supports your opinion. Make a copy of your letter for your files and send your correspondence to the credit reporting agency via certified mail with return receipt requested.

If you're dealing with one of the Big Three, when they send you a copy of your credit report, it usually comes with a *research request* or *investigation request form.* If it does, complete the form and return it, together with a letter if necessary, as well as copies of your supporting documentation. In some parts of the country, instead of sending consumers a form, the Big Three provides them a number to call for instructions regarding how to initiate an investigation into a credit record problem.

After the credit bureau receives your communication, it contacts the creditor or the public agency that reported the information you're disputing so that they can confirm its accuracy. If the creditor or agency says the information is correct, it stays in your credit record. But if the creditor says, "Yes, it's wrong," or if the credit reporting agency can't confirm the accuracy or inaccuracy of the information that you're questioning within 30 days of your letter, the FCRA says that the information must be deleted from your record.

The FCRA does not specify how thoroughly a credit reporting agency must investigate your credit record problem. Generally, if a creditor or public agency says, "I'm right, and the consumer is wrong," the credit bureau will take them at their word.

The FCRA is vague regarding how quickly a credit reporting agency must respond when it's contacted about a credit record inaccuracy. The law says that you must hear back within a "reasonable period of time." Recently however, the Big Three and most other credit bureaus voluntarily adopted a policy of trying to respond to a consumer query within 30 days, and they delete any negative information that they can't confirm within the same period.

If your credit record problem is corrected, the credit reporting agency should send you a revised credit report. But if you are not successful at getting the erroneous or outdated information removed from your credit record and if you continue to believe that your report is in error, here are some other things to try:

- ✔ Provide the agency with new documentation.
- ✔ Contact the creditor directly about the problem and send it a complete set of supporting documentation.
- ✔ Call your state attorney general's office or state consumer protection office to see if any state laws can help you.
- ✔ Send a letter to the FTC and copies of it to the creditor and credit bureau.
- ✔ Consider mediation.

Also, the FCRA gives you the right to prepare a short statement — no more than 100 words — explaining why you think your credit record is wrong. The statement must become a permanent part of your credit record.

Although they may help, written statements are of limited impact. There is no guarantee that anyone will read your statement when you apply for credit, employment, or insurance.

To help make sure that potential creditors, insurers, or employers read the information in your written statement, it's a good idea to give them a copy of it when you're applying for credit, insurance, or a job.

I don't think I owe this!

Check your monthly bankcard and charge card statements to make sure that they accurately reflect the payments you've made, that your account balance is correct, and that they don't show any charges to your account that you didn't make or didn't authorize. If you do find problems with a statement, the federal Fair Credit Billing Act (FCBA) spells out a process you need to use to resolve the problems, and it provides you with special protections while you're pursuing the process.

The FCBA also helps if you have problems with overdrafts from your checking account.

If you discover a problem, write the creditor about the problem within 60 days after you receive the first bill with the incorrect information. Succinctly explain the problem and note the dollar amount involved, all relevant dates, your name and address as it appears on your billing statement, and your account number. Include copies of any sales slips or other documentation that provide proof that you're correct. Make a copy of the letter for your files and send the original certified mail, return receipt requested, to the billing inquiries address listed on your statement.

Calling a creditor about a billing statement problem does not activate the protections of the FCBA. And don't send your dispute letter with your account payment. It may not get to the appropriate person.

While you're waiting for a response from your creditor, keep the following in mind:

- ✔ You don't have to pay the amount you're disputing or any related finance charges. The charge may continue to appear on your bill, however.
- ✔ You must continue making payments on the rest of your account.
- ✔ The amount you're disputing can be applied to your total credit limit.
- ✔ Your creditor cannot report the amount you're disputing to a credit bureau or threaten to damage your credit record.
- ✔ Your creditor cannot close your account or threaten you with legal action.

The creditor must acknowledge your letter in writing within 30 days of getting it. Within 90 days or two billing cycles, the creditor must either tell you why your bill is accurate or correct it, crediting your account for the amount in dispute and for all related finance charges, late fees, and so on.

If the creditor maintains that your bill is correct, the creditor must provide you with a written statement of exactly how much you owe and why. You may also ask to be provided supporting documentation.

If you continue to disagree with the creditor, you have ten days after receiving its explanation of what you owe and why to write back that you will still not pay the amount in dispute. At this point, however, the creditor can begin reporting you as delinquent to the credit bureaus it reports to and can initiate collection action against you. But as long as you've protested in writing within the ten-day time frame, when the creditor reports you as delinquent, it must also report that you don't believe that you owe the money.

Bankcard Holders of America is an excellent organization that offers a wide variety of excellent, low-cost brochures on using bankcards and credit in general. To get a list of its publications, write to 524 Branch Drive, Salem, VA 24153 or call 540-389-5445.

When You Can't Pay Your Bills

If you begin having trouble paying your bills, contact your creditors immediately! Let them know that you're having trouble and ask them if you can make smaller, or interest-only monthly payments for a certain period of time. Also, tell them what you're doing to get your financial situation stabilized. If you don't get in contact and just ignore your bills, hoping they'll just go away (fat chance of that!), you can expect to begin receiving calls or letters from debt collectors, and you'll be damaging your credit record.

If you want help negotiating lower monthly debt payments, contact the Consumer Credit Counseling Service (CCCS). The CCCS is a national, nonprofit organization that can help you get your financial situation under control. It contacts your creditors for you. To locate the office closest to you, call 800-388-2227.

Quality problems with merchandise or services

The sofa you ordered looked so attractive at the furniture store, but when it's finally delivered to your home, its legs are wobbly and there's a tear in the upholstery. You try to get the store to replace the new sofa with another one, but to no avail.

Luckily, because you purchased your sofa with a store charge card, the FCBA can help you. It says that after you've given the merchant an opportunity to resolve the problem, you have a legal right to withhold payment. After you've notified the card issuer of your intention, it cannot report your account to credit bureaus as delinquent or close your account while the dispute is ongoing, but the business can sue you for nonpayment. The FCBA also applies to defective or shoddy services provided by a business.

If you used a bankcard or a travel and entertainment card — not a store-issued charge card — to make your purchase, the FCBA applies only if you made your purchase in your home state or within 100 miles of your current mailing address, and the amount of the purchase must be more than $50. If these criteria don't apply, you may want to sue the business in small claims court.

Dealing with debt collectors

It's 9 a.m. Monday morning and the debt collectors have started calling again. Just what you need! It's bad enough that you've lost your job and are having trouble finding another one and are worried about the stack of unpaid bills on your desk. You don't need debt collectors adding to the stress and worry you're feeling — if you could pay them, you would! But right now, you barely have enough money to buy groceries, put gas in your car, and pay your utility bills!

If you're being hounded by debt collectors, there's a federal law that can help you. It's the Fair Debt Collection Practices Act (FDCPA). The law regulates the activities of debt collectors, including attorneys who regularly collect consumer debts, and gives you certain rights when dealing with them. Here are some of the law's most important provisions:

✔ A debt collector can contact you between 8 a.m. and 9 p.m. But you have the right to indicate in writing that you'd prefer to be contacted at another time, and the debt collector must honor your request. Also, if your employer doesn't want you to be contacted during working hours and you tell the debt collector in writing to stop calling you at work, the calls must stop.

✔ A debt collector can contact you by phone, fax, mail, in person, or by telegram. To protect your privacy, however, a debt collector cannot send you a postcard that mentions your debt or send you an envelope that has anything on it that lets someone know that it came from a debt collector.

✔ After a debt collector contacts you for the first time about your debt, you must be sent a written notice no more than five days later telling you how much you owe, who you owe it to, and what you can do if you don't think you owe it.

✔ You can send a debt collector a letter saying that you don't want to be contacted anymore except to be informed of any additional steps the debt collector or creditor intends to take to collect from you. The debt collector must honor your request.

✔ A debt collector cannot contact anyone about your debt except to find out where you live or work.

✔ A debt collector cannot threaten you with physical harm or harm to your reputation, use profanity, or make false statements as a way to pressure you into paying. Also, you cannot be threatened with deductions from your paychecks or with a lawsuit unless the debt collector or your creditor actually intends to take action and is legally entitled to do so.

Although the FDCPA does not apply to in-house collection departments, your state may have a law that regulates what they can do.

More extreme measures

If a debt collector doesn't scare you into paying what you owe, and serious damage to your credit record doesn't scare you either, your creditor may decide to "turn up the heat, " which can involve suing you and taking legal action to garnish your wages, if your state allows such action, or seizing some of your property and selling it. (Every state exempts certain kinds of property from seizure and sale. Exempt property usually includes most household items and the car you use for work, unless it's collateralizing a loan.)

✔ If a creditor sues you, all of the lawsuit procedures and processes explained in Chapter 1 apply.

✔ If a creditor seizes some of your property, it will probably be auctioned off, and the proceeds will go towards paying your debt. If the property sells for more than the amount of your debt, you get the excess.

✔ If your wages are garnished, your employer must begin paying some portion of your paycheck to your creditor. Federal law, however, limits how much creditors can garnish from each check and the kinds of debts that garnishment can be used for.

If you're having trouble paying off your student loan, don't assume that if you default on it, you get special treatment. The lender can use the services of a debt collector to collect from you, can sue you for nonpayment, and can report your delinquency to credit bureaus. What a way to start life after college!

If you owe what the debt collector is trying to collect, make payment arrangements immediately. Don't delay; otherwise, the creditor may decide to pursue more extreme measures to collect what you owe, and the longer you put off paying the debt, the more damage you'll do to your credit record.

If you don't think you owe the money or if you disagree with how much the debt collector says you owe, write to the debt collector no later than 30 days after being contacted. The debt collector must stop communicating with you. Collection efforts can resume, however, if the debt collector sends you proof of your debt.

If you think your rights have been violated

Here's what to do if you think that your legal rights have been violated:

✔ Make sure that you understand your rights. Call the Federal Trade Commission's Office of Consumer and Business Education in Washington, D.C. (202-326-3650) and the office of your attorney general or state office of consumer affairs to clarify your rights. Be aware of any deadlines you must meet in order to exercise your legal rights or anything special you may need to do to trigger the protection of the law.

✔ After you understand your rights, write or call the creditor or debt collector you're having a problem with and mention the law you feel has been violated. If your problem is serious, always put your concern in writing and keep a copy of your letter. If you call rather than write, keep a record of who you speak with and the upshot of your conversation. This information can be helpful if you have to take further action to resolve your problem.

✔ If your problem is not resolved or if you're unhappy with the solution proposed by the creditor or debt collector, recontact the office of your state attorney general or state consumer protection office. Your state laws may offer you greater protection than federal laws.

Also, file a formal complaint with the Federal Trade Commission's Division of Credit Practices, Bureau of Consumer Protection, Washington, D.C. 20580. Although the FTC will not act on behalf of a individual consumer, if it receives enough complaints about a specific creditor, it may take action. If your complaint is about a financial institution's violation of a credit law, complain directly to the agency that regulates it. (See the following list.)

Under federal law, you also have the right to hire an attorney and sue the creditor or debt collector that's violating the law. Usually, you can sue for actual, and sometimes punitive, damages. If you win, you can collect attorney fees and court costs.

Here's who to contact when you believe that a financial institution has violated your rights:

If the creditor is a nationally-chartered bank, write to

Comptroller of the Currency
Compliance Management
Mail Stop 7-5
Washington, D.C. 20219

If the creditor is a state-chartered bank that is insured by the Federal Deposit Insurance Corporation and is a member of the Federal Reserve System, write to

Consumer and Community Affairs
Board of Governors of the Federal Reserve System
20th and C Sts., N.W.
Washington, D.C. 20551

If the creditor is a state-chartered bank that is insured by the Federal Deposit Insurance Corporation but is *not* a member of the Federal Reserve System, write to

Federal Deposit Insurance Corporation
Consumer Affairs Division
550 Seventh St., N. W.
Washington, D.C. 20429

If your complaint is with a federally-insured savings and loan or federally-chartered state bank, write to

Consumer Affairs Program
1770 G St., N.W.
Washington. D.C. 20552

If your complaint is with a federally-chartered credit union, write to

National Credit Union Administration
Consumer Affairs Division
1776 G Street, N.W.
Washington, D.C. 20456

Taking the pressure off (filing for bankruptcy)

Sometimes, when you're drowning in debt, hounded by your creditors, and maybe even threatened by the IRS, filing for bankruptcy can be your best option. After you file a bankruptcy petition with the U.S. Bankruptcy Court and pay the appropriate fee, an automatic stay will be issued, requiring all of your creditors to cease their collection actions. No more calls from debt collectors; no more threats and letters. Although your financial troubles aren't over, the automatic stay eases the pressure.

Before you file for bankruptcy, schedule an appointment with the CCCS office closest to you to see if the counselors there can help you work out a debt repayment plan that allows you to avoid filing.

Although you can go through bankruptcy without the help of an attorney, it's always best to hire one. Bankruptcy is complicated, and dealing with the court and your creditors can be frightening. A good bankruptcy attorney can help you avoid costly mistakes, help you keep as much of your property as possible, serve as intermediary between you and your creditors, and answer your questions. Some states certify attorneys in bankruptcy.

FindLaw's Web page on bankruptcy law (`http://www.findlaw.com/01topics/03bankruptcy/index.html`) offers consumers a wealth of useful information and resources. You can read about bankruptcy law, learn about federal banruptcy resources, gain information on alternatives to bankruptcy, and access other Internet bankruptcy resources.

Things you should never do before filing

When you're in the middle of a financial crisis, you may be tempted to take the pressure off by doing things that will not be helpful later if you decide to file for bankruptcy. That's why it's always a good idea to consult with a bankruptcy attorney when you're having serious money troubles but may not have decided to file bankruptcy. Here are some of the things the attorney will tell you not to do:

✔ Don't give your creditors postdated checks. If they bounce, you can be charged with a criminal offense, and bankruptcy won't protect you from criminal prosecution.

✔ Don't transfer any of your property to your friends, family, or anyone else with the hope that you can keep it out of your bankruptcy and then get it back later. If you do, the bankruptcy trustee — the court official who supervises your bankruptcy — may cancel the transfer and take the property back. Also, if you try to conceal any transfers and are discovered, you can be accused of fraud.

✔ Don't use your credit cards to run up more than $1,000 worth of debt for luxury goods or services with a single creditor within 60 days of filing. Also, don't get a cash advance of more than $1,000 within 60 days of filing. Neither debt can be wiped out by your bankruptcy.

✔ Don't pay one creditor at the expense of other creditors within 90 days of filing. If you do, the trustee can void that payment and distribute the money more fairly among your creditors.

✔ Don't voluntarily give up an asset you really need, like your car.

Depending on the type of bankruptcy you file, most of your debt will be erased, and you won't have to pay it, or you'll have an opportunity to reorganize your debt. Reorganization involves paying off your debts by making smaller payments — amounts you can afford — over a three- to five-year period.

Despite the undeniable benefits of bankruptcy, you should always consider it your option of last resort. That's because filing for bankruptcy seriously damages your credit record and because the FCRA says it can stay on your credit record for up to ten years. Remember, most credit problems only stay there for seven years. While bankruptcy is on your record, you will find it next to impossible to get new credit, or at least credit with reasonable terms. You may not be able to borrow money to buy a home or to help send your child to college, and you may not be able to get a national bankcard.

Regardless of what type of bankruptcy you file, the legal process is governed by the federal Bankruptcy Code. There are no state bankruptcy laws.

The two most common types of consumer bankruptcies are Chapter 7 and Chapter 13.

Chapter 7

Chapter 7 is a liquidation bankruptcy. It's an appropriate choice when you have so much debt compared to your income that there is no way you will be able to pay back what you owe. When you file Chapter 7, most, but not all, of your debts are wiped out. You also lose some of your property — your nonexempt assets. These assets are sold, and the proceeds are used to help repay your creditors.

Federal bankruptcy law includes a list of the types of property that you can claim as exempt when you file Chapter 7. Your state has its own list. In some states, you can chose between the federal list of exemptions and your state's — whichever is best for you.

In Chapter 7, certain types of debts must be paid off before others. Priority debts must be repaid first. These debts include taxes and the administrative expenses of bankruptcy. In many Chapter 7s, unsecured debts are never repaid because not enough funds are available from the sale of a consumer's nonexempt assets. In fact, often, the only debts that can be paid off are some of the consumer's priority debts.

Chapter 7 does not erase (*discharge* is the legal term) all of your debt — no such luck! You still have to pay off some of them. Although not a complete list, what follows are some of the types of debt that remain after your bankruptcy is over:

- ✔ Alimony and child support payments
- ✔ Most taxes
- ✔ Some educational loans
- ✔ Fines and penalties that government entities have charged you with
- ✔ Any debts you incur after you file

Chapter 13

Chapter 13 is a reorganization bankruptcy. You are allowed to lower most of your debt payments to levels that you can afford to make, and you have three to five years to pay off your debt. Your plan for getting out of debt must be formalized in a reorganization plan and approved by the court. Although you are expected to pay off as much of your debt as possible, some of your unsecured debt — debt that is not collateralized — may be wiped out in Chapter 13.

If you owe more than $250,000 in unsecured debt and more than $750,000 in secured debt, you can't reorganize using Chapter 13 and must use Chapter 11 instead. This type of reorganization bankruptcy is more expensive and complicated, and a high percentage of those who use it end up converting to a Chapter 7 liquidation. Big businesses most often use Chapter 11.

After bankruptcy

After your bankruptcy is behind you, if you're like most consumers, your first thought will probably be "How do I get credit again?" The truth is, you probably won't be able to right away because after you've filed, your bankruptcy can remain on your credit record for up to ten years, and that information scares away most creditors. You don't, however, have to wait ten years to begin the credit rebuilding process — you can start 14 to 24 months after your bankruptcy is over.

While you're waiting to rebuild your credit, make good use of the time: Review your credit record to make sure that it doesn't include any incorrect information and begin saving money.

Don't try to hurry the rebuilding process by working with a credit repair or credit fix-it company. These companies charge exorbitant fees to "clean up" damaged credit records. Some even claim they can make bankruptcies disappear. Don't waste your money! Only time can make negative information on your credit record go away. Many states have passed legislation restricting the activities of credit repair companies. Some states also provide consumers with legal remedies when they get ripped off by one of these businesses.

In an effort to drive credit repair firms out of business, the FTC's new Telemarketing Rule has a provision prohibiting such firms from seeking payment for their services until six months after they provide the services they promise you.

Chapter 9
Smart Spending

• •

In This Chapter
▶ Buying products by mail
▶ Dealing with door-to-door salespersons
▶ Avoiding scams of all kinds
▶ Buying products on warranty
▶ Buying new and used cars
▶ Traveling by plane
▶ Investing wisely

• •

*1*f you're like the rest of us, no matter how hard you work, it seems like there's never enough money to go around! So it's important that you use your money wisely, do what you can to avoid getting ripped off, and be aware of your legal rights if trouble develops. Wise spending involves many things:

✔ Negotiating contracts for important financial transactions, something discussed in Chapter 1

✔ Understanding your legal rights and responsibilities when you use credit (Turn to Chapter 8 for this information.)

✔ Evaluating product and service warranties

✔ Getting the best deal when you buy a new or used car and knowing the laws that can protect you

✔ Knowing the laws that can protect you when you order merchandise by mail

✔ Being alert for scams

✔ Protecting yourself when you invest in a security

And much, much more.

The state of Maryland has an online public information network called SAILOR. *Tough Times,* its excellent monthly consumer information newsletter, is available on SAILOR. Each month, it covers a single topic related to money matters, automobiles, consumer scams, and more. Residents of all states will find *Tough Times* of value. You can read it at `http://sailor.lib.md.us/docs/tip_toc.html`.

The Consumer Law Page at `http://seamless.com:80/talf/txt/intro.html` is an award-winning Web site that features articles of interest to consumers, the text of consumer information brochures, and links to other consumer-related Internet resources.

Shopping by Mail

In today's busy world, many of us let "our fingers do the walking" when we shop. What can be easier and more fun than looking through the pages of glossy catalogues full of tempting merchandise, placing an order by phone any time of the day or night, and then waiting for its arrival. All from the comfort of your home or office!

When you order by mail or phone, the federal Mail Order or Telephone Rule (MOTR), which is enforced by the FTC, says that your order must be shipped when the company says it will. (If the company doesn't give you a ship date, the MOTR assumes your purchase will be shipped within 30 days.) If the company can't meet that deadline, it must give you an *option notice* that offers you the choice of either canceling your order (and receiving a prompt refund) or agreeing to the delay.

The Mail Order and Telephone Rule also applies to fax and computer orders. If you pay for your purchase with a credit card, you're also protected by the Fair Credit Billing Act. For more on the Fair Credit Billing Act, see the " I don't think I owe this!" section in Chapter 8.

Knock Knock

If you invite someone into your home to sell you merchandise or services and you buy what he or she is selling, the federal Cooling-Off Rule gives you three days to cancel purchases of $25 or more and also says that you have until midnight of the third business day to request a full refund. The FTC enforces the Cooling-Off Rule.

The Cooling-Off Rule does not apply to home-sales "parties" or to goods or services primarily intended for personal, family, or household use — a vacuum cleaner for example. Also, it doesn't apply to sales that are the result of prior negotiations made at the seller's permanent business location.

The Cooling-Off Rule requires home salespeople to inform you of your cancellation rights and to give you two copies of a cancellation form — one for you to keep and one for you to send if you decide to cancel the sale — as well as a receipt or contract. The receipt or contract must be dated, indicate the seller's name and address, and explain your right to cancel. In addition, it must be written in whatever language the salesperson's sales presentation was made in.

To cancel the sale, sign and date one copy of the cancellation form and mail it to the address you were provided for cancellation. The envelope must be postmarked before midnight of the third business day after the contract date. Saturday is considered a business day. Send the form certified mail, return receipt requested.

If you're not given a cancellation form, you can write your own cancellation letter.

After you cancel, the seller is required to do the following within ten days:

- ✔ Cancel and return any papers you signed.
- ✔ Refund all of your money and make arrangements to pick up any merchandise that may have been left at your home.
- ✔ Return any trade-in.

Also, the seller must either pick up any items within 20 days or reimburse you for your postage costs if you agreed to ship the merchandise to the seller.

Do I Have a Deal for You!

Susan and her husband Mark are having money troubles. She's been laid off from her well-paying job, and now she and her husband are having trouble making ends meet. Their creditors are demanding to be paid, and at least one bankcard company has canceled their credit card. Susan is worried about how their financial woes will affect their credit histories. Then one day, she gets a call from a friendly-sounding man who tells her about an incredible investment opportunity that she needs to act on right away. If everything the caller says is true, Susan and Mark's financial troubles will soon be over!

Susan is like many consumers who are down on their luck. In desperation, they begin looking for a quick way to make lots of money. Often, they fall prey to wealth-building scams. These scams may be marketed by phone, through the mail or personal sales, and on TV as *infomercials* — program-length ads that seem like real TV shows, not advertising. They are even marketed in cyberspace. These scams promise the following:

- ✔ Easy ways to make a lot of money through real estate or other investments.
- ✔ "Guaranteed" jobs. At most, you'll receive a list of companies to write to.

- ✓ "Guaranteed" loans or credit cards, regardless of your credit history or income.

- ✓ Business opportunities. The only business that makes money from these "opportunities" is the company selling them.

- ✓ Investments of all kinds. Gems, stock offerings, land deals, even ostrich farming!

- ✓ Work-at-home "opportunities" with promises of big money. Yeh, maybe you can make the thousands you're promised — if you worked day and night!

- ✓ Travel deals. That dream vacation is never as cheap or as glamorous as it sounds.

- ✓ Prize offers. These "free" prizes actually cost you a lot of money, and you may end up with nothing to show for the expense.

- ✓ Magazine offers. You don't buy just the magazine you want; you buy multiple subscriptions to magazines you'll never read, sometimes for hundreds of dollars!

In a sad twist on the adage, "you can't get something for nothing," you generally get nothing for something if you respond to a wealth-building ad! Usually, after paying money up front, often a good deal of it, to purchase supplies, computer equipment and software, videotapes, or after attending a sales pitch in the guise of a seminar, you end up with little of real value or nothing more than empty promises.

Steer clear of credit repair firms. These businesses can't do anything you can't do for yourself for little or no money.

The Telemarketing Sales Rule

The federal Telemarketing Sales Rule spells out some basic ground rules for telemarketers and gives consumers the power to stop unwanted calls. It also provides states with the powers they need to crack down on fraudulent telemarketers. The Rule says the following:

- ✓ You have the right to tell a telemarketer not to call you again. If the calls continue, the company is breaking the law.

- ✓ Telemarketers cannot call before 8 a.m. and after 9 p.m.

- ✓ Telemarketers must tell you up front that they are trying to sell you something and must give you the name of the company they're calling for and what they're selling. If they're calling you about a prize promotion, they must tell you that you don't have to pay anything or purchase anything to win.

- ✓ The telemarketer is barred from trying to mislead you about the earnings potential, profitability, or risk of an investment, product, or service that the salesperson is calling you about.

- ✓ You must be given all of an offer's costs and conditions before spending any money on what the telemarketer is selling.

Eleven sure signs of a consumer scam

Every year, Americans lose up to $40 billion in telemarketing fraud. To help you avoid becoming part of the statistics, here are some surefire signs of a scam:

1. The offer sounds too good to be true. It probably is!

2. The caller is very friendly and seems to know a lot about you.

3. You're told that you have to ACT TODAY.

4. You must pay an up-front fee to take advantage of the offer.

5. The investment you're offered is described as "risk free." Don't kid yourself: There's no such thing as a risk-free investment. If there were, we'd all be millionaires!

6. You're congratulated for being chosen for this "special offer" or for "being a winner." Yeh, right!

7. You're told that having bad credit or low income is "no problem."

8. As a condition of getting your discounted or free gift, you must attend a sales presentation or meeting.

9. You're instructed to send money right away, by courier or overnight delivery, not by mail.

10. You're told to call an 800 or 900 number for more information.

11. The telemarketer tries to complete all business transactions by phone, and you're offered nothing in writing — no contract, no guarantee, nada!

 Use the information available at the Consumer Fraud Alert Network's Web site (http://www.pic.net/microsmarts/fraud.htm) to help you avoid being victimized by a scam. You can find descriptions of different scams, solid tips for protecting yourself, and the phone numbers of government agencies and organizations who can help if you become a victim.

Hazards on the Information Highway

According to industry sources, the Internet has more than 15 million users, and that number is growing daily. Millions of consumers also use online services. As a virtually unregulated information and marketing media, cyberspace is now being used by many scam artists.

Cyberspace ads for scams generally fall into two categories: classified advertising and disguised advertising. Bogus classified ads are easiest to spot because they call themselves ads and because they include the usual hype and too-good-to-be-true promises that characterize consumer scams.

As the name implies, disguised ads are harder to spot. Because this kind of advertising is most commonly found on online bulletin boards and in chat groups, it's not always clear whether the ad is an innocent comment by another visitor to cyberspace or the assertions of a scam artist laying the bait to snare another unsuspecting consumer. If you take the bait or if you suspect a scam, contact your commercial online provider as well as the other local, state, and federal offices and nonprofit organizations mentioned in this chapter.

How to Make Yourself Scam Proof

Common sense and a healthy dose of skepticism can help you avoid becoming the victim of a scam. Many con artists use the phone to target unsuspecting consumers, so the following advice can make it easier for you to deal with them:

✔ Assume that if an opportunity is good today, it will be just as good tomorrow, next week, or maybe even a month from now. Don't be pressured into making an on-the-spot decision, especially when money is involved.

✔ Tell a telemarketer that you're not interested and hang up. The longer a good con artist can keep you on the phone, the more vulnerable you may be to the pitch, as con artists can be skilled, convincing liars. Maybe that's why they're in the business they're in!

✔ Don't be lured into trusting the salesperson just because he or she seems to know a lot about you. Con artists often develop their target list from databases that provide them with personal information about you, including your age and income, whether or not you're a home owner, your occupation, the magazines you read, and so on.

✔ Don't agree to or sign anything without first seeing the details of an offer in writing. You should understand exactly what you're agreeing to. Get all your questions answered. If the offer involves a considerable amount of money, ask your financial advisor, CPA, or attorney to review it.

✔ Check out the company and the offer with your state attorney general's office or state consumer protection office and your local Better Business Bureau. Don't wait until after you've been ripped off to contact these offices; it may be too late at that point for them to be of much help.

✔ Call the National Fraud Information Center at 800-876-7060 to find out if the company that contacted you is in the Center's database of fraudulent telemarketers.

✔ Ask about your recourse should you be unhappy with the offer after you've paid for it. Get this information in writing and read the fine print!

✔ Don't give the caller any information about your finances, including bankcard numbers and bank account information.

✔ Know what the FTC's new Telemarketing Sales Rule says a telemarketer can and can't do. See the sidebar, "The Telemarketing Sales Rule," earlier in this chapter.

Charitable scams

Americans are suckers for a heart wrenching plea from a "good cause." But not all good causes are legit. In fact, some bogus charities select names that sound almost identical to the real thing in order to trick you into parting with your money. Here are some tips on how to avoid getting duped:

✔ When a nonprofit organization asks you for money, unless you're very familiar with the organization or with the person who's calling and you know that it's a reputable organization, ask for written information, including a statement of its mission, a review of its current projects, a list of its board of directors, a balance sheet, summary of its sources

and uses of funds, an explanation of how your donation is used, the percentage that goes to support the organization's mission, and the percentage that goes toward its overhead. Also, find out if the organization is approved by the IRS by asking to be sent verification of its 501(c)(3) status.

✔ Check with the secretary of state's office in your state to find out if the nonprofit organization has registered with it.

✔ Never give the representative of a charitable organization your credit card number over the phone.

You can reach the National Fraud Information Center at http://www.fraud.org.

If You Become a Victim

It's such a blow to the ego when we realize we've been duped, especially when there's money involved! But if you've been conned by a scam, it may make you feel a little better to know that there are things you can do to try to recover your money and to help prevent other consumers from becoming victims. You can try doing the following:

✔ Report the company and scam to your local Better Business Bureau.

✔ Register a complaint with the National Fraud Information Center by calling 800-876-7060. The Center logs your complaint onto its national fraud database. Law enforcement organizations around the country use this database.

✔ Contact your state attorney general's office. If it gets enough complaints about a particular company, it may take action.

✔ Report your problem to the FTC. If it receives enough complaints, the FTC will take action. It can seek fines of up to $10,000 per violation against companies that violate its Telemarketing Sales Rule and can even go to court to get refunds for fraud victims.

✔ Talk with an attorney about the possibility of filing a lawsuit against the company that ripped you off. Be aware, however, that these lawsuits are difficult to win because companies that peddle scams are often difficult to locate. After they've worn out their welcome in one area, they often relocate and change names.

Buying a Product on Warranty

Many of the products or services you buy come with a *warranty* — which is the seller's or manufacturer's promise to stand behind its product. It's a kind of contract. Having a warranty gives you an extra measure of protection should something go wrong with what you've bought.

Warranties are not mandated by law; however, the federal Magnuson-Moss Act says that if a product comes with a written warranty, you must be given an opportunity to see the warranty information before you make your purchase. The law also says that the warranty must clearly indicate exactly what it covers, its duration, who pays for any repairs under the warranty, your obligations, and so on.

All warranties are not equal

When you're making an important purchase, compare the warranties of the makes and models you're considering as well as their prices. Read each warranty thoroughly, paying special attention to the fine print — the devil is often in the details! Make special note of the following:

✔ What parts and repairs does the warranty cover or not cover?

✔ What expenses do you have to pay for when you use the warranty?

✔ How long does the warranty last?

✔ Does the warranty cover *consequential damages?* Probably not. Consequential damages are such things as the time and expense you may incur getting the product repaired and having to take off work.

✔ What limitations or conditions does the warranty come with?

✔ What do you have to do to get warranty service?

✔ What will the company do if the product fails?

Don't rely on a salesperson's oral promise about what can be done if there's a problem with a product. The promise may be nothing more than a sales pitch. Get all promises in writing.

Implied warranties

When we think warranty, we usually think written warranty. If a product doesn't come with a written warranty, however, it usually comes with an implied warranty that can last as long as four years. Implied warranties are created by state law (and all states have these laws), so check with your state attorney general's office or state consumer protection office to learn the specifics of its law on implied warranties.

Of the two kinds of implied warranties, the most common is a *warranty of merchantability,* the seller's promise that a product does what it's supposed to do — that a refrigerator keeps food from spoiling, that a vacuum picks up dirt, that detergent cleans, and so on.

The other kind of warranty is a *warranty of fitness.* It applies when you've purchased a product because the seller tells you it's suitable for a particular purpose. For example, the seller tells you that the tent you've bought will keep you dry and warm even in hurricane conditions.

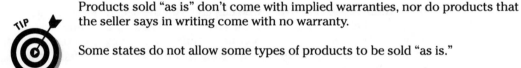

Products sold "as is" don't come with implied warranties, nor do products that the seller says in writing come with no warranty.

Some states do not allow some types of products to be sold "as is."

Resolving warranty problems

If you try to use your warranty and are told it doesn't cover your particular problem, reread the warranty to confirm what it promises. It's back to the fine print! If you still believe you're right, try to resolve the problem with the business from which you bought the product. If necessary, send a certified letter to the manufacturer, return receipt requested. The manufacturer's address should be included on the warranty.

If you get no satisfaction, here are some other things to try:

- ✔ Contact your state attorney general's office or state consumer protection office.
- ✔ Try using mediation or arbitration to resolve your problem. Some warranties require that you try mediation or arbitration before suing a company over a warranty problem. See Chapter 2 for mediation and arbitration advice and resources.
- ✔ File a claim in small claims court.
- ✔ Sue under the Magnuson-Moss Act. At a minimum, you can sue for damages and legal fees.
- ✔ Report your problem to the FTC.

Buying a New Car

As a country, we're famous for our love affair with our cars. In America, cars are not just a means of transportation. They also represent freedom. The car we drive can make a statement about us too — it can say that we're rich (or wish we were), sporty, flirtatious, rugged, and so on.

Shopping

No matter what message you convey with your car, it costs a significant amount of money to own one. In fact, after buying a home, purchasing a car is probably the most significant purchase you'll make. Although it's easy to fall in love with the look and feel of a car, you should always research your options and comparison shop. The following are some tips:

- ✔ Read car magazines and consumer publications that contain new car reviews.

- ✔ Visit several car dealers to see who can give you the best deal. Read the *Monroney* label or sticker on any car you're interested in. This label is required by federal law. It tells you the manufacturer's suggested retail, or base price, for the car. Be aware, however, that the Monroney price is not necessarily the car's sales price because dealers can charge whatever they want.

  The cars you look at also have dealer stickers. The price on these stickers reflects the cost of dealer-installed options, dealer preparation, and other expenses.

- ✔ Find out if the dealer is offering any rebates.

- ✔ Test-drive any cars you're considering.

- ✔ Don't hesitate to negotiate on price. Most dealers are willing to and probably expect to negotiate.

- ✔ If you're going to trade in a car, keep that negotiation separate from the sales price negotiation. After you have the sales price nailed down, then talk trade-in. You'll get a better deal.

If your new car has a chronic problem that you've been unable to resolve by working with the dealer, your state's *lemon laws* — all states have them — can help you get a replacement car or a refund. See the forthcoming sidebar for more on lemon laws.

Lemon laws

All states have lemon laws — laws that can help protect you when the car you buy turns out to be a clunker and is in the shop as much as it's on the road. (Contracts and warranties also help.) These laws define exactly what a lemon is and specify exactly how to trigger the protections of the lemon law in your state. Typically, you must notify the manufacturer, and sometimes your state, in writing about the problems your car is having. Lemon laws require the manufacturer of a defective car to either repair the car within a reasonable period of time and with a reasonable amount of effort or to refund the purchase price of the car, less a deduction for the wear and tear on the car while you owned it. Most lemon laws only apply while a car's express warranty is in effect, or for one year, whichever is longer. Although most of these laws apply to new cars only, some also apply to used cars. When they do, it's usually the dealer's responsibility, not the manufacturer's, to try to repair the car and to refund the money to the buyer if the repair efforts are unsuccessful.

If your car is having a recurring problem or numerous different problems, be sure to save all receipts whenever you take your car to be serviced or repaired. They can help create a record of your efforts to resolve your car's problems, something you need in order to sue the manufacturer.

Usually, before you can have your car replaced or get a refund, you have to go through an arbitration process, either one sponsored by your state or the manufacturer of your car; however, some state laws require arbitration only in certain situations or allow you to bypass arbitration and go directly to court.

Not making your car payments

When you buy a car, until you've made your very last payment, the creditor who financed it for you retains important legal rights to the vehicle as protection against your defaulting on your loan. Those rights are defined by the contract of sale and by the laws of your state. Worst case scenario, if you can't keep up with your payments, the creditor will repossess your car. In some states, the creditor can take back your car without taking you to court and without any prior warning. Now you see your car, now you don't!

The best defense against repossession is to contact your creditor as soon as you are having trouble making your car payments. The creditor may agree to a different payment schedule. If it does, be sure you get the new payment schedule in writing.

If your car is repossessed, your creditor has two choices — keep it or resell it. You have the right to know what the creditor intends to do. Most likely, the creditor will opt to sell the car in order to get back as much of its money as possible. If that's the creditor's choice, you have the right to know whether the car will be sold privately or at a public auction, and if it's to be sold at an auction, you have the right to know the date of the auction, and you have the right to buy your car back.

If your creditor intends to keep the car, you have the right to demand that it be sold. You may want to make this demand if the value of the car is more than what you owe on it because you're entitled to any profit the creditor may make on the car sale.

You can agree to a voluntary repossession as a possible way to reduce your creditor's repossession costs.

If your creditor sells your car for less that what you owe on it, most states allow the creditor to sue you for the difference or *deficiency*. If you don't respond to the lawsuit, the creditor will get a judgment against you for the deficiency. If, however, the creditor violated your state's laws regarding the repossession or sale of your car, you may have a defense against the lawsuit.

Buying a Used Car

Given the cost of buying a new car, more consumers are opting to buy used cars when they need new transportation. If you elect this option, regardless of whether you purchase your car from a dealer or an individual seller, you may be buying a well-maintained vehicle, a car that's been in multiple wrecks, someone else's problems, or even a stolen vehicle. Who knows? If only a used car could talk!

Consumers can now do some of their shopping for a used car from the comfort of their own home on the Internet. Although most of the sites focus on cars for sale in a particular region or state, some sites like Calling All Cars (http://www. carshopper.com) offer nationwide listings. You can learn about new cars for sale at this site too; however, shopping on the Internet is no substitute for physically checking out a car before you buy it.

Knowing what to look for and what questions to ask can increase the likelihood that your new used car will be a deal and not a clunker:

- ✔ Read used car guides to find out the repair records and typical selling prices of the make, model, and year of the cars you're considering. Also get the *Blue Book* value. This price guide to cars is available at most libraries.

- ✔ Drive the car on the highway and in stop-and-go traffic. Test its heating and cooling systems, its lights, interior and exterior, its radio, and so on.

- ✔ Don't assume that a bright, shiny car has been well cared for. The seller may be gambling that if the car looks good, you may be so impressed by its appearance that you won't look under the hood. But remember, beauty is only skin deep!

✔ Ask about the car's repair history and review its repair records if they're available.

✔ Find out if the car has ever been in an accident and look for signs of accident damage yourself — dents, painted areas that don't quite match the rest of the car, crinkled metal, and so on.

✔ Hire an independent mechanic you trust to inspect the car.

✔ If you're buying from an individual, ask why he or she is selling the car.

✔ Ask to see the car's title. If you're buying from an individual, it should be in the seller's name; if the seller is a dealer, the title should either be in the dealer's name or the name of the previous owner. If you suspect a problem with the title, don't accept the seller's explanation. Look for another car.

✔ If you're buying from a dealer, read the car's Buyer's Guide sticker. Dealers — businesses that sell six or more used cars over a 12 month period — are required by the FTC's Used Car Rule to put this sticker on the side window of any vehicle they sell other than a recreation vehicle or motorcycle. Among other things, the sticker tells you whether the car is being sold with a warranty. If it comes with one, ask to read it.

Only a few states require that dealers warrant used cars. When you buy a used car, it's *caveat emptor* (that's Latin for *buyer beware*).

If you negotiate a change in the warranty, make sure that the change is reflected in the Buyer's Guide so that it becomes part of the sales contract.

✔ Call your state attorney general's office or state consumer protection office to find out about any laws your state may have that can protect you when you buy a used car.

Check out the used car you're considering at the Web site of the National Highway Traffic Saftey Administration (`http://www.nhtsa.dot.gov/nsa/nsasearch.shtml`). You can find out about owner-reported problems for a particular make, model, and year, and you can read manufacturer service bulletins about the car.

Warranties

If you buy a car from an individual, the car is probably sold "as is." It may still be covered by its original warranty or by an extended warranty, however. If it is, find out if the warranty is transferable and read the paperwork. If the car isn't covered by a warranty, you can help protect yourself by asking the seller to sign a statement about the condition of the car at the time of sale. You should also be sure you ask questions about the car. Although the seller is not legally obligated to tell you about any problems the car may have other than *hidden defects* — problems that are difficult for you to discover or that only occur under certain conditions — the seller is obligated to respond truthfully if you ask about something.

A private seller is not legally liable for the working condition of the used car he or she sells unless the seller lied or made an express guarantee about its condition.

If your used car turns out to have problems and the car came with an express warranty, the problems may be covered. If there is no warranty but you believe that the seller lied to you about the car's condition and you can prove it, you may be able to sue the seller. Also, your state's lemon law may apply to used cars and to both individual and commercial sellers.

Mileage

Federal law says that every time a vehicle is sold, the seller must give you a written statement of its true mileage. If a seller can't tell you how many miles a car has been driven, look for another car. Also, tampering with a vehicle's *odometer* — the gauge on its dashboard showing the number of miles the car has been driven — is illegal, and both federal and state laws treat such an action as fraud. If you can prove that an odometer has been tampered with, you have the right to get your money back and may also be entitled to punitive damages plus attorney's fees.

Contracts or bills of sale

Any reputable car dealer will ask you to sign a contract or bill of sale when you buy a car. Most states require written contracts whenever an item is sold for more than $500. You should request a contract or bill of sale if you're buying from an individual, especially if you're paying more than $500. Both you and the dealer should sign them. Having the contract signed helps you if the car turns out to be a clunker and you decide to sue the seller.

Organizations that can help you

The **Auto Safety Hotline** maintained by the National Highway Traffic Safety Administration provides information about auto safety and recalls for both new and used cars and other vehicles. Call 800-424-9393. In Washington D.C., call 202-366-0123.

The **Center For Auto Safety** monitors auto defects and can tell you whether a certain make, model, and year car has a history of complaints. Contact this organization at 2001 S Street, Suite 410 N.W., Washington, D.C. 20009 and include a stamped, self-addressed envelope with your request.

The **Automotive Consumer Action Program (AUTOCAP)**, coordinated by the National Automobile Dealers Association and sponsored by state and local dealer associations around the country, is a national dispute resolution program. If you have a problem with a used car purchased from a franchised dealer, you may be able to have the problem mediated. Call your local dealer association.

In some states, you can't register a car without a contract or bill of sale.

The bill of sale should include the following information:

- ✔ The date of sale
- ✔ The year, make, and model of the car you're buying
- ✔ The car's VIN (vehicle identification number)
- ✔ The car's odometer reading — the number of miles it's been driven
- ✔ The amount you're paying for the car and whether you paid in cash, with a check, money order, and so on
- ✔ The seller's name, address, and phone number
- ✔ Any special conditions related to the sale

Leasing Rather Than Buying

Sometimes, leasing a car can be a good alternative to buying one because you often don't have to come up with a down payment, and your monthly payment may be less. You may be able to lease a more expensive car than you can afford to buy. But just how good a deal leasing may be depends on the details of your lease agreement. Although new Federal Reserve Board regulations governing car lease agreements as well as industry reforms have made it somewhat easier to know whether or not the deal you're getting is a good one, you may be in store for some unpleasant surprises at the end of your agreement if you don't do your homework.

Leasing tends to be cheaper than buying if you lease a car for a relatively short period of time, not for many years. So if you're thinking about leasing a car for more than a couple years, you may be better off buying one.

Here are some things you can do to help ensure that you get the best lease possible:

- ✔ Shop around. Talk to car leasing companies associated with car manufacturers, independent lessors, and banks to find out what kind of leasing deals they offer. Frequently, the rates offered by manufacturer-associated lessors can be especially attractive.
- ✔ Don't assume that the company offering the lowest monthly payments is necessarily your best deal. Check to make sure that you're not trading low monthly payments for a substantial down payment or for a large balloon payment at the end of the lease.
- ✔ Understand the difference between an open-end and a closed-end lease. See the following section, "Knowing how to talk the talk," if you don't know the difference.

✔ Avoid low-mileage leases unless you're absolutely certain that you will be doing very little driving in the leased car; otherwise, if you exceed the mileage in your lease, you'll pay dearly for every mile over the maximum — between $.10 and $.15 cents per mile.

✔ Make sure any lease agreement you're asked to sign includes the following:

  • The car's gross capitalized cost

  • The car's net capitalized cost

  • The car's residual value (predetermined value of the car at the end of the lease)

  • The interest rate or lease factor (ask for the annual rate)

  • Whether a security deposit is required and whether it's refundable

  • The amount of the lease-termination fee

  • The number of miles you can put on the car and how much you have to pay if you exceed that amount

  • The dealer's definition of "excessive wear and tear" (ask for specific examples)

✔ Whenever possible, avoid long-term leases. Although your monthly payments may be slightly lower, the longer the lease, the greater the likelihood that your needs will change and you'll want to break your lease. If you do, it will cost you.

✔ Purchase gap insurance from the lessor. If your leased car is wrecked or stolen, gap insurance pays for the difference between what you owe on your lease and the amount that the primary insurer of the car will pay. Gap insurance is relatively inexpensive.

✔ Know your legal rights under the federal Consumer Leasing Act (CLA).

✔ Negotiate.

Most lemon laws do not apply to leased cars. As leasing grows in popularity, though, more states are expanding the coverage of their lemon laws to cover leased automobiles.

Knowing how to talk the talk

The auto leasing industry has its own language. Understanding that language is key to getting a good car lease. Here are some terms you need to be familiar with:

Adjusted or net capitalized cost: The gross cost of a lease less your down payment and any credit you get for rebates or trade-ins.

Capitalized cost: The overall value or cost of your lease according to your lease agreement, as well as the applicable taxes, tags, and any service contracts or insurance.

Capitalized cost reduction: This is equivalent to the down payment on a car.

Closed-end lease: With this kind of lease, you pay a fixed amount of money each month for the duration of your lease. When the lease is up, you don't owe the lessor any more money unless you put more than the usual wear and tear on the car or drove it more than the specified number of miles.

Gap insurance: Insurance that protects you if the car you lease is stolen or totaled. Some lease agreements automatically include it; otherwise, ask for it.

Open-end lease: If you have this kind of lease, you may have to make an "end of the lease" payment if the car is worth less than what the lease estimated it would be worth — its estimated *residual value* — when you return the car at the end of the lease.

Purchase option: A lease with this option allows you to buy the car at the end of the lease for a predetermined price.

Refundable security deposit: A cash deposit paid at the start of a lease. If you meet the terms of the lease, you usually get your deposit back at the end of the lease.

Residual value: This is the amount that a lease agreement estimates a car will be worth at the end of the lease. The residual value is determined at the start of the lease.

The Consumer Leasing Act

The federal Consumer Leasing Act (CLA) requires that a lessor give you certain information when you're leasing property for your personal, family, or household use and when the duration of the lease is more than four months. The CLA covers leased cars, furniture, and appliances. The law does not apply to real estate rentals, certain kinds of daily or month-to-month car rentals, furniture that comes with a rented apartment or home, or property leased for business use.

The CLA says that before you sign a lease, you must be given written information about its costs and terms. This information includes

✔ The amount of any advance payments you must pay

✔ The number, amount, and dates of your regular lease payments

✔ How much you must pay in license and registration fees, taxes, and other miscellaneous costs

✔ The kind of insurance you must purchase

✔ Whether the merchandise you're leasing comes with an express warranty

✔ Who is responsible for maintaining and servicing the property

✔ The lessor's standards for wear and tear on the property you're leasing

✔ The amount and terms of any penalties you must pay and the terms of cancellation

✔ Whether you can buy what you are leasing and at what terms

If you lease property and are not provided with this information, the CLA gives you the right to sue the lessor for 25 percent of the total amount of the monthly payments you've made up to $1,000 plus actual damages. If you win, you can collect attorney's fees and court costs. You must file your lawsuit within one year of the end of the lease, however. The FTC enforces the CLA.

Increasing Your Car Care Confidence

Taking your car to a repair shop can be a humbling experience — and expensive too! Most of us are unfamiliar with the inner workings of our automobiles, so we find it hard to evaluate a mechanic's diagnosis, recommendations, and price. In our car-dependent society, we may feel pressured to pay whatever it takes to get back behind the wheel as quickly as possible. Consequently, many of us end up paying for repairs that don't fix the problem, and we often spend more than we should even when the repairs work.

About half the states have laws relating to car repairs. Most of these laws require that a repair shop prepare a cost estimate for any repairs that need to be performed and that it get your authorization if the actual cost is going to exceed the estimate by a certain amount. If a shop doesn't get your authorization, you don't have to pay for the amount over the estimate.

According to local, state, and federal consumer protection agencies, complaints about car repairs represent one of their top consumer complaint categories.

Car repair tips

The following tips can help you stay out of trouble:

✔ Call your state's attorney general or consumer protection office to find out if it has a law governing car repairs. If your state is one of the approximately 25 that do, ask for information about how the law protects you.

- ✔ Find a reputable car repair shop, preferably before you need one. Get references from people you know or who drive the same kind of car you do.

- ✔ Contact your local Better Business Bureau and your state attorney general's office or state consumer protection agency to find out if the shop you're considering has a complaint record.

- ✔ If your local or state government requires that auto repair shops be licensed, ask to see the shop's license.

- ✔ If your car is under warranty, make sure that the shop is authorized to perform the warranty work.

- ✔ Be sure that you understand a repair shop's diagnosis of your car's problem before you authorize the repair. Don't be embarrassed to ask questions. It's your car! Always get a signed, written cost estimate for the repair. Among other things, it should specify the problem to be fixed, the parts needed, anticipated labor charges, the repair date, and the number of miles presently on your car. It should also state that you'll be contacted if the work to be performed exceeds a specified amount of time or money. By signing it, you authorize the repair shop to make the repair and agree to pay for it.

- ✔ If the first repair shop you go to says your car needs an expensive repair, consider getting at least one more estimate.

- ✔ Never sign a blank repair estimate. It should explain exactly what is going to be done to your car.

- ✔ Tell the repair shop to call you before it performs any work not outlined in the work order.

- ✔ Get all warranties in writing. If your repair is covered by a warranty, be sure to follow its instructions for how to get a warranty repair done.

- ✔ After your car has been repaired, get a completed repair order that details all the work that was done, the parts that were provided and their costs, labor charges, and so on. Keep the repair order with other car-related records in case you run into a problem later.

- ✔ Ask to get back all replaced parts. Your state may require this practice.

The Car Care Council is a nonprofit organization dedicated to educating motorists about vehicle maintenance and repair. At the Council's Web page (http://www.peoplevision.com/carcare/), you'll find a quiz that you can take to find out just how much you don't know about car care, and then you can review its informational resources so that you'll score better the next time!

When you and the mechanic disagree

If you're unhappy with a mechanic's work and don't want to pay the full amount of the bill, in most states, the mechanic has the right to keep your car until you pay and to charge you storage fees as well. If you're adamant about not paying the bill, your only recourse may be to sue the mechanic in small claims court. But in the meantime, you're without transportation! In a few states, you can get your car back by paying a court clerk the amount the mechanic says you owe. That way, you have your car while you're trying to resolve your dispute.

If you're unhappy with your car's repairs but can't be without your car, pay the charges with a credit card and exercise your rights under the Fair Credit Billing Act (covered in Chapter 8) by withholding payment when it comes time to pay the bill.

Air Travel

Finally, after months of scrimping on extras and stashing every extra dollar in their savings account, Bob and Betty are going to enjoy a romantic second honeymoon! They've just landed on the exotic little island they've been dreaming about for a year, but where's their luggage? As the luggage carousel moves in endless circles, they notice that everyone else on their flight is walking away, suitcases in hand. This is not the way Bob and Betty imagined their vacation would begin! Now what?

Although air travel can whisk us away to locations that our great grandparents could only dream about by turning the pages of *National Geographic,* it can also present us with problems we never encounter when we travel by auto, bus, and train! As a result, air travel brings with it stresses and anxieties not associated with more "old fashioned" modes of travel. Knowing your rights when air travel-related problems happen can alleviate some of that stress and worry.

If your luggage turns up missing

Do not leave the airport without talking to the airline and completing a form describing your luggage and how you can be reached. The form should also indicate the name of the person who filled it out. Also, get a phone number other than the reservations number so that you can call to monitor the airline's progress in locating your luggage.

Depending on the policy of the airline, you may be entitled to receive some money to pay for your immediate needs before you leave the airport. Also, if you have to purchase clothing and other items while you're away from home and waiting for the airline to find your luggage, you may be entitled to reimbursement for those expenses. Keep your receipts.

The small print on your airline ticket should tell you about your air carrier's responsibility if it loses your luggage.

If your luggage is declared officially lost

You have to complete a reimbursement claim and possibly another form as well. After the airline receives your information, it begins negotiating with you about how much they will pay you for your lost luggage and its contents. Most likely, you will not be reimbursed for the items' original costs because the airline takes into consideration how much their value has depreciated. Generally however, if your luggage is lost on a domestic flight, the airline's liability is limited to no more than $1250 per passenger. On international flights, an airline's liability is limited to no more than $9.07 per pound. These limits also apply to missing and delayed luggage.

If you don't meet the airline's deadline for submitting your claim and the other form, you may have waived your right to reimbursement.

About 98 percent of all missing luggage is tracked down and returned to its owners within hours.

If you get bumped

Frequently, airlines overbook their flights to compensate for possible no-shows because they want their planes to be as full as possible when they take off. Airline economics aside, getting bumped from a flight can ruin a good day!

To decrease your chances of getting bumped, check in and get your boarding pass well before departure time.

The airline must give you a written statement describing your rights. Often, you may be entitled to on-the-spot compensation. The amount depends on the cost of your ticket and how long it will be before you can get on another flight to your destination. The longer the delay, the bigger your compensation, up to $400. Getting bumped doesn't have to be all bad if you're not in a rush! But to be eligible for any compensation, you must have had a confirmed reservation on the flight you got bumped from. Also, these rules do not apply to charter flights, scheduled flights on planes that accommodate 60 or fewer passengers, or international flights coming to the U.S.

If the airline gets you on another flight to your same destination and that flight will arrive within an hour of your original flight's scheduled arrival time, the airline doesn't need to pay you anything.

If you offer to be bumped from a flight, the airline will compensate you for the inconvenience. Your compensation may include a free ticket as well as money for food and lodging. The airline must follow certain rules regarding what they can offer you, however. Also, you don't have to accept what an airline offers. You can try to negotiate something better for yourself.

If the weather's bad and your plane is delayed

The airline is not required to compensate you if the weather or mechanical problems delay your plane. Many airlines, however, in the interest of good public relations, offer to buy you an airport meal if the delay means you have to sit around for a couple hours. If you are delayed overnight, the airline may also pay for a room at the airport hotel.

Investor Rights

If you have sufficient income, you may want to increase your net worth by investing in securities — stocks, bonds, mutual funds, and so on. To protect yourself, before investing in anything, familiarize yourself with how various investments work, your rights as an investor, and with the responsibilities of the broker, financial consultant, or sales representative you may work with.

Under federal securities law, the companies and organizations that buy and sell securities enjoy a great deal of autonomy and have responsibility for regulating their own behavior through SROs (self-regulatory organizations) under the federal oversight of the Securities and Exchange Commission (SEC). For example, brokers register with the National Association of Securities Dealers (NASD) — an SRO — and with the states in which they conduct business. Other SROs include the American Stock Exchange, the New York, Boston, Chicago, and Pacific Exchanges, the Municipal Securities Rulemaking Board, and miscellaneous organizations that set the rules for buying and selling securities, mandate the qualifications for industry professionals, regulate the activities of those professionals, and discipline those who fail to abide by the rules.

Federal securities law also gives you certain protections, which include the right to sue if you've been harmed by a broker or a brokerage firm that has violated the law. Many brokerage firms require, however, that their customers sign contracts agreeing to use binding arbitration rather than sue when problems develop. Each state also has laws governing the buying and selling of securities within its boundaries.

The SEC is responsible for ensuring that the organizations and individuals who make up the securities industry operate in a fair and ethical manner and that the public is provided with the information it needs to make informed investment decisions. To accomplish these goals, the SEC requires that certain kinds of information be disclosed to the public and has adopted rules to govern the buying and selling of securities. It also files lawsuits and takes other enforcement actions when someone violates the law. Neither the SEC nor any broker or brokerage firm, however, can guarantee that you will make money from your securities investments. Investing is always somewhat of a gamble, and it's up to you, as an investor, to make informed decisions based on your willingness to take risks.

If you're an investor, check out the Securities and Exchange Commission Web site at `http://www.sec.gov/`. If you suspect securities fraud, you can use this site's link to the SEC Enforcement Complaint Center electronic mailbox to report the problem.

The Rules of Fair Practice

Many of your most important rights as an investor are defined by the Rules of Fair Practice established by the National Association of Securities Dealers. This set of rules gives you the right to the following:

- ✔ Complete and accurate information about any investment you are considering, including the potential risks and rewards. You may also have a legal right to written disclosure of an investment's risks. The disclosure may come in a prospectus or a disclosure statement, but if you need more information, you can write to request additional information.

- ✔ Up-front information about the obligations and costs of an investment you're considering.

- ✔ Full disclosure of all the costs you will or may incur, including commissions, sales charges — also called *loads* — transaction expenses, service charges, penalties, and so on.

- ✔ Responsible advice from your broker.

- ✔ Background information about the company you're considering doing business with, including whether it's ever been in trouble with a government regulatory agency.

- ✔ Information about where your money has been invested and what your investments are worth.

- ✔ Access to the investment firm or advisor who has invested your funds.

If you're working with a professional in the securities industry, investment advisors are bound by *suitability* rules that require them to provide you with appropriate advice. If you're working with a professional in the commodity futures industry, professionals are expected to abide by a "know your customer" rule, which means that they're supposed to make sure that you are adequately informed of the risks involved.

As I've already said, a broker can't guarantee that you'll make money through an investment he or she may recommend, but a broker does have an ethical and legal obligation to manage your funds responsibly, which means that a broker must abide by these guidelines:

- A broker must recommend investments that meet your financial goals.

- A broker can only make investments that you've authorized.

- A broker cannot make investments just to generate additional commissions for him or herself.

- A broker cannot take your funds for his or her personal use.

Contact your state's Securities Board or Department of Banking and Finance (the name of the right office depends on your state) to obtain a written report on the employment and disciplinary history of a broker. This report is free in most states.

If troubles develop

If you lose money in an investment or don't make as much money as you expected, you may not have a legitimate beef with the investment firm or advisor because investing is all about risks. Sometimes you win and sometimes you lose. But if you believe that an investment firm or advisor has not been honest with you or that you've been treated unfairly, you may have something to gripe about. As with any other problem that can end up in court, your first step should be to bring your concerns to the attention of your broker. If you get no satisfaction, write a letter to the broker's branch manager and send copies to the broker and the firm's compliance office. It's the job of this office to help resolve reasonable client complaints.

Assuming these steps don't resolve your problem, write to your state's securities regulator and send copies of your letter to the brokerage firm's branch manager and compliance office. To get the address and phone number of your state securities regulator, call the North American Securities Administrators Association, Inc., at 202-737-0900. The state regulator may be able to resolve your problem relatively quickly.

You should also contact the federal Securities and Exchange Commission (SEC) at

Office of Consumer Affairs/Investor Services
450 5th Street, N.W.
Washington, D.C. 20549
202-942-7040

The Securities Investor Protection Act

This federal law helps protect the securities and cash that your brokerage house may be holding for you. The law is administered by the nonprofit Securities Investor Protection Corporation (SIPC). It says that if the brokerage firm you're working with goes bankrupt or goes out of business, the securities and cash held in your account are protected, up to $500,000; however, only $100,000 of the $500,000 apply toward any cash that may be in your brokerage account. The SIPC does not protect you from any losses you may incur as a result of market changes.

The SEC will not help you get your money back. But if it receives enough complaints against a specific business or broker, it may take action.

You may also try to resolve your dispute through binding arbitration. In fact, depending on your agreement with a brokerage firm, you may have signed an agreement stating that if problems developed, you will resolve them through binding arbitration rather than with a lawsuit.

If your problem goes to arbitration, it's a good idea to get the help of an attorney familiar with securities law because the broker will have legal representation.

If a problem is decided in your favor, and history shows that it probably will, you may be awarded financial damages and possibly reimbursement for your legal fees. Depending on the situation, you may be entitled to punitive damages too.

Chapter 10

Buying and Selling a Home

· ·

In This Chapter

▶ Hunting for a home

▶ Dealing with real estate agents

▶ Finding a mortgage

▶ Closing the deal

· ·

*A*fter years of saving and sacrifice, you finally have enough money for a down payment on your dream house! Or maybe you already own a home but want to sell it because your dreams have grown bigger or your family is expanding. For most of us, buying and selling a home represent the two most important and most complex financial and legal transactions we ever make. If you want to get the most for your money and avoid the potential legal pitfalls and problems that both buyers and sellers can face, you need to understand the home buying and selling processes, including how to work with a real estate broker or agent. This chapter explains all of that stuff.

Finding a Home to Buy

Most people begin their house hunting by driving through the neighborhoods where they'd like to live, looking for "for sale" signs. They also read newspaper real estate ads and may tour open houses. And sooner or later, most home buyers begin working with a local real estate agent or broker.

The Internet is another house hunting resource, especially for consumers who are relocating to a new community or state. Many real estate companies not only post home listings on the Web but also provide helpful information about their communities.

When you schedule an appointment with a real estate agent or broker, it's important for you to realize that no matter how helpful that person may be, he or she usually works for the seller, not for you. In fact, an agent cannot work for you and the seller of a home at the same time.

Sellers list their homes with real estate companies who employ agents who attempt to find home buyers. When a house is sold, the agent receives a *commission* — or percentage of the sales price — paid by the seller. So agents have a financial incentive to get the highest price possible for the home, not to help you, the buyer, receive a good deal! Furthermore, it's unlikely that an agent will voluntarily offer information about any problems that a home in which you're interested may have because doing so might discourage you from buying the home or help you negotiate a reduced price.

You should know, however, that there are agents who work just for buyers, although they are fewer in number than the traditional real estate agent. If you work with a *buyer's agent* (sometimes called a *buyer's broker*), you may have to pay the agent by the hour or on a fee basis.

Call the Buyers Broker Registry at 800-729-5147 to locate a buyer's agent in your area.

Steer clear of so-called buyer's agents whose fees are based on a home's sales price, which means that they don't have a financial incentive to get the best deal for you.

http://www.coldwelbanker.com/QA/buy/index.html is a good Web site for home buyers. It addresses a wide variety of subjects, from how to find a home, to home inspections, to dealing with warranties, to negotiating and closing a deal. It also features information about many different kinds of homes, from fixer-uppers and new homes to condos and townhomes.

The Step By Step Guide to Home Buying, http://www.maxsol.com/homes/steps.html, is another helpful Web site for home shoppers. You are not only led through the home-buying process but are also referred to other Web sites for additional information on home sellers, inspectors, and more.

If You're the Seller

As a seller, you will probably contract with a real estate agent to help you find a qualified buyer for your home. This agent can also help you set a realistic asking price, advise you about the things you can do to help your home sell quickly, and help you close the deal. One of the key benefits of working with an agent, assuming he or she is a member of the Multiple Listing Service (MLS), is that information about your home will be in the MLS, providing your home exposure to countless other brokers and agents as well as to buyers who might otherwise never know about your home.

Real estate broker, agent, listing agents: Who are these people?

When you're in the market for a home, you may find yourself dealing with a number of different real estate professionals. To help you understand who's who, here's a list of the roles of the broker, agent, and listing agent:

✔ A real estate broker is a real estate professional who is licensed by your state to run a real estate business and is paid a fee for negotiating real estate transactions. A broker can have other real estate agents working for him or her and can sell homes too.

✔ A listing agent formally puts a seller's home "on the market" and also tries to sell the house.

✔ A real estate agent sells real estate for a real estate firm, often as an independent contractor.

Listing your home: what to expect

When you list your home, you are expected to sign a legally binding contract, or *listing agreement,* that gives the listing agent certain rights and defines the terms of your relationship, including the amount and conditions of the sales commission — usually between 5 and 7 percent of your home's selling price. There are three basic types of listings:

✔ **Exclusive Right to Sell listing:** If an agent other than the one you listed your home with sells it during the time that your listing agreement is in effect, the listing agent splits the commission with the other agent. The listing agent also gets paid if you sell your home yourself. Listing agents like this type of listing best.

✔ **Exclusive listing:** If you sell your home yourself, you may not have to pay the listing agent a sales commission depending on your state.

✔ **Open listing:** You can list your house with any number of agents, and the first one to sell it gets the commission. You can sell your house as well without paying a commission.

The listing agent may suggest that both of you sign the standard listing agreement used by the real estate firm for which he or she sells. If you want the agreement to include special provisions, you may want to hire an attorney to draft a listing agreement for you. If you do use the standard agreement, you can have an attorney review it before you sign and suggest possible changes so that you can be assured that it's fair to you. The attorney can even negotiate the changes. For example, the standard agreement usually entitles an agent to a commission if he or she locates a "ready, willing, and able" buyer for a home, regardless of whether or not the sale actually takes place. You may want to try negotiating an agreement that says that the agent will be paid only if the sale goes through.

Regardless of the type of listing agreement you use and whether or not you hire an attorney, the agreement should include the following:

- ✔ Its duration. You may not want to sign an agreement that lasts for a long period of time — more than 90 days — or that automatically renews. If you don't believe that the agent is doing enough to sell your home, you want the freedom to list it with someone else.

- ✔ Your asking price.

- ✔ How the agent's commission is calculated — it's usually a percentage of the selling price.

- ✔ Whether you have to pay a commission to the agent if you, not the agent, sell your home, and other conditions related to the payment of the commission.

- ✔ The agent's rights and responsibilities to you.

- ✔ Your obligations to the agent.

- ✔ Who pays to advertise your home.

- ✔ How any disputes between you and the agent will be resolved. Most agreements include a binding arbitration provision for resolving problems that may lead to lawsuits.

Check out this Web site for useful information if you're selling your home: `http://www.coldwelbanker.com/QA/sell/index.html`. You can find advice about pricing your home to sell, information about closing costs, and common questions and answers about selling a home.

When problems develop

Misunderstandings or other problems may develop between you and your real estate agent. For example, you may expect the agent to do something that the agent doesn't do, or you may be displeased with something the agent does do! When a problem develops, here's how to handle it:

- ✔ Talk to the agent and try to resolve the issue together. If that doesn't work, talk to the broker that the agent is working for.

- ✔ Try mediation.

- ✔ If you still don't get any satisfaction and the issue is serious enough, file a complaint with your local real estate board. It may hold a hearing to resolve the problem.

- ✔ Especially if you feel that the agent has acted unethically or even broken a law, contact the agency in your state that regulates real estate professionals. If it decides to investigate and finds wrongdoing, the agent may be fined, his or her license may be revoked, or the agent may be ordered to provide you with restitution.

A home typically receives the most attention from agents and potential buyers just after it goes on the market. So be sure yours is priced to sell. The longer it stays on the market, the more it will appear that something is wrong with your home and the more likely that you will have to drop the price.

Truth is on your side

You probably know your home inside and out, warts and all. You may know that its heating system is faulty, that its foundation is cracked, that it has a termite problem, or that it has some other problem that might affect how readily your home will sell and the price you can get for it.

When you're selling a home with structural defects or other problems, you have several options. If you have enough money and time, you can fix the problem before you put your home on the market; otherwise, you can be up-front about the problem with potential buyers and offer to reduce your asking price if necessary; or you can opt not to volunteer any information about the problem, hoping that the buyer won't discover it until the sale has been consummated and the problem isn't yours anymore.

If your home has serious structural or other problems that might not turn up in an inspection and that would most likely lower the value of your home, most states require that you tell a potential buyer about them. For example, you may have to complete a disclosure form and provide it to potential buyers. Your state may also require you to inform a buyer about certain environmental hazards your home may have, such as lead-based paint and asbestos.

If your state has no laws requiring that you voluntarily disclose any defects or other problems your home may have, from a legal, not to mention a moral perspective, it's best to be forthcoming about them because your dishonesty may come back to haunt you. For example, the buyer may have the right to sue you because you were not forthright about the condition of your home and in essence sold the buyer "damaged goods." You should know that the law tends to favor buyers in these situations.

Your real estate agent should be aware of your state's disclosure requirements and should help ensure that you comply with them. In fact, if you are sued by the buyer over a problem with your home after the closing, your realtor may be sued too and may be held liable for nondisclosure.

If You're the Buyer

After you've found your dream home, or something close to it, and you want to buy it, you have to make the seller a formal offer — usually the offer is for something less than the asking price. You should present your offer and all of its terms in a written contract or *purchase and sale agreement;* sometimes you may have to use a *binder* or *earnest money agreement.*

Although the seller's agent can help you draw up the contract and will probably have a standard form you can use, the agent has a financial motivation to draft a contract that benefits the seller. So unless you're working with a buyer's agent, you may want to get legal help preparing a purchase and sale agreement. If you don't, you should hire an attorney to review a proposed contract before you sign it.

In some areas of the country, when you agree to buy a home, you and the seller sign a *binder,* in which case, you have to pay a small deposit on the house. A binder includes much of the same information as a purchase contract, but it's not an enforceable contract.

At a minimum, your purchase and sale agreement should include the following:

✔ A legal description of the property you're buying.

✔ The home's purchase price, including the size of your down payment.

✔ The amount you're paying in earnest money.

Don't sign a contract that doesn't require that the earnest money be held in a trust account or given to a title company, escrow company, or an attorney.

✔ A provision for the return of any deposit or earnest money you've paid if the contract is canceled. The provision should also specify how quickly you can get it back.

✔ A statement that the seller must provide you with an unencumbered deed and clear title to the property.

✔ An itemization of all other documents that you want the seller to provide at closing, such as a survey of the property or title insurance.

✔ Who is responsible for risk of loss due to fire, water damage, and so on until the title to the property has been transferred into your name or until you've taken possession.

✔ Whether the property is being sold "as is" or whether the seller is making any promises about the condition of the property.

✔ Whether the seller must make certain repairs prior to closing.

✔ The appliances, fixtures, air conditioning units, hot tubs, furniture, and so on that the seller conveys with the house.

✔ A closing date and the date you take possession of the house — they don't have to be the same. There should also be a provision requiring the seller to pay you rent if he or she can't vacate the property by the date of possession.

✔ A provision discussing how expenses, such as the taxes, utility bills, and insurance that the seller may have prepaid, will be prorated or apportioned between you and the seller at closing.

✔ A financing contingency clause, assuming you need financing to buy the house. At a minimum, this clause should state the general terms of the financing you will try to find and indicate a deadline by which you must find it. If the clause is worded properly, you should be able to cancel the contract if you're unable to secure the financing.

✔ A home sale and closing contingency clause. In short, this clause should say that you can cancel the contract if you need to sell your current home to buy the new one but you're unable to.

✔ An inspection contingency clause. Be sure to include this clause if you want the house to be inspected by a professional for termites, as well as for mechanical, structural, and environmental problems, including the presence of radon, lead paint, or asbestos in the house. Include this clause so that you can cancel the contract if the house doesn't pass muster. This clause is absolutely essential in my opinion.

✔ The date after which the agreement is no longer valid.

It's a good idea to include a walk-through provision in your purchase and sale agreement giving you the right to literally walk through the house you're buying just prior to closing, often 24 hours prior, so that you can inspect the house. During the walk-through, you can make sure that any repairs that the seller agreed to make have been completed to your satisfaction and that nothing that was to convey with the house has been removed.

Depending on the reasonableness of your offer and how badly the seller wants to sell, the seller can accept your offer, reject it, or make a counter offer. If the seller counters, "the ball is in your court." You can agree to the seller's counter, respond with a new offer, or you can keep house hunting.

If you live in a state where it's customary for buyers and sellers to sign a purchase and sale agreement before it's been reviewed by attorneys, protect yourself by including the following phrase on the document: "Subject to the Approval of the Attorneys for The Parties Within _____ Days."

After both you and the seller have signed the agreement, you are expected to cement the deal with some earnest money — a tangible symbol of your intention to live up to the terms of the contract. Later, when you close on the house, the amount you paid in earnest money is deducted from your down payment.

If your purchase doesn't go through, you can usually get back your earnest money, plus interest. If you fail to live up to the terms of your contract, however, you may forfeit that money.

Never make your earnest money check payable to the seller. Make it payable to the real estate agent or to the real estate firm handling the deal. To prevent the check from being cashed and used for the wrong purpose, write the words "fiduciary agent" or "escrow agent" after the name of the payee.

What to Put in the Contract If You're the Seller

Naturally, if you're the seller, when you're negotiating a purchase and sale agreement, some of your interests are different from the buyer's. The most obvious difference is that you want to get the highest price possible for your home, and the buyer wants just the opposite. But if you're concerned about selling your home as quickly as you can, you may be more open to giving the buyer a good deal.

As the seller, be certain that the contract you sign adequately protects you. This issue is something that your agent should help ensure, assuming you are working with one. Your contract should have some of these provisions:

✔ The earnest money will not be returned to the buyer if he or she fails to live up to the terms of the contract; you get to keep it.

✔ You and the seller set a reasonable time period for the fulfillment of any contingency clauses in the contract — the buyer obtaining adequate financing or selling his or her current home, for example.

✔ You specify any serious problems or defects that you are aware your home has. Spelling them out helps protect you from the possibility of being sued later by the buyer. For the same reason, if your home is in mint condition, you may also want to include a clause stating that to the best of your knowledge, your home has no serious problems or defects.

If there is a possibility that you may want to remain in your home after closing (for example, you're building or renovating a new home and it may not be ready for you by the date of closing), you should include a provision in your contract allowing you to continue living in your home for a specific period of time in exchange for paying the buyer rent and possibly other expenses as well.

Finding a Mortgage

If you're like most people, after you've signed a purchase and sale agreement, your shopping has just begun. Now you have to find a lender willing to finance your purchase. Depending on your income and credit history, that might be harder than finding a house to buy.

The best place to start your search is with your current bank or credit union. But don't stop there. Other banks, as well as mortgage companies and savings and loans may offer you a better deal. The real estate agent may also be able to recommend lenders to contact.

Figure out how high of a mortgage you can afford by checking out this Web site: `http://www.maxsol.com/homes/qualify.hom.html`.

Dealing with lenders

Although all lenders tend to have two basic categories of mortgage loans — *fixed rate* and *adjustable rate* — they often differ in regard to the specific types of fixed and adjustable rate loans they make. Also, they may offer different interest rates and may have different down payment requirements.

Most mortgage loans, regardless of whether they're fixed rate or adjustable rate, are made for 15 or 30 years. Usually, the longer the term of the loan and the bigger the down payment you make, the smaller your monthly payments will be.

Some lenders offer federal guaranteed mortgages. These loans, which are backed by a federal agency like the Federal Housing Administration (FHA) or the Department of Veteran's Affairs (VA), require lower than average down payments, so they tend to be attractive to buyers who might not qualify for a conventional loan. Guaranteed mortgage loans may only be available, however, for certain categories of home buyers, certain types of housing, or only for property that falls within a certain price range. Loans that are not backed by an agency are called *conventional loans*.

If you're a first-time home buyer or if you meet certain income criteria, your local or state government may sponsor a home-buying program in which you can participate.

Some sellers offer their own financing. If you go this route, the seller essentially loans you money to buy his house. You make direct payment with interest to the seller.

Learning about loans

Many types of mortgage loans are available. What follows are brief descriptions of some of the most common.

Fixed rate mortgage

This is the traditional type of mortgage loan. Its interest rate and your monthly payment are determined at the start of your loan and usually remain the same throughout its duration.

Graduated payment mortgage

This loan is a type of fixed rate mortgage. At the start of the loan, your payments are relatively low, but they will rise at a set rate over a specified period of time — 5 to 10 years usually. Then they remain fixed for the remainder of the loan. You may want this kind of mortgage loan if you expect that your income will be rising in coming years.

Adjustable rate mortgages

This kind of loan usually starts out at an interest rate that is somewhat lower than what comes with a fixed rate mortgage. Throughout the life of your loan, however, the rate changes as market conditions change. Usually, the rate is adjusted annually at a predetermined date. Look for an adjustable rate mortgage that allows your monthly payment to decrease as well as increase. Also, find one that limits the amount your monthly payment can change at any one time and the amount your payment can increase or decrease over the life of your loan. Most adjustable rate mortgages come with such limits or caps.

Balloon mortgages

This kind of mortgage loan requires you to make a series of equal monthly payments, often for interest only, followed by a large final payment — the *balloon* — which is usually due just 3 to 5 years after the loan begins. If you're unable to make the balloon payment when it comes due, you have to refinance your home or sell your home.

Assumable mortgages

Sometimes the seller's mortgage loan can be assumed or taken over by the buyer at the seller's interest rate, which may be lower than the current prevailing rate. But when interest rates are high, lenders don't like to make this kind of loan because they can usually make more money writing a new one. If a seller's mortgage loan is assumable, read the mortgage agreement carefully to make sure that it doesn't include a *due on sale* clause that gives the lender the right to raise the interest rate to the existing rate if you take the loan over.

Applying for a loan

Brace yourself if you hate paperwork! You see a lot of it when you apply for a mortgage loan.

Most loan applications ask you for information about

- ✔ Your debts and assets.

- ✔ Your credit history, including a list of the account numbers and outstanding balances for all of your bankcards, retail charge cards, and for any other loans you may have.

- ✔ Your employment history. You may be asked to provide proof of your income including IRS W-2 forms and copies of recent federal tax returns.

- ✔ Information about where your down payment will come from.

- ✔ Information about the home you want to buy.

The lender also reviews your credit record to see if you have or have ever had any debt problems.

Before you begin the mortgage loan application process, order a copy of your credit report from each of the Big Three credit reporting agencies: TRW, Equifax, and Trans Union. Review the reports to make sure they don't contain any erroneous information that can prevent you from getting a loan or getting one with good terms.

After you've provided the lender with all the information it needs to process your loan application, it can take as much as 30 days to find out whether or not you've been approved. If you apply for an FHA or VA mortgage, you may have to wait a little longer.

According to the federal Real Estate Settlement Procedures Act (RESPA), which applies to most real estate lenders, the lender must provide you with an estimate of your closing costs when you apply for a mortgage loan or must send you an estimate within three days after you file your application. You must also be given a copy of *Settlement Costs and You*, a brochure produced by the U.S. Department of Housing and Urban Development (HUD).

If you're approved for a mortgage loan, you have to formally promise the lender to repay it by signing a promissory note. You also have to sign a mortgage or deed of trust giving your lender a security interest in the home you're buying. If you fall behind on your payments, your lender can repossess your home. You may also be required to purchase mortgage insurance if you're considered somewhat of a financial risk.

In addition, you may be expected to buy title insurance. This insurance helps protect the lender against the existence of any liens or other encumbrances on the property you're buying that could take priority over its loan to you. Typically, you pay for this insurance in a lump sum at the time of closing. Sometimes, a purchase and sale agreement requires the seller to pay for this insurance.

Federal agencies that regulate lending institutions

If you're denied a mortgage loan and think that you may have been discriminated against, you can file a complaint with the particular agency that regulates the lender. Here's a list of possible agencies to contact:

For nationally chartered banks (banks with NA or NTSA in their names):

Comptroller of the Currency
Compliance Division
250 E Street,
S.W."National", Washington, D.C. 20219
202-622-2000

For banks with state charters that are insured by the FDIC and are part of the Federal Reserve System:

Federal Reserve System
Division of Consumer and Community Affairs
20th and C Street, N.W. Washington, D.C. 20551
202-452-3000

For banks with state charters that are members of the Federal Reserve System but are not insured by the FDIC:

Federal Deposit Insurance Corporation
Office of Consumer Affairs
550 17th Street, N.W.
Washington, D.C. 20429
800-934-3342

For savings and loan institutions that are federally chartered or insured:

Office of Thrift Supervision
Consumer Programs
1700 G Street, N.W.
Washington, D.C. 20552
202-906-6237

For federally chartered credit unions:

National Credit Union Administration
1775 Duke Street
Alexandria, VA 22314-3428
703-518-6300

For state-chartered credit unions, government lending programs, state-chartered banks, S & Ls that are not insured by the FDIC, and independent mortgage companies:

Federal Trade Commission
Bureau of Consumer Protection
Division of Credit Practices
6th and Pennsylvania Ave.
Washington. D.C. 29580
202-326-3758

If your loan is denied

If a mortgage lender turns you down, federal law requires that the lender tell you why in writing. Common reasons include the following:

- ✔ You have a bad credit history.
- ✔ Your income is not large enough to support the mortgage for which you've applied.
- ✔ You can't come up with a big enough down payment.
- ✔ The house you want to buy didn't appraise high enough to justify the size of the mortgage for which you applied.

The federal Equal Credit Opportunity Act (ECOA) bars lenders from rejecting your loan application or treating you differently from other loan applicants because of your race, color, national origin, religion, sex, marital status, age, or handicap. In addition, a lender can't disallow any public assistance funds you may receive or any alimony, child support, or maintenance payments you may be receiving regularly when evaluating your loan application.

Closing the Deal

The end is in sight! You've gotten your mortgage loan, and now it's time for the closing, also called the *settlement*. But before you close, sit down with your lawyer and review all of the documents that you have to sign and exchange with the seller at the closing. Make sure that they've been properly prepared and accurately reflect the terms of your purchase and sale agreement.

RESPA gives you the right to review a settlement sheet, prepared by your lender or by your attorney, that details all of your closing costs the day before the closing. You'll see another copy at the closing.

At closing, all the final legal formalities required to transfer title from the seller to you take place. You have to sign so many documents that you may feel as though you're literally signing your life away, especially if you're a first-time buyer!

Checks with a lot of zeros will have to be written at closing. The biggest one is your payment to the seller for the price you both agreed less the earnest money you've already put up. Checks may also have to be written to pay for the following:

- ✔ Your lender's title insurance
- ✔ House-related taxes that the seller may have prepaid
- ✔ Certain other house-related expenses that the seller may have already paid for that you will benefit from, such as insurance and utility bills
- ✔ Other expenses that the purchase and sale agreement obligates you to pay

Sometimes there is no formal closing. Instead, an escrow agent handles the closing after the buyer and the seller have provided the agent with the necessary documents and funds.

The federal Fair Housing Act

The federal Fair Housing Act (FHA) protects you from being denied the opportunity to buy the home you want or get the mortgage you need because of discrimination. It prohibits discrimination in housing sales and mortgage loans on the basis of race, religion, color, national origin, and sex. The FHA also protects you from discrimination based on familial status, which means that you can't be discriminated against because you have children under the age of 18 living with you, you are working to get custody of children under the age of 18, or because you're pregnant. (The law also protects prospective tenants from discrimination practiced by landlords.) The FHA also bars real estate brokers and agents from steering certain categories of buyers to particular neighborhoods.

Your state and local governments may have their own anti-discrimination laws related to housing. For example, some localities bar discrimination on the basis of sexual orientation.

If a mortgage lender denies you a loan or a seller refuses to sell to you and you believe you're being discriminated against, you can do the following:

- ✔ Call the federal Department of Housing and Urban Development (HUD) at 800-669-9777 to file a formal complaint. You must do so within one year of the incident. HUD will look

into your allegation. If it feels that there has been a violation of the FHA, it will try to negotiate a conciliation agreement with the violator. (If HUD determines that your local or state agency has the same powers that it has to address your complaint, your complaint is turned over to that agency and HUD's involvement ends.) If it's unsuccessful, an administrative hearing will be held before a judge — you'll be represented by a HUD attorney. If the judge finds that discrimination did occur, the defendant can be ordered to do the following: compensate you for actual damages, including pain, suffering, and humiliation; provide injunctive or other equitable relief (injunctive relief stops someone from doing something); and/or pay the federal government a civil penalty on behalf of the public interest. The defendant can also be ordered to pay "reasonable" attorney fees and expenses.

- ✔ File a formal complaint directly with your state or local agency if it has the same housing powers as HUD.

- ✔ File a lawsuit at your own expense in federal district or state court within two years of the incident.

Words and phrases that you should be familiar with

When you buy or sell a home, you may hear unfamiliar words and phrases. Not knowing what they mean can be stressful. To reduce your anxiety, here are definitions of some of the most common:

Buyer's affidavit: When a buyer signs this document, he or she is swearing to a lender that there are no pending or existing lawsuits of any sort against the buyer. The buyer is also swearing that there are no tax liens or judgments against him or her that attach to the property after the buyer purchases it.

Deed: A written legal document that transfers title to a property from one owner to another. The two most common types of deeds are *warranty deeds* and *quit claim* deeds. A warranty deed guarantees that no one else has a legal claim to the property you're buying. This is the best kind of deed. A quit claim deed makes no such guarantees.

Encumbrance: A claim or restriction on the title to a piece of property.

Lien: A financial claim against a piece of property.

Mortgage deed or deed of trust: When you sign this document, you give the mortgage holder or lender a lien on your home.

Seller's affidavit: When a seller signs this, he or she swears that no liens or encumbrances are on the property for sale.

Title: Title equals ownership. If you have clear title to a piece of property, you own it and have the legal right to use it, control it, and sell it without any restrictions or encumbrances.

Title insurance: Insurance protecting you and the lender against losses that may result from any title-related problems that didn't show up during the title search.

Title search: Research into a piece of property to find out if there are any liens on the property, unpaid taxes, restrictive covenants or easements, and so on that can affect your right and ability to use the property as you would want. The title search is conducted by a title company, abstract company, or attorney. Although it's not legally required, if you're a buyer, a title search helps protect you from buying a property that has other owners, liens, and encumbrances. You should require the seller to correct any title defects as a condition of sale.

Closing and the Seller

If you're the seller, don't expect that you get to sit idly by at closing while the buyer does all the work. You will have to sign documents, including a document transferring title to the home from you to the buyer, an affidavit of title, and a bill of sale transferring any personal property that conveys with the home you're selling.

If you're buying your home with someone else

Before you take title to your new home, if you're buying it with someone else — a spouse, friend, or live-in partner — you need to decide how to structure ownership so that you can live with the legal implications if you end your relationship. The structure of ownership also affects your estate planning.

Your legal ownership options are as follows: Own the home as *tenants in common* or as *joint tenants with right of survivorship*. In some states, if

you're buying your home with your spouse, you can own it as *tenants in the entirety*.

If you're in a heterosexual or same-sex unmarried relationship and want to be certain that the home you're buying together will automatically convey to the surviving partner when one of you dies, consider owning the home as *joint tenants*.

If any of this talk about ownership options confuses you, turn to Chapter 16 for the details on the legal ways to own property.

You have to write a few checks too. Here are some of the things you have to pay for:

- Your agent's commission
- Any taxes owed on the property you're selling
- The outstanding balance on your mortgage loan
- Any other outstanding liens on your property
- Other expenses you agreed to pay in the purchase and sale agreement

You have to pay Uncle Sam a capital gains tax on any profit you may make from the sale of your home unless you purchase a new one to live in within two years of the sale. (You may also have to pay a state capital gains tax.) If you're at least 55 years old, you get a onetime capital gains tax exemption of $125,000.

Buying a New Home or Building One

New home buyers including those who build a home from the ground up — a *custom* home — must deal with issues that buyers of older homes don't have to consider. You should pay close attention to the reputation of the builder you hire to build your home or the builder who built the home you're thinking about buying. Check out the builder's references; inspect other homes the builder has constructed; and evaluate the builder's warranty. If you're building from the ground up, you also need to consider the terms of the builder's contract and how willing the builder is to negotiate. Here are a few more things to consider:

✔ **The warranty:** Many home builders offer insured ten year warranties that protect home buyers from faulty materials, structural defects, and shoddy workmanship in a home's electrical and heating systems, plumbing, and roof, among other things. (Most states and many local governments have laws requiring a warranty to last for a minimum of a year after purchase. To enforce them, you may have to sue the builder.) Read the warranty carefully so that you understand exactly what it does and doesn't cover, what you must do to activate it, and whether the warranty conveys if you sell your home while the warranty is still in effect. Be aware that warranties tend to protect builders more than buyers.

✔ **The contract:** Although most builders use a standard contract, consider it negotiable. A contract should include the following:

- The price you're paying the builder and any other charges.

- The amount of your deposit, whether it's refundable, and under what conditions. Most deposits are about 5 percent of the purchase price.

- The times you can inspect the house during the building process and what the builder must do when you find problems. You should have the right to visit the house periodically while it's being built and just before closing.

- The date your home will be completed, including a financial penalty clause that costs the builder money for every day after that date that the home is not finished.

- All of the provisions in your builder's warranty.

Chapter 11

Your Home Is Your Castle — Well, Almost

*Y*ou may feel like the king or queen of your castle, but in fact, you don't have complete control of your domain even if your name is on the title and you're making the monthly mortgage payments. What you can do with your home may be limited by covenants, zoning ordinances, building codes, easements, neighborhood association rules, and so on.

As a property owner, you may have other legal concerns as well, including liability issues, potential problems with neighbors, and home repair and remodeling contractors who don't do their jobs. And if you decide to lease your home to someone else, you face a whole other set of legal considerations. This chapter is meant to guide you through all of these potential problems.

Ordinances

Local zoning ordinances often limit what you can do with your home and property. For example, an ordinance may limit the height of a privacy fence to six feet; limit how close to the street you can build; or prohibit you from running a business out of your home. Some towns and cities have many restrictive zoning ordinances; others have very few. If you want permission to not comply with a zoning ordinance, you can ask your local government's planning department for a zoning variance. If you do, you may have to attend a public hearing about your request, and your neighbors can speak for or against your request.

As a home owner, you are required to meet certain city or county codes or standards in regard to the way you build a home, remodel it, and maintain it. These codes are designed to help protect the safety and health of those who live in or visit your home as well as your neighbors' well-being.

Covenants

Private entities, often subdivision builders, not governmental bodies, create *covenants,* which may set a minimum size for the lots and/or homes in your subdivision, prohibit certain architectural styles, ban satellite dishes, and so on. Covenants are usually established to help create and maintain a certain ambiance or visual appeal in a subdivision in order to help maintain the property values of its home owners.

You should have been informed of the covenants attached to your property when you purchased it; otherwise, your homeowners' association should tell you about them. If you sell your home, the buyer has to comply with the covenants.

Covenants may impose restrictions or requirements not imposed by municipal zoning ordinances, but they cannot violate state or federal law.

Easements

An *easement* gives someone the right to use a particular part of your property. The most common type of easement is a public utility easement, but your neighbors may have one as well. For example, a public utility may have an easement to come onto your property so that it can work on power lines; or your neighbors may have an easement to drive down your driveway to get to their home.

Easements may be recorded on the plats and deeds related to your property and may also be reflected in your mortgage documents. Also, the title search that should have been conducted prior to the purchase of your home should also reveal any easements that may exist on your property. You can also learn about easements on your property by visiting your county courthouse.

If a utility or neighbor no longer needs an easement, you can probably get it released.

Eminent domain

The government has the right of *eminent domain* when it comes to your property. Eminent domain is limited by the Bill of Rights, which gives you the right of due process and the right to be fairly compensated. Eminent domain enables the government, under certain conditions, to take some of your property if it's needed for a public purpose in exchange for paying you money. For example, your county may decide to widen the road in front of your home, and to do the job, it needs a ten-foot-deep strip of your front yard.

You usually learn about the government's plans to exercise its right of eminent domain through a written notice and at least one public hearing. You and others affected by the government's plans may be able to negotiate some changes in the plans that make them more acceptable to you.

At some point in the process, the government has your property appraised and makes you an offer. You can accept or reject it. If you refuse to accept it, you can sue the government for more money, but it's advisable to get the assistance of an attorney who's experienced at dealing with eminent domain issues.

Home Owners' Associations

If you live in a community with a home owners' association, the association's by-laws may give it a lot of power over what you can do with your home. You should have read these by-laws as well as the association's rules prior to purchasing your home so that you were aware before you paid any money exactly what kinds of restrictions you were agreeing to. Usually, your home owners' association can sue you if you refuse to follow its rules. Also, if you don't pay the association the dues or fees you're obligated to pay, the association may even be able to put a lien on your property. The association

Co-ops and condos

If you live in a cooperative (co-op) apartment or townhouse, you don't actually own your unit; instead, you're a shareholder of the corporation that owns all of the units in the apartment building or townhouse development. An elected board of directors manages the co-op and sets the rules regarding how you must maintain your property, who can buy shares in the cooperative, and other such rules. Co-op boards typically wield considerable powers. If you're approved to become a shareholder in a co-op, you have to sign a document agreeing to abide by the corporation's rules and to pay monthly co-op fees, which include your share of the co-op's property taxes.

When you live in a condominium, you actually own your residence, but typically, a condominium association or board of directors sets rules for the maintenance and appearance of the outside of your home. Although you are free to decorate the interior of your home any way you want, you usually have to get approval to make significant changes to it, such as major additions.

uses these fees to help maintain your neighborhood's common areas, such as parks, pools, biking trails, the clubhouse, and so on.

Home Insurance

Maintaining adequate insurance on your home is another responsibility of home ownership and is something most mortgage lenders require.

Coverage and reimbursement

Home owner's insurance reimburses you for the cost of repairing and replacing your home and its contents when it is damaged due to fire, storms, theft, and so on. It also protects you in the event you're sued by someone who is injured on your property. Depending on your coverage, your insurer may also pay for your hotel and other living expenses if the damage is so serious that you have to live elsewhere while your home is being repaired.

Home owner's insurance varies in its comprehensiveness and the basis of your *reimbursement* — the cash value or the replacement value of your home and its contents in the case of loss. As for injuries to persons on your property, this insurance helps pay for medical costs, up to a point, and also pays for the costs of an attorney if you and the injured party end up in court.

If your home is located in a high-crime area or an area subject to frequent hurricanes or earthquakes, or if other factors make your home relatively risky to insure, you may have trouble getting the home owner's insurance you need at a reasonable rate. To get the coverage you need, you may have to purchase a rider for your policy. A rider amends your insurance policy in some way. Also, many states have established insurance pools to help make insurance affordable to homeowners living in areas with a high risk for earthquakes, hurricanes, and so on.

It's illegal in every state for an insurance company to commit *redlining*, which happens when a company discriminates against a neighborhood because of the personal characteristics of its residents or because it's a low-income neighborhood.

If you begin a home-based business, check with your insurance agent to find out if you need additional coverage. Your current policy may not be sufficient.

Problems with a claim

If you file a claim with your insurance company and it's denied, or if you feel that your reimbursement is not fair, talk with your agent. If that conversation doesn't resolve your problem, place a call to your insurance company's customer service office. You may also want to call your state's insurance commission to see if it can help you. If you have a lot of money at stake, you may also want to hire an independent claims adjuster who can assess the dollar value of your damage or loss. Should the adjuster's assistance result in a bigger settlement than what you were originally offered, however, you have to pay the adjuster 10 to 15 percent of that amount. Other possible options for resolving home owner's insurance problems include dispute resolution and small claims court (both of which are covered in Chapter 2) if the dollar value of the damages is not large.

When you have a problem with your insurance, the National Insurance Consumer Helpline may have some suggestions for what you can do. Call it at 800-942-4242.

Steer clear of independent claims adjusters who try to contact you if your home has been damaged by a fire or a natural disaster. They may be con artists looking to make money from your misfortune.

Trouble in Paradise

If you have neighbors living close to you, and you probably do unless you live in the country or own a large amount of land, you may get along with them just fine. But on occasion, you're likely to experience problems. Your neighbor's barking dog or loud music is keeping you up at night; your neighbors like to have raucous parties at all hours; a tree limb from your neighbor's yard knocks down your fence; or your neighbor is accumulating junk and old cars in his driveway.

Living next door to an enemy can be hell, so you should always try to resolve problems with neighbors by talking neighbor-to-neighbor in a friendly manner. If a low-key conversation doesn't resolve your problem, you may be able to get help from your neighborhood association or condominium owner's group. Or a letter from a number of your neighbors may put pressure on the person to take care of the problem.

Your local or county government may also be able to help you resolve the problem you're having with your neighbor. For example, your neighbor may be violating a local ordinance of some sort. Sometimes, just alerting your neighbor to that fact is enough to resolve the problem. If not, you may be able to file a formal complaint with the appropriate local government agency, or even with the police, depending on the problem. Your neighbor may be formally notified of the ordinance violation and told what he or she must do to fix the problem, and may be fined as well.

Depending on the nature of the problem, ordinance violations may be treated as a civil or a criminal offense. For example, some nuisance laws say that people have a right to reasonable comfort in their own home and a reasonable right to enjoy themselves in their own home. Your neighbor can therefore be accused of violating a nuisance law if she chooses to mow her lawn at 5 a.m. on a Saturday morning; or you can be accused of the same if you insist on cranking up your CD player after midnight and ignoring your neighbors' requests to "turn it down!"

When a neighbor violates a nuisance law, your local law authority may arrest your neighbor or require the person to appear in court. In addition, you have the option of initiating a civil lawsuit against your neighbor. If you win your lawsuit, you're able to collect monetary damages as well as court costs and attorney fees.

Remember, regardless of whether you or your government sues your neighbor, if your case goes to trial, you may have to testify in court. Living next to someone you testified against can be an uncomfortable experience, and your neighbor may try to get revenge against you. Suing a neighbor should always be considered your option of last resort. Lawsuits don't make for good neighbors!

If your neighbor has painted his house bright purple or has filled his yard with plastic pink flamingos, you're probably going to have to live with your neighbor's choices even if they offend your sensibilities. Your neighborhood association or condo complex may, however, have specific rules about paint colors, and your neighbor's choices may be in violation of the covenants in your subdivision. But if your neighbor is neglecting his or her home and yard, and if that neglect is creating a safety or health hazard, your neighbor may be in violation of an ordinance, and your local or county government may step in to deal with the situation.

Maybe your neighbor is having money or health problems and can't afford to keep up his or her yard or perhaps doesn't have the right tools and equipment. If you think that any of these situations apply, try being a good neighbor instead. For example, consider offering to help clean up the trash, paint the house, trim the trees, and so on.

Your home owner's association may have rules that outlaw what your neighbor is doing or not doing. So if you're not able to resolve a problem directly with your neighbor, the association may be of help.

Home Repairs and Improvements

Remember the movie *The Money Pit* about a couple who buys a fixer-upper and ends up spending countless dollars trying to transform it into a jewel? Although your home may not drain your pocketbook like the home in that movie did, you'll find that buying a home is just the start of what you'll spend on it as a home owner. Over the years, if you want to maintain and maybe enhance the value of what is probably your single most important asset, you'll no doubt write at least a few checks for home repairs and improvements. If you're handy with a hammer and know the difference between a crescent wrench and a Philips head screwdriver, you may be able to perform minor repairs and improvements yourself. But for difficult or big jobs that require special skills, know-how, and equipment, (such as adding a room or putting on a new roof), you will probably hire a contractor to do the work for you. You may even hire an architect who in turn will hire the contractor.

Before you decide to tackle a remodeling job yourself, call your city or county building inspection department to find out what permits you need and what building codes you have to comply with. A reputable contractor already knows this information and can take care of getting the necessary permits.

Handy with a hammer? If you are, you can put to good use the information you'll find at Home Improvement Nettips, a Web site located at `http://www.nettips.com/homepage.html`.

Protecting yourself

The Better Business Bureau lists problems with home remodeling firms as number two on their complaint list. Home repairs also showed up as the number-two source of consumer complaints in a 1992 Consumer Federation of America national study (auto repairs were number one.) To avoid becoming one of these statistics, whenever you let someone you don't know work on your home, be absolutely certain that the individual or firm you hire is qualified to do the job; otherwise, you put yourself at risk for hiring a plumber, roofer, or contractor whose cost overruns, shoddy workmanship, or missed deadlines can turn your life into an expensive nightmare. The following can help you protect yourself and get your money's worth too:

- ✔ To locate a reputable repair person or contractor, get references from friends and neighbors.

- ✔ Especially for big jobs, get detailed written estimates from more than one contractor or repair person and check their references. Find out if the quality of their work was satisfactory, completed on time, and for the contract amount.

- ✔ Never hire a contractor who works on a cost-plus- or time-plus-materials basis.

- ✔ Find out if your local Better Business Bureau or your state or local consumer protection office has any complaints on file about the individual or company you're considering hiring.

- ✔ Check with your local or state consumer protection office to find out whether there are any laws that can protect you if troubles develop.

- ✔ Don't automatically go with the lowest bidder. A bid may be low because it assumes the use of inferior quality materials, subcontractors, and other cost-cutting shortcuts that may sacrifice quality.

- ✔ Ask for proof of a contractor's liability insurance and workmen's compensation insurance. If a contractor doesn't have adequate insurance, you may be liable for any on-the-job injuries. You should also check with your insurance agent to find out what your home owner's policy does and does not cover should accidents happen.

- ✔ Make sure that a contractor is bonded and know what the bond covers. This means that if the contractor does not meet the terms of your agreement regarding the work to be performed, the contractor's insurance company will pay for some other contractor to finish the job.

- ✔ Find out if your state or local government has any laws that can help protect you. State and local governments are pretty tough on unscrupulous contractors and repair people. Small claims court or dispute resolution may be options, depending on your problem.

The American Homeowners Association (AHA) is a membership organization that produces helpful publications on subjects related to owning a home, including getting your home renovated or repaired. It also maintains referral services for legal assistance, contractors, realtors, discounts on insurance, mortgages, moving costs, and so on. To obtain written information on the AHA, call 888-470-2242. You may also want to request a free brochure on finding a home remodeler by writing the National Association of Home Builders, Remodelers Council, at 1201 15th Street, N.W., Washington, D.C. 20005.

Getting down to details

If the repair work you need done is relatively minor — your toilet or air conditioner needs to be fixed, for example — all you may need is a signed written estimate before you authorize the work. But if the work required is major, after you've decided on a contractor, you need to make sure that the details of your agreement are in writing. Your contract should include a complete description of the work to be done, the materials to be used, the starting and completion dates, and the names of any subcontractors to be used. It should also spell out the payment schedule, any warranties the contractor is offering, cleanup and financing arrangements, as well as the contractor's full name, address, phone number, and the contractor's license or registration number if your state requires either.

If your job is going to cost more than $500, your contractor is legally required to put it in writing.

If the contractor is going to be providing appliances or equipment, be sure the contract specifies the exact models. Don't accept a contract that includes the phrase "or the equivalent." If your first choice for an appliance or other equipment is not available, the contract should specify what will be substituted.

To help ensure that the work you've contracted for gets done, never pay a contractor the full amount of the job up front; a 10 to 30 percent down payment is usually reasonable. It's better to pay in installments, perhaps tying each payment to the completion of certain milestones. Also, never release the final payment until the job is completed to your satisfaction.

To end this section, here are some miscellaneous tips:

✔ Some states place ceilings on the percentage of the total contract price a contractor can require up front.

✔ Never pay for materials and supplies up front. After the contractor buys them, ask for the receipts, review them, and then, assuming there are no surprises or discrepancies, reimburse the contractor.

✔ If the contractor is going to use subcontractors, ask for lien waivers from each of them. That way, if the contractor fails to pay them, they cannot place a lien on your home in order to get payment from you.

✔ The federal Truth in Lending Act gives you three business days to cancel a contract that you sign in your home that gives the contractor any kind of financial claim to your home.

Don't get conned

Fly-by-night contractors are in the business of preying on unsuspecting consumers. Here are some common signs of these con artists:

✔ They come looking for you, unsolicited.

✔ They drive up to your home in an unmarked truck or van.

✔ You're approached by a door-to-door salesperson who claims to be offering you a great deal.

✔ The "contractor" has a post office address with no street address or a phone number with an answering service.

✔ The contractor or salesperson promises to use your home as a demonstration model and in return, to charge you a reduced price.

✔ They use high-pressure sales tactics to get you to commit to hiring them.

✔ They refuse to give you a written estimate or contract, or you're promised one but it's never delivered.

Renting Out Your Home

If you've decided to buy a new home, you may choose to rent out your old house rather than sell it. If you do, it's important for you to understand your legal responsibilities as a landlord and find out what you can do to protect yourself.

Choosing a tenant

Perhaps the most significant challenge of being a landlord is finding a good tenant. You want one who will treat your property with care and pay the rent on time. The better the tenant, the less likely you and your tenant will end up in court.

To help you identify the ideal tenant, whether you advertise that you have a place for rent, put up a sign, or use a rental service, always ask prospective tenants to complete a rental application. The application should provide you with the applicant's full name, current address, day and evening phone numbers, and Social Security number. It should also provide you with information about an applicant's recent — past three to five years — employment and rental histories, current income, and credit and financial history. Get personal references as well as the names and phone numbers of former employers and landlords. At a minimum, call former landlords to find out whether the applicant was a good and reliable tenant, and verify the applicant's current income and employment.

Because screening rental applicants can be time-consuming, if you own a lot of rental property, you may want to use the services of a tenant reporting service. Tenant reporting services function much like credit reporting agencies but collect and report information specifically related to property rentals, such as evictions. Although these services cost money, they can help save you the hassle and cost of having to go to court to get a tenant evicted or to enforce certain aspects of a lease.

The federal Fair Credit Reporting Act allows landlords to check a prospective tenant's credit history by ordering a copy of that individual's credit record from one of the national credit reporting agencies. This report can tell you whether an applicant is having money troubles, has a history of not paying debts, and so on.

When you're looking for a tenant, the federal Fair Housing Act prohibits you from discriminating on the basis of race, color, sex, national origin, religion, or marital status. You're also barred from discriminating on the basis of an applicant's mental or physical disability. Your state and local government may also prohibit housing discrimination on the basis of sexual orientation.

Be wary of prospective tenants who want to pay their rent in cash or with money orders. This practice may be a sign that they are earning their income illegally or have had serious financial troubles. If, however, you're renting to low-income people, prospective tenants may want to pay in cash because they don't have a bank account.

Leases

Don't rent to anyone without a signed agreement or lease. A lease is essentially a contract that spells out your obligations and the obligations of your tenant — the rules of the game. At a minimum, a lease should include the following:

- The address of the rental property.
- The amount of the monthly rent and who is responsible for utility bills, taxes, and other charges.
- The date the rent is due.
- Whether a late fee will be assessed and the amount of that fee. Your local government may limit your ability to charge a late fee. Also, nearly all states prohibit excessive or *usurious* late fees.
- The amount of the security deposit. Your state may limit how much you can charge; may require that you keep the deposit in an escrow account; or may require that you pay your tenant interest on the money.
- Whether or not pets are allowed, and if so, whether you require an additional deposit to cover potential pet damage.
- Who is responsible for repairs and maintenance.
- Under what conditions a landlord can gain access to the rental property. Normally, a landlord cannot have unlimited, unannounced access to a rental property unless a tenant says it's okay.
- Whether or not a tenant can sublease the property.
- Provisions for rent increases.
- Provisions for move-in and move-out inspections of the property.
- What the landlord can do if the tenant defaults on the rent. Check your local laws to find out what you can and cannot do to collect and what the process is for evicting a tenant.
- Who has responsibility for paying attorney's fees and court costs that the landlord must incur in trying to enforce the terms of the lease.
- What kind of notice the tenant must give before moving out.

Most office supply or stationery stores sell sample rental applications and leases.

Many states have adopted the Uniform Residential and Tenant Act. Among other things, this law says that if, without good reason, you fail to return a tenant's security deposit, the tenant has the right to sue you for triple damages, court costs, and attorney fees.

Your obligations and rights

You have a responsibility to maintain your rental property so that it's safe for your tenant and hazard free. You're also responsible for ensuring that your property complies with all state and local housing and building codes and with appropriate health and safety ordinances too. For example, you may have to provide certain types of locks, peepholes, and other kinds of safety devices. If you don't meet these obligations and your tenant is injured or harmed as a result, you're opening yourself up to a lawsuit.

In most states, rental property comes with an *implied warranty of habitability.* This warranty obligates you, regardless of what your lease says, to keep your rental property safe and livable. If you fail to do so, your tenant can take you to court, and you can be required to do the necessary repairs and maintenance. Also, depending on your state and local laws, your tenant may have the right to withhold rent, ask for a reduction in rent, cancel the lease, or even sue you in small claims court.

You also have an obligation to respond within a reasonable period of time to tenant requests for the maintenance and repairs you have agreed to make. But you're probably not responsible for repairing problems or damage resulting from your tenant's carelessness.

You have the right to expect your tenant to live up to the terms of your lease, to take good care of your home, and to make a reasonable effort to protect from harm guests and others who visit the property.

You also have the right to evict a tenant who fails to live up to the terms of your lease. Before initiating an eviction, however, be sure you understand your state's eviction procedures. You can learn about them by calling your local, nonprofit tenants or landlord-tenants council or your local housing authority. Generally, you must provide your tenant with a written notice demanding that the tenant take care of problems by a certain date. This notice should also state that if the tenant doesn't take satisfactory action, you will initiate eviction proceedings. Often, eviction requires that you file a complaint or petition in court; a court hearing will follow. If the court says that you can proceed with the eviction, depending on your state, you may be able to enter your rental property and physically remove your tenant's furniture and other belongings after giving your tenant notice that you intend to do so, or a sheriff or other law official may have to do the evicting.

Some areas have special landlord-tenant courts.

Chapter 12

Driving and the Law

. . . .

In This Chapter

▶ Getting your license

▶ Understanding the rules of the road

▶ Knowing your rights when a cop pulls you over

▶ Dealing with accidents

▶ Fulfilling your responsibilities as a driver

. . . .

D riving is simple. Just turn the ignition key and step on the gas, right? Wrong. Before you can get behind the wheel, you have some legal hoops to jump through first. Namely, you must get a driver's license and have insurance. And to maintain your right to get behind the wheel, you must demonstrate your willingness and ability to obey the rules of the road.

Getting Your Driver's License

In about half of the states, 18 is the magic age for getting a regular driver's license. In some states, you can get one as early as 15, while at least one state makes you wait until you're 21. That said, most states allow young people to get their licenses at an earlier age if they meet certain conditions such as passing a driver's education class or getting the consent of their parents.

Although the exact process for getting a driver's license differs slightly from state to state, it typically includes passing the following tests:

✔ A written test about the basic rules of the road. Pretty much a no-brainer.

✔ A behind-the-wheel test of your ability to drive. Passing this test can be a little trickier, especially if you're intimidated by having a stranger in the seat next to you watching your every move!

✔ A vision test.

Your driver's license may come with restrictions, or sometimes restrictions may be added later. The restrictions can be as insignificant as requiring that you wear your glasses or contact lenses whenever you drive, or if you have a chronic and potentially dangerous medical condition, the restrictions may limit when you can drive. If you ignore your restrictions and get pulled over by a police officer, your license can be suspended.

Your driver's license does not last forever. You have to renew it periodically. If you're lucky, you can do it by mail and avoid the hassle of making a personal appearance at the department of motor vehicles and having a new photo taken (and who looks good in those photos anyway!) and/or a vision test. If you're a senior citizen over a certain age, your state may require that you pass an eye exam and a driver's test every time you renew your license.

If you move to a new state, you may have to apply for a new driver's license within 30 days of your move, or you may be able to wait until your old license expires.

The Rules of the Road

Keeping your right to drive requires that you demonstrate that you're a responsible driver. If you don't, your license may be *suspended* — that means you lose it temporarily — or *revoked* — you're grounded for good. Grounds for suspension or revocation can include the following:

- ✔ Causing "too many" traffic accidents (every state has its own rules for what "too many" is)
- ✔ Getting a lot of tickets for moving violations
- ✔ Driving without insurance
- ✔ Being convicted of driving while under the influence of alcohol or drugs

States share information on the records of their drivers. So if you move, your new state may refuse to license you if your previous state has suspended or revoked your license.

If your license has been suspended or revoked, don't even think about driving. If you do and a police officer pulls you over, you'll be arrested and charged with either a misdemeanor or a felony depending on why you lost your license.

Facts about buckling up

✔ Most, but not all, states have seat belt laws pertaining to adults.

✔ All states require that children be restrained when they're passengers in a moving vehicle.

✔ In some states, drivers can be fined if their passengers don't wear their seat belts.

✔ If you're injured in a traffic accident and weren't wearing your seat belt, you can probably still collect for your injuries.

Stopped by the Cops

Your three-hour drive to the beach is almost over. It's been an easy one — beautiful scenery and little traffic. You've been making great time. Life couldn't be better! Then all of a sudden, out of nowhere, a cop car with its lights flashing is right behind you in your rear view mirror. Talk about putting a damper on your trip!

If this happens to you, pull off the road as quickly and safely as possible and remain in the car unless the police officer tells you to get out. The officer will ask to see your driver's license and possibly your vehicle registration and proof of insurance. The officer should tell you why you've been stopped — it's your legal right. If the officer doesn't provide this information, ask.

If you're not sure that the person who stops you is really a police officer, ask to see his or her photo I.D. Don't settle for a badge. If the "officer" refuses to show you an I.D. or, after seeing it, you're still not convinced, ask that the officer's supervisor be called or offer to follow the officer to the police station.

You can be stopped by a police officer if he or she has a *reasonable belief* or *reasonable suspicion* that you or someone in your vehicle is committing or has committed a crime. The crime can be any number of things — driving too fast, driving with an expired license plate, reckless driving, driving while intoxicated, driving with a headlight out, leaving the scene of a crime, robbery, murder — you get the picture.

After you've been stopped, the police officer cannot search your car unless you give your permission or unless the officer has *probable cause*. Probable cause is a kind of gray area; its definition varies widely among states, and those definitions are constantly changing. Generally, an officer has probable cause when he or she believes that your car contains incriminating evidence — evidence that you and/or your passenger are committing or have committed a crime. With probable cause, your vehicle can be searched without a search warrant.

Why you're stopped by a police officer affects when an officer has probable cause. For example, being stopped because your head light is out may provide less probable cause for a search than being pulled over because you've been driving erratically or at a high rate of speed.

The Fourth Amendment of the U.S. Constitution protects you and your belongings from unreasonable searches and seizures. Law enforcement officials must usually obtain a search warrant in order to search your home. But the Supreme Court has ruled that the Fourth Amendment provides you less protection when you're in your car.

If an officer looks through your vehicle window — a *plain view* search — and spies something that he or she considers to be possible evidence of a crime — an open container of beer is sitting on your seat or a half-smoked marijuana cigarette is lying in the ash tray, for example — the officer can take it as evidence. After spying potential evidence, the officer has the right to conduct a full-scale warrantless search of your car.

If an officer begins searching your vehicle without apparent probable cause, ask to see his or her search warrant, but don't try to stop the search. If you are not shown a warrant and he or she continues the search and takes something from your vehicle, you can challenge the seizure in court.

The police have the right to frisk you or "pat you down" without a warrant if they have a reasonable suspicion that you may possess drugs or weapons and can articulate their reasoning to the courts. Although they cannot search your clothes or your pockets, if they feel something suspicious, they can seize it; otherwise, the police need probable cause to search your clothing and your pockets. This restriction also applies to warrantless searches of your car.

Getting Tickets

Even the most careful and conscientious drivers are likely to get a ticket for a traffic violation of some sort at some point in their driving career. If you're lucky, your tickets will be for non-moving violations — parking tickets and tickets for mechanical defects, for example. You have to pay fines on these kind of violations, but they do not damage your driving record. But tickets for moving violations like speeding, reckless driving, and driving while intoxicated do go on your record and possibly increase your insurance costs. If you get two of them within a certain period of time, expect to have your license suspended or revoked for a period of time.

Parking tickets may not be a big deal, but don't ignore them. If you accumulate enough unpaid tickets, a warrant for your arrest may be issued or your car may be immobilized by the infamous Denver Boot. The Boot is essentially a mechanism that locks a wheel on your car so that you can't drive it. The only way to get it removed is to pay your tickets.

When you get a ticket, you can either pay it by the due date or fight it. If you decide to fight, you have to be arraigned in court on a certain date. At the arraignment, your rights are read to you and you are asked to plead guilty or not guilty. Because you're fighting the charge, you say "not guilty." (Some states let you do this by mail.) If you've been charged with a serious moving violation, it's a good idea to hire an attorney to represent you. If you don't get an attorney, your case is a matter of your word against the police office who ticketed you, which means that you will probably be at a serious disadvantage.

If you are ticketed for a moving violation and you decide not to fight it, you're pleading guilty when you pay the fine. That means that the cost of your insurance premium may go up, and the violation goes on your driving record.

Accidents Happen

If you're involved in an accident, regardless of whom you think is at fault, stop your vehicle and inspect the damage. Not stopping is a criminal offense. If you're convicted of a "hit and run," your driver's license may be suspended, or you may be fined and sentenced to jail.

If no one is injured and damage to the vehicles involved is very slight to nonexistent, you and the other driver can handle the situation yourselves without calling the police. Exchange your names, addresses, phone numbers, the names of your insurance companies, your policy numbers, your driver's license numbers, license plate numbers, and the makes, models, and years of your cars. If, however, someone is injured or killed, or if property damage is substantial, you must call the police, and they will file an accident report.

Most insurance companies do not pay claims without a police report. Do not sign any insurance forms related to an accident-related injury without consulting an attorney first.

Although all states require accident reports in the case of death or injury, each state has its own criteria for when an accident report is required.

If you hit a parked car, you're expected to make a reasonable effort to locate the owner or at least to leave your name, address, and phone number on the car you hit and to notify the police.

When the police arrive, you must answer any questions the officers may ask. If, however, there are witnesses, get their names and phone numbers but don't talk with them about what you think happened. If you end up in court as a result of the accident and the witness testifies, what you said at the scene can be used against you.

If you have the presence of mind to do so, make some notes about your accident while everything is still relatively fresh in your mind. For example, you may want to draw a diagram of the accident and describe the weather, street conditions, and any other pertinent factors. This information can be helpful if you are sued over the accident or end up suing the other driver.

Drinking and Driving

Drinking and driving don't mix. To deter drivers from using alcohol, states' laws have become harsher in recent years. Presently, depending on your state, if you're convicted of drinking and driving, your license may be suspended or revoked, you may be jailed, fined, put on probation, forced to enroll in a rehab program, and so on. If you've been convicted before for drunk driving, your penalty will be especially serious.

Every state has its own standard for determining when a driver is under the influence of alcohol and should not be behind the wheel, and the laws governing drinking and driving also apply to driving while under the influence of illegal drugs.

If you're stopped by a police officer and the officer suspects that you've been drinking, he or she will probably ask you to take a number of roadside impairment or sobriety tests, which can include walking in a straight line, reciting the alphabet backwards, or standing on one leg. You may also be asked to take a preliminary breath test, which gives the officer a measure of the level of alcohol in your blood. The results of these tests may provide the officer with sufficient probable cause to arrest you.

If you're arrested and taken to the police station, you may be asked to take a Breathalyzer test, which provides a more precise measure of your intoxication level.

Legally, you can refuse to take a roadside sobriety test. But the officer can arrest you anyway if he or she suspects that you're intoxicated because your speech is slurred, your eyes are bloodshot, you're weaving when you stand still, and so on. At the police station, you can also refuse to take a Breathalyzer or a urine or blood test; however, your refusal to take any of these tests can be used against you in court, and you may be subject to stiffer than usual penalties if you're convicted. Also, depending on your state, a blood sample can be forcibly withdrawn if you've been involved in a traffic accident in which someone was killed or seriously injured.

When you get a driver's license, your state assumes that you've given implied consent to be tested for alcohol use. Usually the concept of implied consent also applies to testing for the use of drugs while you're driving.

If you're involved in a car accident that results in death or serious injury, the officer may want a sample of your blood. Testing your level of intoxication by sampling your blood provides stronger evidence in court than the results of a Breathalyzer test.

The Responsibilities of Owning a Vehicle

If you own a vehicle, you must follow certain rules if you want to keep your vehicle on the road and keep yourself out of legal hot water.

Register your car

When you buy a vehicle, you must register it right away. Also, you probably have to renew the registration every year. In most states, registration is contingent on proof of liability insurance.

Get it inspected

To help ensure that your car meets minimum safety standards as established by your state, you must have your car inspected regularly — usually annually — either at a state-authorized repair shop or dealer, or at a government inspection station. Your car also may have to meet certain environmental standards. If your car doesn't pass muster, you will have a specified period of time to bring it up to standards and to get it reinspected; otherwise, you can't continue driving it. If you don't get your car's problems fixed and you keep it on the road, you will be subject to fines.

Have insurance

All states have financial responsibility laws. Most of these laws require that drivers have liability insurance, but others allow drivers to provide proof that they have other means of paying for a state-specified amount of damages in the event of an accident.

Liability insurance helps protect you legally and financially if an accident is your fault and someone is injured or killed and/or you cause serious property damage. Your insurer pays the legitimate claims of the injured party and defends you in court if you are sued. Usually, your insurer also protects you if someone driving your car with your permission is involved in an accident.

You can purchase additional insurance, such as uninsured motorist coverage (pays your expenses when you're hit by an uninsured driver); collision coverage (pays for the physical damage to your vehicle); and comprehensive coverage (pays for non-accident-related damage to your vehicle — a tree falls on your car, your car is pounded by hail, your car is stolen, and so on).

Some states have no-fault laws for liability insurance. In these states, policy holders are reimbursed by their own insurance companies when they are injured in an accident regardless of who caused the accident. But this kind of insurance restricts the ability of anyone injured in an accident to sue the person at fault.

Although most no-fault insurance policies apply only to personal injury claims, a few also apply to property damage.

Part III

Tough Stuff: Being Sick, Getting Older, Dying

The 5th Wave — By Rich Tennant

"As you know, your uncle died intestate, and in this State we have our own way of distributing assets to the heirs. Now, do you all know what a piñata is?"

In this part . . .

The chapters in this part cover some pretty tough issues, stuff you may find difficult to deal with, but stuff that all people face at some point in their lives. I'm talking about health care, social security, estate planning, and other legal issues related to growing old. The purpose of the chapters in this part is to help you plan for the future so that you and your loved ones can avoid legal and financial troubles.

Chapter 13
Your Health Care Rights

. . . .

In This Chapter

▶ Understanding your rights as a patient

▶ Filing a malpractice claim

▶ Paying for medical expenses

▶ Filing health insurance claims

▶ Challenging an insurance claim denial

. . . .

*W*hy is something so fundamentally important so frustrating and difficult? I'm talking about dealing with the health care system — doctors, hospitals, health insurance companies, and increasingly, managed care organizations. Doctors often discourage us from playing an active role in our own health care. Medical terminology sounds like gobbledy-gook and seems designed to keep us in the dark. Rules, restrictions, and delays commonly associated with insurance providers and managed care organizations would test even Job's patience!

Our feelings of frustration and confusion are exacerbated by a changing health care industry and the fact that things we used to take for granted are disappearing. Here are some examples of what I'm talking about:

✔ Their bottom lines under pressure, fewer and fewer employers are providing their employees with fee-for-service health insurance. Those that do often make their employees pick up a greater share of their premium costs than in the past.

✔ The costs of medical care and other market forces are pushing consumers into managed care organizations with strange sounding acronyms like HMOs (Health Maintenance Organizations) and PPOs (Preferred Provider Organizations).

✔ Both insurance companies and managed care organizations are getting tougher on preexisting conditions, whether serious or minor, making it more difficult for many of us to get the health coverage and care that we need.

Although there's talk at both the state and federal levels about finding ways of addressing some of these problems through legislation, at least for the near future, consumers must become more actively involved in all aspects of their health care and be ready to assert their rights when they feel they're not getting the care they need or are not being treated fairly by a medical provider, insurance company, or managed care organization. If pushed, push back. If you don't get your questions answered, keep asking. If you don't get what you think is fair, complain. Doing this stuff may not be easy. In fact, you may feel like David did when he fought Goliath. But remember, David won!

Power to Patients!

Here's a run-down on your basic legal rights when dealing with doctors, hospitals, and other health care providers.

Informed consent

You have a right to a "plain English" explanation of any medical treatment or surgery your doctor suggests and the right to agree or not agree to it. Exactly what you must be told varies by state, but at a minimum, you should expect an explanation of your health problem, your treatment options, including their pros and cons, and your prognosis. Informed consent also gives you the right to refuse to participate in any medical research projects you may be asked to be part of.

If you agree to what your doctor recommends, you are asked to sign a consent form. Read it carefully before you sign — there may be something in it you weren't told about. If you have any questions, ask them. If there's anything on the form that you don't want to agree to, cross it out and initial it.

A doctor who fails to get your consent can be charged with a criminal offense.

Generally speaking, you don't have to sign a consent form for a simple, routine treatment or procedure like getting an inoculation or having your blood drawn. It's usually assumed that when you roll up your sleeve or stick out your finger, you're implying your consent. In many states, however, if the blood is being drawn for an HIV test, implied consent is not enough.

If your condition is life-threatening or if you're in the middle of a medical emergency, the doctor responsible for your care doesn't need your permission, or anyone else's, to do what's necessary to save your life or end the emergency.

Generally, parents have the right to consent to medical treatment for their minor children.

You cannot give your informed consent if you're drunk, high on drugs, or emotionally out of control and beyond reason. In these situations, the law assumes that your judgment is impaired. Also, you may not be able to give your informed consent when you are mentally incapacitated. But a close relative is usually allowed to give or withhold his or her consent on your behalf.

Some managed care organizations require doctors under contract to them to sign confidentiality clauses or *gag clauses.* Many doctors have been critical of these clauses, arguing that they restrict their ability to provide patients with information about all of their treatment options. Some doctors also criticize gag clauses because they restrict the ability of doctors to recommend specialists and to provide second opinions. These restrictions essentially undermine a patient's right to informed consent. States are beginning to pass laws to help address this problem.

All of the major national online service providers offer a wealth of health and medical information as well as medical support groups. Use key word "health" to get to these resources, or try the name of the particular medical or health issue you want to learn more about.

The right to treatment

If you're one of the more than 35 million Americans who are uninsured and the 60 million plus who are underinsured, you may live with a gnawing fear that some day you or a dependent will need hospital emergency care and will be turned away because you can't pay for it. So you should sleep a little better knowing that federal law and most state laws require that all public and private hospitals treat anyone with a medical emergency, including women in labor, regardless of their ability to pay. Hospitals as well as doctors who turn emergency patients away can be accused of "patient dumping" and risk government fines, lawsuits, and the loss of their accreditation.

It can be a different story if you need routine medical care and you don't have any way to pay for it. For example, you can be turned away by a private hospital. But you can probably receive care if you go to a public hospital because federal law requires most public health facilities receiving government grants and loans to care for anyone regardless of their ability to pay.

If you schedule a doctor's appointment for a non-emergency medical problem, in most states, you can be refused treatment if you have no insurance or any other means of paying for your care. If, however, you have an established relationship with a doctor, your doctor can't legally "abandon" you or refuse to continue treating you without giving you sufficient time to locate a new doctor.

When you can't speak for yourself

Life is full of surprises, both good and bad. Sometimes, even if you're the healthiest person, you can suddenly become seriously ill with no hope of recovery or can be critically injured and literally lose the ability to speak for yourself and make your own decisions. Unless you've planned for this possibility, you may be kept alive indefinitely, hooked up to expensive life support systems that could quickly deplete your assets and take an emotional toll on your family members and close friends. Also, someone else you may or may not trust may be appointed by the court to handle your legal and financial affairs.

You can use three key legal tools to plan for the possibility of becoming incapacitated: a durable power of attorney, a durable power of attorney for health care, and a living will. Each of these tools is legally recognized in every state, but each state has its own criteria for what makes them valid. You can prepare them yourself or you can use an attorney. You can amend or cancel these documents whenever you want. Review them each year to make sure that they continue to reflect your wishes.

Here's a brief overview of each of these important legal tools:

✔ To handle your legal and/or financial affairs, give someone you trust a durable power of attorney. Do so by preparing an agreement in accordance with the legal requirements of your state that spells out exactly what powers you're giving to your representative and under what conditions the power of attorney is activated.

Be sure that you give this person durable power of attorney as opposed to power of attorney; otherwise, that individual's power is automatically voided as soon as you become incapacitated — just when you need help!

✔ To make decisions regarding your medical care, give someone a durable power of attorney for health care. Again, in your agreement, stipulate under what conditions you want this legal power to be activated and spell out exactly what powers you want your representative to have or not have. It's a good idea to give this person the power to help enforce your living will.

✔ To spell out the life-sustaining medical care you do and don't want when you're sick or injured and near death with no hope of recovery, write a living will.

Most states require that you let your doctor know about a living will. Better yet, review it with your doctor so that you increase the chances that it will be activated when the time comes.

If you spend a lot of time in more than one state, prepare a legally valid durable power of attorney for health care and a living will for each state. You may also need to prepare multiple durable power of attorney documents for your legal and financial affairs.

Contact the nonprofit organization Choice in Dying to obtain fill-in-the-blanks living wills and durable power of attorney for health care forms that are legally valid in your state. Write to 200 Varick Street, New York, N.Y. 10014. Or call 800-989-WILL.

The Patient's Bill of Rights

The Patient's Bill of Rights, drafted by the American Hospital Association, has been adopted by most hospitals. It sets out your basic rights when you're hospitalized. They include the right to

✔ "Considerate and respectful care."

✔ Be provided understandable information about your medical condition and proposed treatment as well as the outlook for your recovery from your doctor and others involved in your care. You also have the right to review the pros and cons of your treatment options, including the risks.

✔ Refuse a certain medical treatment, surgery, or plan of care assuming your refusal is not in conflict with your state's law or the policies of the hospital.

✔ Expect that the directives in your durable power of attorney for health care and your living will will be honored by your hospital, assuming that your requests are not in conflict with the laws of your state or hospital policies.

✔ Expect that the information in your medical records is treated as private, confidential information by your hospital except when your state law requires or allows certain information to be reported.

✔ Review your medical records and have anything you don't understand explained to you.

Hospitals and doctors cannot refuse to treat you because of your race, ethnic origin, sexual orientation, and so on. That's called discrimination and if they discriminate, they can be sued.

If you're HIV-positive or have AIDS

Acquired Immune Deficiency Syndrome (AIDS) is caused by the virus known as HIV. If you carry the virus, you're HIV-positive and you can give the virus to others.

Even as this book was being written, laws regarding the rights and obligations of HIV-infected persons are evolving to reflect the growing understanding of HIV and AIDS within the medical community and within society in general. The challenge as the law develops is to find a balance between the privacy rights of those who are HIV-positive and the obligation of the medical community to protect the public health.

Presently, almost all states have laws relating to the confidentiality of an HIV-positive person's health condition; however, those laws vary widely. Here are the general rules:

✔ If you test positive for HIV, your state may have no policy regarding public health reporting; others require that doctors report anyone who tests positive to their health departments. Some states require doctors to name names; others allow use of a Social Security number or another identifier. Regardless, no matter where you live, your state prohibits its health department personnel from naming you as someone who is HIV-positive — the information is *supposed* to remain confidential. Realistically speaking though, there is no way of guaranteeing that it will.

✔ A majority of states require that once your state's health department is notified of your health problem, the department must try to locate and notify your sexual partners as well as anyone you may have shared needles with if you're an IV drug user. Obviously, your cooperation is essential. Again, your anonymity is supposed to be maintained, but in many instances, it is probably not very difficult for someone to figure out that you're the one with the health problem.

✔ Health care providers may be permitted to notify blood banks and organ transplantation companies that you're HIV-positive without your permission. It's a matter of protecting the public health.

✔ If you're applying for insurance, an insurance provider may have the right to know about your health problem, depending on the kinds of questions you are asked. As with other preexisting conditions, however, you do not have to offer up information unless you are specifically asked.

✔ If you're a health care worker, you may have an obligation to notify your employer of your health status if you're HIV-positive.

If you want to learn your state's policy, call the National AIDS Hotline at 800-342-AIDS. The national AIDS hotline provides callers with free information and referrals about HIV and AIDS — no questions asked.

If you're HIV-positive or have AIDS, you have a moral obligation, if not a legal one, to inform your sexual partners about your health problem. If you use drugs and have shared needles with others, let them know too. If you refuse to do so, depending on your state, your doctor may have a legal obligation to do the notifying for you.

A growing number of professional medical organizations as well as many professional licensing agencies have formal policies giving doctors an ethical obligation to treat HIV/AIDS patients.

It's illegal to discriminate against an adult or child with AIDS. If your child's school is reluctant to let your infected child come to class, the federal All Handicapped Children Act may be of help. It says that if a child doesn't pose a health threat to other children, he or she must be allowed to attend regular classes. If your school refuses, you can sue it. Given the history of such lawsuits, you have a good chance of winning.

You can spend literally hours exploring all of the HIV- and AIDS-related information and resources available at http://pubpages.uhe.edu/~jfa/aids.html.

Organizations you should know about

If you're HIV-positive or have AIDS, these organizations may help you with legal problems related to your diagnosis:

The Lambda Legal Defense and Education Fund
666 Broadway, 12th Floor
New York, New York 10012-9996
212-995-8585

Lesbian/Gay Rights and AIDS Project of the American Civil Liberties Union
132 West 43rd Street
New York, New York 10036
212-944-9800

The AIDS Action Council
1875 Connecticut Avenue, N.W., Suite 700
Washington. D.C. 20009
202-986-1300

National Association of People With AIDS
1413 K Street, N.W.
Washington, D.C. 20005
202-898-0414

The right not to be released before you're ready

There's a lot of pressure on today's hospitals to minimize their costs by releasing patients as soon as possible. Utilization review companies set standards for hospitals, insurance companies, and managed health care organizations regarding when someone should be hospitalized as well as what's an appropriate length of stay for a particular medical problem. If you stay longer than the "appropriate length of stay," it is usually at your expense.

If you're told that it's time to vacate your hospital room and you don't feel that you're well enough to leave, you can appeal your discharge. Start by talking with the hospital's patient representative who can fill you in on the appeal process. Try to get your doctor involved too because doctors typically have more clout than patients in the hospital hierarchy.

After your appeal has been filed, the utilization review company should respond within two working days. If your appeal is denied, and especially if you become much sicker or are injured after you leave and you can attribute it to a premature discharge, you may be able to sue the hospital, your doctor, insurance company, and the utilization review firm, depending on the circumstances.

The right to refuse medical treatment

Although your decision may be misguided, you have the right to refuse any medical treatment or surgery you don't want. You also have the right to leave a hospital at any time, assuming you're mentally competent. Before you leave, however, the hospital can ask you to sign a form releasing it of any legal responsibility should your medical condition take a turn for the worse later on.

The right to see what's in your medical records

In less enlightened times, your medical records used to be considered your doctor's property. But that attitude is changing. Nearly 30 states give patients a limited right to know what's in their records. For example, in some states, you must put your request in writing. If you're dealing with a hospital or large medical clinic and you want the information in your file photocopied, you may have to pay — often an outrageous price per page. A call to your state's medical society should fill you in on your state's laws regarding patient access to medical records.

Save money on photocopying the information in your medical file by asking your doctor to make the request for you — your doctor can probably get it for free.

If you don't live in one of the 30 states that give you an explicit right to see your medical records, you still have an implied legal right to see them although doing so may take a lawsuit.

The right to privacy

Unless you give your permission, your doctor may not share the health and medical information that you've given to him or her nor anything else in your medical records with anyone. This ban extends to current or potential employers and insurance companies. There are exceptions, however:

- ✔ If you sue your doctor, your doctor can use your medical information against you.
- ✔ If you have a contagious disease, to help protect others, your doctor must report the fact to the health authorities.
- ✔ If you're treated for a gunshot or a stab wound, your injury must usually be reported because it's assumed that your wound is crime-related.

✔ Generally, if information you've shared with your doctor leads him or her to suspect that you're going to commit a crime or hurt someone, your doctor must notify the appropriate legal authorities.

✔ If you have a sexually-transmitted disease like syphilis or gonorrhea, your doctor must report your condition to the health authority in order to protect the health of others.

Also, if a doctor treats a child who he or she suspects is the victim of child abuse, the doctor is legally required to report the suspicion to help protect the child.

Prescription for Problem Solving

Now that you have a basic understanding of your rights when dealing with your doctor, if you think that your rights have been violated, your first step should be to express your concerns directly to your doctor. If you get no satisfaction, try the following:

✔ File a complaint with your local and/or state medical association, either of which may be willing to help you resolve your problem, perhaps through mediation.

✔ Contact the board that licenses doctors in your state — your state health department can give you the phone number. Depending on the nature of your problem, the number of complaints already registered against the doctor, and the results of any investigation that the board initiates, among other things, the doctor's license to practice medicine may be suspended or even revoked.

Find out about organizations that can provide you with emotional support as well as information when you're dealing with a particular health or medical problem by going to the Patient Advocacy List at `http://infonet.welch.jhu.edu/advocacy.html`.

Medical Malpractice

Although modern medicine often seems miraculous, doctors are not miracle workers. You can't sue your doctor for medical malpractice just because a prescribed treatment or surgery doesn't cure what ails you. But if you believe that your doctor failed to follow accepted medical practices in diagnosing and/or treating you, and if you suffered serious harm as a result, you may have the basis for a lawsuit in your state's civil court.

Most states have a one year to three year statue of limitations for medical malpractice lawsuits.

If your case is strong enough, you may be able to find an attorney willing to take your case on contingency; however, medical malpractice is a very specialized area of the law, so not just any attorney can take your case.

Medical malpractice cases tend to be tough to win. If you lose, depending on the terms of your contingency agreement, you may be liable for your attorney's expenses, which can run well over $5,000. Also, some states have capped the amount you can win in a malpractice lawsuit or require that you try arbitration before suing.

Paying for Your Medical Expenses

Federal law prohibits the federal government from regulating the activities of health insurance companies. That's the province of your state government. In the absence of a similar law regarding managed care companies, the federal government has also adopted a similar hands-off policy towards this growing industry.

To find out your state's laws, call your state insurance commission or your state attorney general's office.

Employers are not usually required to provide health insurance to their employees although a handful of states require it. Those employers that do are expected to comply with the provisions of the federal Employee Retirement Income Security Act (ERISA). In addition, if employers have at least 25 employees, they must offer their employees the option of enrolling in a managed care plan instead of a traditional health insurance plan.

When you're interviewing for a new job, you can't be asked whether you have a preexisting medical condition.

If you're covered by the insurance plan of your spouse's employer and you get divorced, the employer must allow you to remain on the plan at the group rate for up to three years.

Generally, health insurance companies and managed care organizations can establish their own criteria for determining who they cover and the kinds of medical treatments, procedures, and medications they pay for. So if you have a health problem — a preexisting condition — they can refuse to cover that problem for a specified period of time, or even forever. And if your health is really bad, they can refuse to cover you at all.

A crash course in managed care

Presently, more than 123 million Americans are enrolled in some sort of managed care health plan. These plans integrate the financing and delivery of health care services to consumers via contractual arrangements with health care providers. Consumers who participate in a managed care plan are given financial incentives to use the services of the plan's providers.

The two most popular types of managed care organizations are HMOs and PPOs. HMOs provide consumers who enroll in their plans with a prearranged set of medical services for a fixed annual price. Usually, members also make a very small co-payment when they use an HMO service. Typically, HMO members are limited to using the providers within the HMO's network.

All HMOs are state-licensed. HMOs participating in the federal Medicare or Medicaid programs must also be federally licensed.

PPOs are groups of doctors and other medical providers who negotiate with employers, insurance companies, or other sponsoring groups to provide their employees or members with discounted medical services. PPO members are able to use providers who are not part of the PPO, but they are not reimbursed for their expenses at the same rate as if they'd used a PPO provider.

Although the verdict's not in yet on whether managed care provides patients with better care than the traditional fee-for-service system, it does have its benefits:

✔ Lower out-of-pocket costs. When you visit a doctor, have a diagnostic test, go to the hospital, have a prescription filled, and so on, you usually pay just a small co-payment.

✔ Less paperwork to deal with.

✔ Better coverage for preventative health care.

On the downside however, especially if you're a member of an HMO, your choice of doctors and other medical providers is limited and your access to specialists is restricted because to get to them you must go through a "gatekeeper" or primary care physician who has to make a referral.

Increasingly, patients, consumer groups, nurses, and doctors are decrying certain policies of some HMOs. They are criticial of the following:

✔ HMOs can jeopardize a patient's health by limiting someone's access to the specialists, treatments, and procedures that he or she may need — all in the name of cost cutting.

✔ Some HMOs are not being 100-percent forthcoming with consumers about the rules of their plans.

✔ Some HMOs use financial incentives or the threat of penalties, including dismissal, to pressure doctors into not providing their patients with complete information about all of their medical care options. This practice is in direct conflict with the concept of informed consent. As a consequence, some doctors feel pulled in two directions: Should they be loyal to the HMO they're working for in order to assure their financial well-being, even if it means not providing their patients with the best possible care, or should they risk antagonizing the HMO by being honest and open with their patients, even if what they recommend is expensive and is going to cost the HMO more money?

As a consequence of the criticism that many have leveled against some HMOs, more than 34 states have passed laws outlawing or restricting certain industry practices. These practices include dramatically limiting the length of hospital stays (including requiring that new mothers leave the hospital within 48 hours of giving birth) and restricting what doctors can tell their patients about their medical care options. Some of these laws also require that doctors tell patients about any HMO financial incentives or penalties that may affect the care they receive.

If you're "uninsurable," don't lose heart. You may be able to purchase coverage through a state insurance pool for high risk people. The coverage is limited and expensive, but it's better than nothing! Also, in many states, Blue Cross/Blue Shield offers *open enrollment* periods during which anyone who applies, regardless of their health status, can get coverage.

If you're getting on in years and you're shopping for health insurance, make sure that the policy you're considering doesn't include a clause stating that it won't be renewed once you turn 65.

If you have health coverage, you can breathe a big sigh of relief because you can't lose your insurance if you file a lot of claims or develop a serious health problem that costs the insurer a lot of money. You can be dropped, however, if you don't keep up with the payments for your coverage or if your insurer discovers that you lied on your application.

Don't forget that if you have health coverage through an employer with more than 20 employees and you quit or are fired, COBRA allows you to continue that coverage for up to 18 months, assuming you weren't fired for gross misconduct. The only hitch is that you have to pay the full cost of your coverage — no more employer subsidies.

To become HMO-smart, check out the HMO SmartPages at http://www.buysmart.com. This site provides information on more than 160 HMOs, including the type of coverage provided, the number of board-certified doctors working for an HMO, as well as how they are compensated.

If You Have Problems with Your Insurance Claims

If you file an insurance claim and the company refuses to pay it, or if you think your reimbursement is too small, you have a right to challenge the company's decision. Insurers do make mistakes, and surveys show that claim reimbursement calculations are frequently wrong!

Here's how to challenge an insurer's decision:

- First, reread your policy to make certain that you are not confused about your coverage; however, reading yours may leave you thoroughly confused because policies don't tend to be written in straightforward English.

- Then call your insurance provider's customer service office for an explanation. The company may provide an 800 number.

The Medical Information Bureau (MIB)

Sounds intimidating, doesn't it? Most people are unaware of the MIB, but if it's maintaining a medical file on you in its computerized database, the MIB's information could affect your ability to get adequate health coverage, as well as life insurance and disability insurance.

If your health insurance company is a member of the MIB, the insurance company sends information about any claim that you file to the MIB. Also, if you're seen by a health insurance company doctor, the doctor may also send information to the MIB. Then, when you apply for insurance with an MIB member company, the insurer can access the information in your file to help it decide whether or not to cover you.

You can write the MIB to find out if it has a file on you. Send your letter to

Medical Information Bureau
P.O. Box 105
Essex Station
Boston, MA 02112
617-426-3660

The MIB will write back to tell you whether or not you're in its database. If you are, you can send it a check or money order for $8, and the MIB will send you a copy of the information in your file.

If there's an error in your file, you have the right to have it corrected. To get that accomplished, you must put your request in writing and provide proof that the information is in error. The MIB must correct its database after it has verified your information.

If you're denied insurance due to MIB information, the insurer must give you the name and address of the company providing the negative information and let you know where the information came from — probably the MIB. Also, because the FTC is beginning to hold the MIB to the same legal standards as credit reporting agencies, you can get a free copy of your MIB report by requesting it in writing within 30 days of your denial.

If you're not satisfied with what you learn, and you're not covered by an employer's health insurance plan, try the following:

- ✔ Write a letter to your insurance provider explaining your problem and asking for a written clarification of its policy regarding your claim. Send it certified mail, return receipt requested. Compare the company's explanation to what's in your policy.

- ✔ If you still "can't get no satisfaction," write to the person in charge of your insurer's claims department and carbon copy (cc) your state's insurance commission.

- ✔ If the problem still remains, write to your state's insurance commission and copy both the president of the insurance company you're dealing with as well as the head of its claims department.

- ✔ If the commission can't help you, you may want to hire an attorney, assuming the amount of money in dispute is substantial. You can sue for actual and punitive damages, attorney fees, and pain and suffering.

If your insurance plan is regulated by ERISA, you have to follow ERISA's appeal process. This process should be described in the information booklet you received when you enrolled in the plan. If you have questions about the process, talk to the person at your place of work in charge of the plan.

If you follow the appeals process and your appeal is denied, ERISA gives you the right to sue for actual damages and attorney fees.

The National Insurance Consumers Organization can offer you advice and guidance when you're "doing battle" with an insurance company. Contact it at 121 North Payne Street, Alexandria, VA 22314. Or call 703-549-8050.

Government-sponsored health programs

Medicare and Medicaid are large government-sponsored insurance programs. Medicare covers elderly people, certain disabled people, and those with permanent kidney failure. Medicaid provides coverage for low-income people with few assets.

Once you turn 65, you are automatically eligible for Medicare, regardless of your income. Chapter 15 discusses Medicare in detail.

Medicaid is a federal-state program. People receiving public assistance like Aid For Dependent Children (AFDC) and Supplemental Security Income (SSI) are automatically entitled to receive Medicaid benefits. So is anyone else who meets the income and asset eligibility criteria of his or her state.

Apply for Medicaid at your local social services or welfare office. Be prepared for the usual inefficiencies and red tape of government bureaucracy — lots of paperwork and long delays. You have to provide proof of your financial status.

If you're approved, at a minimum you are entitled to the basic package of benefits and services that the federal government requires all states to offer Medicaid recipients. Some states can offer more if they want. Basic Medicaid benefits and services include the following:

- Doctor care
- Clinic visits
- Family planning services and supplies
- Prenatal care
- Hospital services — inpatient and outpatient
- X-rays and other diagnostic tests
- Prescription drugs
- Nursing home care and some home health care

Chapter 14

Social Security: A Social Safety Net

. . . .

In This Chapter

▶ Determining whether you are eligible to receive benefits

▶ Figuring out how much your benefits will be

▶ Applying for benefits

. . . .

*Y*ou may be tempted to flip right past this chapter thinking, "What's the point of reading about Social Security? There won't be any money in the system when I'm ready to retire! Why should I care?" You may be right given projections that the system may be insolvent as early as the middle of the first decade of the 21st century. But given the critical role that this program plays in the lives of many people, it's likely that Washington will do what's necessary to keep Social Security alive and that it will be there in some form or fashion to help you when you retire. Because you will help fund this program throughout most of your working life, it's important that you know what benefits your Social Security taxes are helping to pay for and how you can collect your retirement benefits when the time comes.

Also, although most people tend to be less aware of them, your Social Security taxes also fund other benefits that you or members of your family may need to use before you're even thinking about retirement. They include disability and Medicare benefits.

Medicare is a health program for people over 65. When you become eligible for Social Security retirement benefits, you automatically become eligible for Medicare. Turn to Chapter 15 for a discussion of Medicare.

And finally, if your parents are nearing retirement age or are already there, you have another reason to become familiar with the benefits and rules of Social Security. (These rules are about as complicated and confusing as the government can make them, so every little bit of incentive to learn them will be to your benefit.) If your parents have problems collecting what they're entitled to, you'll be able to help them. Have I convinced you yet to read this chapter?

Am I Eligible?

Anyone who earns enough and works long enough at a job covered by the Social Security system — most jobs are — can collect Social Security benefits. That probably includes you.

Federal workers, some state and local government employees, as well as railroad workers are not covered by Social Security.

Each quarter throughout your career, whether you work for someone or are self-employed, you accumulate Social Security *credits* based on your earnings. You can earn a maximum of four credits each year. Most people must accumulate 40 quarters worth of credits (ten years of work) to qualify for benefits.

At the same time that you're earning your credits, you're also paying into the Social Security system. If you're employed, your payments are made as deductions from your paycheck — they're the FICA (Federal Insurance Contributions Act) deductions you see on your check stubs. If you're self-employed, you contribute to the Social Security system through the self-employment taxes that you must pay.

How Much Will I Earn When I Retire?

A complicated Social Security formula adjusted for inflation determines exactly how much your monthly retirement checks will be. According to the Social Security Administration, your retirement checks should replace about 42 percent of your lifetime earnings, assuming yours were "average." The formula is weighted, however, so that low-income workers receive a higher rate of return on their payments into the Social Security system than more highly paid workers.

Social Security payments are intended to provide retirees with a base level of retirement income — not to be their only source of income. Payments do *not* finance a comfortable standard of living. So be sure you do what you can to fund your retirement with savings, pensions, insurance, and other investments.

To get a more precise idea of exactly how much, or how little, you will collect when you retire, ask the Social Security Administration to estimate your benefits. Call 800-772-1213 for a Personal Earnings and Benefit Estimate Statement. When you receive the form, fill it out and return it to the SSA. You should hear back in about six weeks.

Request a Social Security benefits estimate each year. Not only does the information help you plan your retirement, but it also helps you ensure that your current employer is paying and your past employers have paid into the system for you.

When Do My Retirement Benefits Begin?

Presently, although most people begin collecting their Social Security retirement benefits at age 65, you can start receiving them as early as age 62. But if you chose this option, your monthly checks will be smaller than if you wait three more years.

To help deal with the projected financial pressure that the baby boomer generation is going to begin placing on the Social Security fund, the SSA has begun pushing back the age when retirement benefits can begin. So if you were born between 1943 and 1959, you won't be able to begin collecting your full benefits until about age 66, and if you were born in 1960 or later, you shouldn't expect to see benefits until you reach the ripe old age of 67.

Although you can work and collect Social Security benefits too, there are limits on how much you can earn when you're younger than 70. If you exceed the limit, your benefits are reduced. But after 70, you can work as much as you want. Between 1996 and 2002, the limits are being increased gradually.

When you begin thinking about retiring, the SSA suggests that you talk with the SSA about a year before you plan to stop working because it may be to your benefit to start your retirement benefits before you actually quit your job.

Social Security Disability Benefits

Regardless of your age, but assuming you've earned enough Social Security credits to be eligible, you can collect disability payments from the Social Security system if you become physically or mentally disabled and expect that you'll be unable to perform "substantial" work for at least a year, or worse yet, that you'll die. (The SSA generally considers earnings of at least $500 per month to be "substantial.") To begin receiving these benefits, however, you have to prove to the SSA that you meet its criteria for being truly disabled, which can take time and patience.

After you qualify for disability benefits, you receive the benefits until the SSA decides that you can return to work. Your readiness is assessed periodically. And to encourage you to return to work as soon as possible, the SSA offers you special incentives.

The federal government's own brochure on the Social Security program describes disability as "one of the most complicated of all Social Security programs"!

If you're certified as disabled, those same family members who may be eligible to receive Social Security retirement benefits once you are eligible may be entitled to receive disability benefits. Those family members are reviewed in the following sidebar.

Other information you should know about Social Security retirement and disability benefits

✔ Your spouse may be able to start collecting retirement benefits when you do, assuming that he or she is at least 62, even if your spouse has never worked. Your spouse's benefits will probably be about 50 percent of yours. If, however, your spouse also earned benefits, your spouse can collect whichever is higher — his or her own benefits or a percentage of yours. Your spouse is also eligible if he or she is younger than 62 but is caring for a child under age 16.

✔ Your unmarried children may be able to begin receiving retirement benefits when you do if they're not married and are younger than 18, under 19 and still in school, or 18 and older and disabled.

✔ If you're divorced, you may not want to contribute one more red cent to the support of your ex-spouse. But the SSA may have the last word. Assuming you were married for at least ten years and your former spouse has not remarried, your ex can begin collecting retirement benefits at age 62. Your divorce must have happened, however, more than two years before the benefits begin.

✔ If you delay retirement, you'll be rewarded with a special credit which will be added to your monthly Social Security benefit.

✔ You may have to pay federal and state income taxes on your Social Security benefits if you earn substantial income in addition to your retirement benefits.

What about Survivor Benefits?

When you die, certain members of your family may be eligible to receive Social Security survivor benefits if you were eligible to receive Social Security payments even if you weren't old enough yet to collect retirement benefits. These family members include the following people:

✔ Your spouse, if he or she is at least 60; however, your spouse can be as young as 50 if he or she is disabled.

✔ Your spouse regardless of his or her age if your spouse is caring for a child under 16 or for a disabled child receiving Social Security benefits.

✔ Any of your unmarried children under 18 and any unmarried children who are under 19 as long as they are full-time elementary or secondary school students.

✔ Any of your unmarried children who are severely disabled and at least 18 as long as they became disabled before they turned 22.

✔ Your parents if you provided at least half of their support.

Your widow or widower can remarry after your death and still collect survivor benefits.

How Do I Apply for Benefits?

The SSA suggests that when you want to apply for Social Security benefits — retirement, survivor, or disability benefits — you call 800-772-1213.

You have to provide the SSA with proof of your eligibility to receive the benefits for which you're applying. Although exactly what you have to provide depends on what you're applying for and on your circumstances, here are some typical examples:

- ✔ Your Social Security card or a record of your number
- ✔ Your birth certificate
- ✔ Your children's birth certificates if they're applying for benefits
- ✔ Your marriage certificate if you're applying for benefits based on your spouse's employment history, or your divorce decree if you're divorced

If you can't locate everything you need for your initial appointment, don't delay applying for retirement benefits. Personnel at the Social Security office may be able to help you locate those items you can't seem to find.

After the SSA has everything it needs, you'll probably see your first check two to three months later.

What Do I Do If the SSA Says "No"?

If the SSA denies your claim for benefits, or if the benefits you've been receiving are going to be reduced or terminated, the SSA must notify you in writing. You have the right to appeal the SSA's decision within 60 days of the date of the notice. To learn about the appeals process, call the SSA's 800 number and ask for its fact sheet, "The Appeals Process."

You don't need an attorney to appeal, but if there's a substantial amount of money at stake, the cost of legal help may be relatively insignificant, especially if you have little patience with government bureaucracy and the convoluted rules of Social Security. Take heart, though: Appeals are often decided in favor of taxpayers!

To help you locate an attorney familiar with the ins and outs of the Social Security appeals process, call the National Organization of Social Security Claimants' Representatives at 800-431-2804.

Most appeals are resolved by filing a request for reconsideration or, failing that, through an administrative hearing before an administrative law judge employed by the SSA. At the hearing, you are expected to present evidence supporting your position, and you can even subpoena witnesses.

About two to three months after the end of the hearing, you will receive a written notice of the judge's decision. If it's in your favor, you may be able to collect retroactive payments beginning with the date that you first filed your claim. If the judge decides against you, you can appeal again, and ultimately, you can sue the SSA in federal court.

Changes in Your Life That Can Affect Your Social Security Benefits

Certain events in your life can affect the continuation of your Social Security benefits or the amount of those benefits. Here is a partial list of possible changes that you should tell the SSA about:

- You move.
- You get married or divorced.
- You change your name.
- Your income increases or decreases.
- You become a parent or an adoptive parent.
- You are imprisoned.
- You leave the United States.

The SSA should also be informed if a Social Security beneficiary dies or becomes unable to manage his or her own funds.

At the Social Security On Line Web site (http://www.ssa.gov/), you can get benefit information, compute your own benefits, download forms, learn about legislation affecting Social Security, and research various Social Security topics.

Supplemental Security Income

The Supplemental Security Income (SSI) program makes monthly payments to individuals who make very little money and have very few assets. You're eligible for this program if you're over 65 or you're disabled; children are also eligible.

SSI is administered by each state with money channeled through the Social Security Administration; however, federal money for SSI comes from general tax revenues, not from the Social Security fund, and the amount of your monthly SSI check is based on your financial need and not on your past earnings. (Most states supplement the basic rate that the federal government pays to SSI recipients.) Your local Social Security office can tell you what you can expect to receive.

Apply for SSI benefits at your local welfare or social services office. If you qualify, you will be automatically entitled to begin receiving Medicaid health benefits, food stamps, and other assistance in addition to your SSI checks.

Chapter 15

Getting Older: We All Do It

• •

In This Chapter

▶ Financing your retirement

▶ Winding your way through the Medicare maze

▶ Obtaining nursing home care

▶ Finding home health care

• •

You're getting older, like it or not. And sooner or later, you need to begin planning for your "Golden Years" if you want them to be truly golden. At a minimum, that planning should include the following:

✔ Laying the groundwork for financing your retirement — no small feat given that financial experts estimate that to sustain a retirement lifestyle comparable to the one you may be enjoying now, you'll need 70 to 80 percent of your pre-retirement income.

✔ Familiarizing yourself with the residential options available to those 65 and over should your health fail and you need to move out of your home or apartment into a different sort of residence. This planning includes considering how you are going to pay for nursing home care if it becomes necessary. Adequate planning and good health insurance can mean the difference between being able to pay for the care you need with your own resources or having to deplete your life savings before Medicaid kicks in.

✔ Knowing your options should your health or physical condition necessitate home health care.

Those of you with older parents in failing health may already be dealing with some of these issues. If you are, you understand how financially and emotionally difficult they can be, even when they've been preceded by solid planning. You also understand that pension plans, Medicare, and Medicaid are governed by complex, confusing webs of rules and regulations that can quickly overwhelm older people and prevent them from getting what they're entitled to receive.

Don't count on Social Security to provide you with a comfortable retirement lifestyle. At best, your monthly checks will fund a subsistence living.

Software programs can help you determine your retirement financial needs and how to meet them. Quicken Financial Planner and Rich and Retired are easy to use, educational, and flexible because they let you test a number of what-if scenarios.

Financing Your Retirement

How our expectations have changed! We used to expect that after 40 plus years of working, we'd retire to enjoy hobbies, travel, family, and friends and live comfortably on an employer-funded pension plan — a *defined-benefit* pension plan — and Social Security, augmented by whatever personal savings and other investments we'd been able to accumulate during our working years.

Although that carefree vision of our "Golden Years" may still be attainable, increasingly, it's up to us to make it a reality: At best, Social Security only covers your most basic expenses, and defined-benefit pension plans are becoming perks of the past, replaced by *defined-contribution* pension plans. This type of pension places much if not all of the burden for building a retirement nest egg on you, not on your employer.

The retirement nest egg you're able to amass may have to finance as much as 30 or more years of living if you retire at 65. So if you have a pension, it's critical that you make sure that its funds are managed wisely and, when pension problems develop, that you know your legal rights. Doing so can mean the difference between a relaxed, comfortable retirement and one full of worry, stress, and even poverty. These days, nothing is guaranteed, not even a financially secure old age!

Defined-benefit and defined-contribution pension plans — what's the difference?

If you're lucky, you have a defined-benefit pension plan. If you do, your employer automatically enrolled you in it once you met certain eligibility requirements. You have been guaranteed either a specific amount of retirement income, $1,000 per month for example, or more commonly, a monthly pension based on a formula that takes into account the number of years you work for your employer, your age, and the size of your salary. Your employer is legally obligated to contribute enough money to its pension plan each year and to manage and invest the money in its pension fund in a manner that will guarantee that you and other participating employees receive the income you were promised when you retire.

A key advantage to participating in a defined-benefit pension plan is that it's probably insured and protected by the Pension Benefit Guaranty Corporation or PBGC. If your employer terminates its pension plan or encounters financial difficulty and can't make good on its promises to you, the PBGC guarantees payment of your vested pension benefits, up to a certain dollar limit set by law. The maximum benefits it pays changes annually.

To find out if your defined-benefit plan is PBGC-insured, ask your employer or its plan administrator. If you have questions about the PBGC or about your pension plan should it be taken over by the PBGC, write to the agency: Pension Benefit Guaranty Corporation, 1200 K Street, N.W., Suite 930, Washington, D.C. 20005-4026; or call 202-326-4000. If you're hearing impaired, call 202-326-4179.

If you've begun participating in a pension plan through your employer, it's probably a defined-contribution plan. There are several important distinctions between this kind of plan and a defined-benefit plan:

- ✔ Participation in a defined-contribution plan is not automatic — it's voluntary and you have to enroll.

- ✔ Your employer makes no promises regarding how much retirement income your pension will provide you.

- ✔ Your active involvement is required if you want your pension plan to be a success. Although your employer may or may not contribute to it, *you* decide how to invest the money in your retirement account. (In defined-benefit plans, your employer makes this decision.)

Examples of defined-contribution plans, a.k.a. *retirement plans*, include employee stock ownership (ESOP), profit sharing plans, and 401(k) plans. Of the three, the most popular is the 401(k).

If your employer is deducting money from your paychecks and depositing those funds in your 401(k) account, federal law currently allows your employer to delay actually making that deposit for up to 90 days! This legal loophole can tempt cash-strapped employers who may need some extra operating capital. Some of the employers who take advantage of the loophole are unable to replace the money by the 90-day deadline. When they can't, they are in essence defrauding their employees. At the time this book was written, the Department of Labor had proposed a new regulation to address this problem, but the regulation was met with fierce business opposition.

How 401(k) plans work

About 22 million workers have approximately $855 billion in 401(k) and 403(b) plans — the non-profit equivalent of a 401(k) for those of you working in the public or nonprofit sectors. Here's a brief overview of how a 401(k) plan works. When you're eligible to begin participating in your employer's 401(K) plan, instead of getting the full amount of your salary, you defer some of it — there's a limit on how much you can defer each year — and have the deferred amount deposited in your 401(k) retirement account. You aren't taxed on the amount you defer nor on any interest your account may earn until you withdraw it.

Your employer is legally required to give you at least three different investment options for the funds in your account. If you're unhappy with the performance of the option you chose or want your funds to be invested more or less aggressively, you can select another option whenever you want or at periodic points throughout the year, depending on how your plan works.

Being "vested" is not a fashion statement

Whether your plan is a defined-contribution or a defined-benefit plan, you won't lose what money you've accumulated if you decide to leave your current employer before you've reached retirement age and you're *vested* in your pension plan. When you're vested, you've been participating in a plan long enough to have a non-forfeitable right to your pension benefits no matter where you work. If you're not vested, you are still entitled to 100 percent of whatever you have contributed to the plan and to whatever interest your contributions have earned. But you aren't entitled to whatever your employer has contributed.

If you're vested and you leave your current employer, you can either keep your retirement dollars in your current pension plan or take them out. If you decide to cash out, you receive your money in a lump sum payment. If you decide to keep your retirement dollars where they are and your former employer was contributing to your plan, those contributions stop.

The federal government has established two schedules that employers can use to determine the rate at which their employees become vested. But employers are free to use a more generous schedule if they want.

Employers are prohibited from changing their vesting schedule in order to deny their vested employees the retirement benefits they've accumulated when they retire.

The Employee Retirement Income Security Act (ERISA)

Although your employer is not legally required to establish a pension plan for you, if it does and you work in the private sector, your employer's plan must meet the requirements of the federal Employee Retirement Income Security Act (ERISA). This law was enacted in 1974 to address some of the key abuses occurring in the private employer pension system by creating minimum standards for pension plans and by giving both plan participants and their beneficiaries certain rights. For example, ERISA requires that your private sector employer do the following:

✔ Provide you with written information about your pension plan and your pension benefits. Some of this information is free and should come to you automatically on a periodic basis. It includes the following:

- A summary plan explaining the basic facts about your employer's pension plan — its benefits and how they are calculated, eligibility requirements, when you can begin receiving retirement benefits, what you must do to begin collecting them, and so on. You should get this information within 90 days of enrolling in a plan.

- A summary annual report telling you where the money in your pension fund has been invested and how well it's done. This report is a condensed version of the report that most pension plans must file with the U.S. Department of Labor each year. You should receive your summary report no later than 90 days after the end of each plan year.

Annual reports and summary annual reports don't make for exciting reading; even so, read them carefully! They can reveal important information about the health of your pension fund and can highlight potential problems that may have a direct bearing on how much retirement income you end up with.

ERISA also spells out other pension-related information you can request in writing and says that you employer must provide it to you, for free or for a charge depending on what you ask for. This information includes an individual benefit summary giving you the total value of the retirement benefits that you've accrued so far and whether those benefits are vested.

✔ Abide by certain rules in establishing a process that you can use when you retire and want to begin collecting your pension benefits.

✔ Establish an appeals process that you can use when you have problems with your pension. For example, you may have trouble collecting your benefits or the amount of your monthly benefit may be wrong. ERISA also gives you the right to sue your pension plan in state or federal court if you exhaust your plan's claims and appeals processes.

✔ Provide survivor's benefits to your surviving spouse if you have a vested right to your pension no matter whether you die before or after you retire.

ERISA also does the following:

✔ Sets out standards of conduct for pension plan fiduciaries (a *fiduciary* manages a pension plan and is responsible for investing its assets) and establishes penalties for those who don't meet the standards. For example, fiduciaries generally cannot use money earmarked for a pension plan for any other purpose, and they cannot mix pension funds with other funds. Also, fiduciaries cannot put pension fund dollars in high-risk investments or in only one or just a very few investments. Although you can sue your plan's fiduciaries for mismanagement or misuse of funds, the fund, not you, gets the monetary award if you win.

If you — and only you — make all investment decisions for your employer-sponsored pension plan, the plan's administrators and others with responsibility for it do not have fiduciary responsibility for the consequences of your decisions.

✔ Prohibits employers from firing you or laying you off just to avoid paying you pension benefits.

✔ Gives you the right to sue your pension plan to get the benefits you're due and to enforce your pension rights in general. The Secretary of Labor can also sue a plan if there's sufficient cause.

Getting what you've earned

ERISA says that you must be allowed to begin receiving your pension benefits by the 60th day after the end of the plan year in which the latest of the following occur:

✔ You turn age 65 (unless your plan specifies an earlier retirement age).

✔ The 10th year you began participating in the plan ends.

✔ You stop working for your employer.

How you receive your pension benefits depends on what kind of pension you have. If you have a defined-benefit plan, you will probably receive payments over time in the form of an annuity. If you have a defined-contribution plan, you may get your funds in a lump sum, or your plan may make some other provision for payment.

Although you may be eligible to begin receiving your pension benefits, you may not receive them immediately because your pension plan may need time to value your account balance, liquidate your investments, calculate your monthly payment, and so on.

After you file a claim to begin collecting your pension benefits, your plan must respond to your claim in writing within 90 days. If your claim is denied, the pension plan administrator must send you a written notice explaining why. (If you don't get a response to your claim by the deadline, the law says that you should assume that your claim has been denied.) You have the right to appeal your denial by requesting a formal review. Again, put your request in writing.

Ordinarily, your plan must respond in writing to your appeal within 120 days of receiving it. It should spell out the exact reasons for its final decision specifically referencing the rules of your pension plan.

Although the law does not say that a hearing must be held in the event of an appeal, it does allow you to support your appeal with written documentation.

If you're unhappy with the outcome of your appeal, you can ask the Department of Labor's Pension and Welfare Benefits Administration (202-219-8776) for help. You may also want to talk with an attorney about a lawsuit in state or federal court.

Many attorneys specialize in pension problems. If your case is strong, an attorney may take it on contingency. The nonprofit Pension Rights Center in Washington, D.C., (202-296-3776) can refer you to a lawyer in your area.

When an employee sues his or her pension plan, the courts have shown themselves to be more likely to decide for the plan.

It's estimated that more than half of the approximately 60 million Americans covered by retirement plans are not getting the benefits they've earned. The highest error rates are associated with 401(k) and profit-sharing plans. If left uncorrected, even a small error in calculating a pension can add up to a substantial amount of lost retirement income, which is a good reason to stay on top of your pension benefits as they're accrued by reading and understanding the reports you receive about your pension.

Although certainly a percentage of the errors in pension benefit determinations can be attributed to the deliberate effort of some employers to cheat their workers out of money, most of the mistakes are caused by the sheer complexity of the law and by the fact that ERISA gets amended nearly every year. It's especially difficult for small employers to keep up with the law and to incorporate its ever-changing provisions into their pension plan administration systems. Mathematical errors and mistakes in data entry also contribute to the errors.

The best and cheapest way to ensure that you get what you deserve is to keep tabs on your pension benefits as they accumulate: Read your summary plan description, check your yearly benefit statements, and match pension contributions through the year with your year-end statement.

If you think someone made an error in the calculation of your pension benefits, contact your employer's plan administrator in writing and ask for a detailed explanation of how your benefits were calculated. The administrator must respond in writing within 90 days. If you don't agree with the response, use the appeals process as you would use for appealing a pension claim denial.

The Center for Retirement Benefits (800-666-1000) can act as your pension detective — for a price. It can determine what your pension should be and can help you get what you may be missing, on contingency. It takes 50 percent of what it collects. Although a 50-percent cut may sound excessive, it can be worth the price if an error is significant.

Other things you should know about pensions

- ✔ Your employer can limit its pension program to certain categories of workers, or it can offer different options to different employee categories. All employees within a particular category must be treated the same, however.

- ✔ Your employer can establish requirements for how long you must work before you can begin participating in its pension plan and accruing pension benefits and for when you can become vested in your retirement plan. Generally, you must be allowed to participate once you've reached age 21 and have put in one year of service with your employer. This one year translates into 1,000 hours. For part-timers, that equals about six months of full-time work or twelve months of part-time work.

- ✔ Your employer is not required to continue offering a pension plan.

- ✔ Depending on your plan, your monthly pension benefit may be reduced if you're receiving Social Security benefits.

- ✔ Depending on the laws of your state, if you divorce, your ex-spouse may be entitled to a share of your pension benefits.

- ✔ If your employer is acquired by or merges with another company and your current pension plan is continued, your new employer cannot set new "years of service" standards for becoming vested. This restriction does not apply if your plan is discontinued and replaced with another.

- ✔ Under certain conditions, your pension plan can be suspended if you return to work after retiring.

Medicare

Medicare is a federal health insurance program available to nearly everyone 65 or over, regardless of income. The federal Health Care Financing Administration administers the program establishing its benefits, rules, and conditions. But it contracts with private health insurance companies to process claims and make payments. The money to fund the Medicare program comes from your pay-checks in the form of payroll deductions as well as from the premiums and coinsurance payments that Medicare participants pay.

You can enroll in the Medicare program even if you continue working as long as you meet the program's age requirement.

Like the Social Security program, Medicare is in financial trouble. Part A of the Medicare program is projected to be bankrupt by 2001. To avoid insolvency, Congress will probably decide to increase the amount that program partici-pants must pay and to reduce the amount that Medicare pays its medical providers.

Help! I'm lost in the Medicare maze

The Medicare program is extremely complex, full of confusing rules, exceptions, procedures, and processes that make the program difficult to understand and use effectively. In fact, having a Ph.D. in bureaucracy would be a real asset when dealing with Medicare. Adding insult to injury, the program doesn't cover many basic types of medical care, and its long-term care benefits are very limited. You should therefore buy additional medical insurance if you can afford it.

Although this chapter cannot fill you in on all of Medicare's twists and turns, this overview should give you at least a hint of what a challenge the program can be.

Medicare Part A

The Medicare program has two parts: Part A, Hospital Insurance, and Part B, Medical Insurance. If you're eligible for Social Security or Railroad Retirement benefits, you are automatically eligible to receive Part A benefits free of charge; however, "free" isn't really free because you still have to pay a deductible and coinsurance payments.

If you're 65 but not automatically eligible to receive Part A benefits, you can get them by paying a monthly premium. Also, if you're under 65 but you've been receiving Social Security or Railroad Retirement program disability benefits for more than 24 months, or if you've been on dialysis for permanent kidney failure or had a kidney transplant, you may be eligible for Medicare.

A summary of your Part A benefits

Part A covers the cost of "medically necessary" care in a hospital, psychiatric hospital, or skilled nursing facility participating in Medicare, as well as medically necessary home health care and hospice care.

Hospital benefits include the following:

- ✓ A semiprivate room and all your meals.

- ✓ Regular nursing services and the drugs you receive.

- ✓ The cost of special care including intensive care and coronary care.

- ✓ Blood transfusions.

- ✓ Lab tests, X-rays, and other radiology services billed by the hospital.

- ✓ Medical supplies such as casts, splints, and so on.

- ✓ The use of a wheelchair and other appliances.

- ✓ The cost of operating and recovery rooms.

- ✓ Rehabilitation services such as physical, occupational, and speech therapy.

- ✓ Skilled nursing facility benefits. Medicare pays the cost of skilled nursing care if you enter a skilled nursing facility within 30 days of leaving the hospital and if you were hospitalized for at least three days prior to your admittance. For Medicare to pay, the care you receive must be something that only a skilled nursing facility can provide and must be ordered by your doctor.

- ✓ Home health care benefits. Medicare pays the full cost of covered home health services if you're confined to your home and need intermittent skilled nursing care, physical therapy, or speech therapy. If you need durable medical equipment, you must make a 20-percent coinsurance payment. To be covered, your home health care must be ordered by a doctor, and the care provider must be participating in Medicare.

- ✓ Hospice Care. If your doctor certifies that you're terminally ill, Medicare pays for home hospice care or care in a hospice facility if it's provided by a Medicare-participating provider. These services include doctor and nursing care, individual and family psychological help, prescriptions, and social services. Medicare also pays for "appropriate" custodial care including homemaker services. Although you don't have to pay any deductibles for this benefit, you are responsible for 5 percent of the cost of outpatient drugs or $5 toward each prescription, whichever is less. Also, if you're in a hospice facility, you have to pay 5 percent of the Medicare-allowed rate, which varies by area of the country.

Medicare Part B

When you turn 65, you also become eligible to participate in Medicare Part B, but it will cost you. You have to pay a monthly premium that changes annually. Usually, after you enroll in Part B, your premiums are deducted automatically from your Social Security checks.

Summary of your Part B benefits

The Medicare Part B program typically covers about 80 percent of the cost of the "medically necessary" Medicare-covered services you receive from your doctor. It also covers inpatient and outpatient medical and surgical services and supplies, physical and speech therapy, diagnostic tests, durable medical equipment, lab services, home health care, and blood transfusions. You must pay the remaining 20 percent — that's your coinsurance payment.

At first glance, the preceding list of covered services may seem pretty comprehensive. You may change your mind, however, when you look at what Part B doesn't pay for:

- Most routine physical exams
- Most prescription drugs
- Most immunizations
- Exams for prescribing and fitting eyeglasses or hearing aids
- Dentures
- Most routine foot care and dental care

More about Medicare

You can enroll in Medicare during one of two enrollment periods — the initial period or the general period. The initial period begins three months prior to your 65th birthday and continues for three months. The general period occurs every January 1 through March 31.

Although you can enroll in Medicare Part B when you're older than 65, you pay a 10 percent premium penalty for every year you delay enrolling, with one exception — if you're still working and are covered by your employer's group health insurance plan. Once you do retire, you have seven months to enroll without penalty.

If you try to enroll in Medicare and are denied participation, you have the right to appeal to the Social Security Administration. Depending on how far you take your appeal, you can request a hearing before an administrative law judge and even file a lawsuit in federal court.

The devil is in the details

It's time for just a small taste of how confusing and complicated Medicare can be. Brace yourself!

Benefit periods

Medicare measures your use of Part A services in terms of benefit periods. Your first benefit period begins the first time you receive inpatient hospital care under the Medicare program. And it ends after you've been out of the hospital or a skilled nursing or rehabilitative facility for 60 days in a row. Your second benefit period begins whenever you receive inpatient hospital care again. There is no limit on the number of benefit periods you can have for hospital, skilled nursing facility care, and rehabilitative care.

Within each benefit period, Medicare pays up to 90 days of all medically-necessary inpatient hospital care covered by Part A. For example, in 1996, from the first day through the 60th day of your hospital stay during a benefit period, Part A pays for all covered services once you've paid your inpatient hospital deductible — $736 in 1996. From the 61st day through the 90th day of a hospital stay during the same benefit period, Part A pays the full cost of all covered services except for $184 per day — your coinsurance payment. You pay that amount.

If you need to be hospitalized for more than 90 days and want Medicare to pay for it, you can use some of your *reserve days*. Medicare gives you 60 extra or reserve days to use during your lifetime if necessary to help pay for Medicare Part A services. There is a coinsurance payment for reserve days.

Medicare has a different set of criteria for both the maximum number of days of stay in a skilled nursing facility and for the cost of that stay it pays for. Confused yet?

Medicare-approved charges and Medicare providers

Medicare sets approved charges for each medical service it covers. These charges represent the most that it is willing to pay for a service. If you're charged more than the Medicare-approved amount, you have to pay the difference. And doing so can get expensive because Medicare's approved charges often fall far short of actual costs.

To minimize your medical costs, try to use medical providers who accept the Medicare-approved amount as full payment. Doing so is called "taking on assignment." You can find out which medical care providers in your area take on assignment by reviewing the *Medicare-Participating Physician Directory* available free from your local Social Security office, your local or state office on aging, and from most hospitals.

If you can't afford to pay your Medicare costs, your state's Medicaid program may be able to help you. The final sidebar in Chapter 13 discusses Medicaid.

Although doctors are not required to treat Medicare patients, they cannot charge Medicare patients more than they charge other patients. Also, if a doctor doesn't take on assignment, Medicare generally limits how much he or she can charge to about 15 percent more than the Medicare-approved amount. Doctors who charge more than this amount can be fined. Medicare also places similar limits on some suppliers.

If you feel that you've been overcharged, ask for a reduction in your bill or a refund if you've already paid. If you don't get either, call your Medicare carrier for help.

Connecticut, Massachusetts, Minnesota, New York, Ohio, Pennsylvania, Rhode Island, and Vermont all have laws limiting your out-of-pocket charges to less than 15 percent of the Medicare-approved amount.

Filing claims

When you use Part A of the Medicare program, your medical provider submits a claim for reimbursement to the appropriate insurance company. The provider also charges you for any coinsurance payment or deductible you may owe.

It is possible that your medical provider may decide not to submit a claim to Medicare if it believes that the service it provided will not be covered; however, you can request that it file a claim. If Medicare refuses to pay, you can appeal. The appeals process is described in the next section of this chapter.

When you use Part B of the program, your medical provider usually submits a Medicare claim to the appropriate insurance company if it takes on assignment. Medicare pays you 80 percent of the approved amount after subtracting any part of the deductible you've not already met. Your medical provider can charge you for that amount plus your coinsurance payment — the remaining 20 percent of the approved amount; otherwise, you are responsible for paying the full amount of your bill and for submitting your own claim to Medicare.

After your Part B claim has been filed, you are notified of its status via an *Explanation of Medicare Part B Benefits*. This notice tells you what your co-payment is and how much Medicare is paying. It also gives you a toll-free number for getting in touch with the insurance company that processed your claim should you have any questions.

A growing number of older people are receiving their Medicare-covered health care through an HMO. If you're one of them, you have no claims to file unless you go outside your HMO.

If your claim is denied

If your Medicare claim is denied or if the amount of your reimbursement is less than what you think is fair, you can appeal. Part A and Part B have different appeals processes. The appeals process may also differ depending on what you're appealing. You didn't think it would be simple, did you?

Regardless of which appeals process you must use, you have a certain number of months to file your appeal. If your initial effort doesn't satisfy you and the dollar amount in question exceeds a certain minimum, you are eligible to have your problem decided by an administrative law judge. You may also be eligible to sue in federal district court.

The Medicare appeals process is cumbersome, slow, and inadequate. Take heart, however. If you can wait for the "wheels of government justice" to turn, ever so slowly, and especially if you can get your doctor actively involved in your appeal, your chances of winning are good.

While your appeal is being processed, you are liable for the medical bills relating to it.

Purchasing Medigap insurance

Because so many essential medical services are not covered by Medicare, those with the financial resources often purchase Medicare supplemental insurance or *Medigap* insurance. In fact, about half of the Americans covered by Medicare have Medigap insurance. The best time to buy this extra insurance coverage is during your Medigap open enrollment period, which occurs during the first six months that you're 65 or over and enrolled in Medicare Part B. During this time period, you cannot be turned down for Medigap insurance due to any health problems you may have, nor may a Medigap insurer place special conditions on your policy or increase the cost of your insurance because of your health or claims history. This open enrollment period is a one-time opportunity — use it or lose it!

If you have a pre-existing condition, no matter when you buy Medigap insurance, an insurer can impose a waiting period of up to six months.

Although Medigap can certainly help you pay your medical bills, it doesn't take care of everything. For example, Medigap insurance does not pay for long-term care; you need to purchase yet more insurance for that. Also, if Medicare refuses to pay the costs of a medical service or item because it's "unreasonable and unnecessary," your Medigap insurance won't pay for it either.

If you get your Medicare benefits through a managed care organization like an HMO specifically designed to serve Medicare beneficiaries, you may not need to purchase Medigap insurance. These organizations often provide many of the services not covered by Medicare for little or no extra cost. To find out if there's an HMO is your area that contracts with Medicare, call 800-638-6833.

Federal and state laws regulate the sale of Medigap insurance. Insurance companies and agents who violate these laws may be subject to criminal and/or civil penalties. For example, most states limit the sale of Medigap insurance to no more than ten standard policies. Policy A is the basic or core policy; it's available in all states. Policies B through J each include the benefits in the core policy plus additional benefits. The costs of these policies range from about $500 to more than $3,000. To find out what's available in your state, call your State Insurance Department or Commission.

The cost of Medigap insurance has been increasing rapidly in recent years — despite the fact that the rate of increase in inflation and the cost of other types of health insurance has slowed. It therefore pays to comparison-shop. Also, if a Medicare HMO is available in your state, check out its costs and coverage.

If your doctor offers you a *retainer agreement* that provides you with certain non-Medicare-covered services and that waives your Medicare coinsurance and deductible payments, beware. The agreement may violate Federal Medigap laws. Also, if a doctor refuses to see you as a Medicare patient unless you pay him or her an annual fee and sign a retainer agreement, report the doctor to your State Department of Health. You can also report the doctor to the federal government by calling 800-638-6833.

Nursing Home Care

As the elderly population grows, the private sector's involvement in providing nursing home care has grown — today, about 70 percent of all nursing homes are privately owned. The nursing home industry has become a big and profitable business fueled in part by the fact that the federal and state governments pay about 60 percent of the bills and demand relatively little in return from nursing home providers. As a result, the quality of care being provided by nursing homes in the U.S. ranges widely, from excellent to abysmal.

The sooner you begin planning for the possibility of nursing home care, the better chance you have of locating a good one. Too often, people end up selecting a nursing home in the middle of a medical crisis when they may have little or no time to comparison-shop.

Here are some basic tips for locating a nursing home providing quality care:

✔ Talk to your state's Ombudsman program. If they're unwilling to come right out and say which homes are especially good, they may steer you away from the really bad ones you may be considering with phrases like "There are better ones" or "We've not gotten too many complaints about them recently" or "I wouldn't want my mother there." You can obtain the number for the Ombudsman program by calling your local or state Agency on Aging.

✔ Shop around — visit a number of nursing homes in your area. Make a couple of unannounced visits at different periods of the day. Keep your eyes open.

✔ Ask to see a home's *Statement of Deficiencies and Plan of Correction* from its most recent state or federal inspection. The report should be on file at the nursing home and you have a legal right to look at it. Don't expect a perfect report. But you may want to eliminate a home from your list if it was cited for some serious problems that could affect your health, safety, or quality of life, and it appears as though the problems have not been corrected.

✔ Pay careful attention to the physical appearance of the nursing home. Is it clean, well lit, well maintained, and decorated attractively? Does it smell bad?

✔ Take note of the residents. Are they clean, neatly dressed, and is their hair combed? Are residents interacting with one another and with the staff?

✔ Eat the food if possible.

✔ Find out what kind of regularly scheduled activities are available for residents.

✔ Ask for a copy of the contract you will have to sign and read it carefully. Sometimes it's called a financial or admissions agreement. It should clearly state all costs and services the nursing home provides as well as the facility's legal responsibilities.

It's illegal for nursing homes to use *duration of stay* contracts. These contracts require residents to continue paying out of their own funds even if they've used up all of their personal resources and have become eligible for Medicaid.

Avoid contracts that let a nursing home "off the hook" with waivers of responsibility for a resident's lost possessions, injury at the home, and so on. Also avoid those that include clauses giving the home blanket approval for certain treatments. Both types of clauses are illegal.

✔ Talk with the staff. Are they friendly and courteous?

✔ Talk with residents and with their family members if possible.

✔ Check out the compliance history of a nursing home by contacting your state's Department of Health or whatever agency is responsible for licensing nursing homes in your area.

✔ Find out if Medicaid, Medicare, Medigap, or your long-term care insurance will pay for any of your care.

All nursing homes must be licensed by the state and must meet certain state standards. Homes participating in the Medicare and Medicaid programs must also meet federal standards and must comply with the Nursing Home Reform Act (which is covered in the next section).

The increase in the number of elderly has helped create a new profession — geriatric care managers. For a fee, these professionals assess an older person's needs and even arrange necessary care. Although many geriatric care managers provide invaluable help to older people and their families, the profession is unregulated. So shop carefully for a geriatric care manager, check all references, and get all agreements in writing.

The Nursing Home Reform Act

The federal Nursing Home Reform Act was enacted in the late 1980s to help raise the standards of nursing homes participating in the Medicare and Medicaid programs. States are required to monitor the compliance of nursing homes with this law.

States frequently drag their feet when it comes to carrying our their Nursing Home Reform Act monitoring responsibilities, and the federal government has been lax in enforcing the law. Making matters worse, the process for resolving problems can take months.

Despite its shortcomings, the provisions of the Nursing Home Reform Act represent an important step in the right direction. Although the list that follows is by no means a comprehensive overview of the law, it highlights some of the law's most important provisions:

✔ Sets minimum standards for nursing home construction, safety, nutrition, recreation, and medical services, among other things.

✔ Requires that nursing homes have a registered nurse on duty at least eight hours per day, every day of the week, and a licensed nurse on duty at all times.

✔ Requires that nursing homes be open and honest about their costs. You have a right to know the basic costs of staying at a nursing home and what services cost extra.

✔ Mandates periodic state nursing home inspections. The law requires that these inspections focus on the quality of life that the nursing home is providing the residents. So that the inspections involve more than just a review of a home's records, inspectors must also talk to and observe residents. Nursing homes that don't pass muster can lose their license and their right to continued participation in the Medicare and Medicaid programs.

✔ Establishes a Bill of Rights for nursing home residents.

Nursing home residents' Bill of Rights

When you enter a nursing home, you don't check your rights at the door. You're still entitled to vote, to enter into contracts, to marry, to practice your religion, to control your own health care, and more. To help underscore your rights, the Nursing Home Reform Act guarantees residents the right to

✔ Participate in developing an individualized plan of care for their nursing home stay

✔ Select their own doctor

✔ Have their personal preferences and needs respected

✔ Express their grievances without fear of reprisal and make recommendations for improvement

✔ Privacy in their medical treatment and their medical and personal records

✔ Be free of abuse and physical restraints, tranquilizers, and other mind-bending drugs, except when they're doctor-ordered

✔ Receive their mail unopened

✔ Manage their own finances and to have a full accounting of their finances if their nursing home is managing them

✔ Participate in resident councils

✔ Associate freely with the people and groups they choose

✔ Visit privately with their spouses and to have family visits

✔ Share a room with a resident spouse and be informed in advance of any change in room or roommate.

Long-term care Ombudsman Program

Federal law requires all states to run an Ombudsman Program for nursing home residents. You can get information about this program from your local or state Agency on Aging; you should also receive information about it when you move into a nursing home.

Ombudsmen advocate for nursing home residents and investigate and try to resolve problems. They have the legal power to inspect nursing home records, to talk with residents, and to do what's necessary to respond to complaints.

If you need an ombudsman's help but you're concerned about possible reprisals, the ombudsman must maintain your anonymity if you request it.

Protecting your rights

If you're having a problem with your nursing home, try resolving it on an informal basis by raising it with the nursing home staff person who is in a position to fix it — a nurse, nurse's aid, doctor, or facility administrator, for example. If informal methods don't work, talk with the home's resident or family council — most nursing homes have one. They may be able to help you resolve the problem.

If the problem remains and it's serious enough to continue pursuing, use the nursing home's grievance process — all facilities regulated by the Nursing Home Reform Act must have one and must make it known to their residents and to their families.

Sources of assistance outside the nursing home include

- ✔ Your state's Ombudsman program.
- ✔ The agency that licenses and certifies nursing homes in your state. It may send someone out to investigate your complaint, order that the problem be corrected, and impose penalties.
- ✔ An attorney who specializes in elder law. Depending on the nature and seriousness of your problem, you may have the basis for a lawsuit.

Paying for nursing home care

At today's prices, the annual cost of a nursing home can reach as much as $70,000 per year. If you're not good at math, that means it can cost close to $6,000 a month! Obviously, without adequate insurance, time in a nursing home can wipe out your life savings in no time, leaving little for your surviving spouse or children.

Medicare pays for relatively little of your nursing home care, which means that you may need Medicaid's help unless you have significant financial resources and/or a good long-term care policy. Even if you have the bucks to pay for your care out of your own pocket, you may eventually need Medicaid's help if your stay is long enough.

Medicaid cannot be of help unless your income and the value of your assets are extremely low, as it's a health insurance program for indigent people. If you're not Medicaid-eligible when you enter a nursing home, to become eligible, you have to spend most of your income and other assets paying for your care until you've become poor enough. This process is called *spending down*.

When you apply for Medicaid, don't try to hide any of your assets and income. If you do and the government discovers it, you can be denied coverage, forced to repay anything Medicaid's already paid for you, and you may even be liable for civil and criminal penalties.

If you plan far enough in advance, there are legal ways to "have your cake and eat it too." In other words, you can preserve much of your wealth and also become eligible for Medicaid. Although planning to become eligible for Medicaid is something you should discuss with an attorney who understands the rules of Medicaid inside and out, some of the things you can do to protect your assets include the following:

- Transferring them to others
- Placing them in an irrevocable trust
- Investing in your home

If you transfer any assets from your name within 36 months of applying for Medicaid, Medicaid will deny your application for as long as 30 months. Exactly how long depends on the value of the assets and the cost of the nursing home care. There are exceptions, however.

Purchasing long-term care insurance is a way to preserve your assets and pay for much of your nursing home care, but it's quite expensive. Also, the long-term care insurance industry has a history of abuse because long-term care insurance is not as well regulated as other types of insurance: Agents have misrepresented the policies they sell, and consumers have had trouble collecting benefits and getting refunds when they canceled their policies. The industry is cleaning up its act, though. You should be able to find a number of good long-term care insurance policies. About 35 states have passed laws regulating these policies.

Don't wait until you are elderly to buy a long-term care policy. It may be unaffordable at that point.

To ensure that the long-term care policy you buy pays for the care you may need, educate yourself about possible features of such policies, work with a trusted insurance broker, and consider several different policies before selecting one. Be sure the one you choose offers broad coverage.

Many long-term care insurance policies pay little or none of the costs of less skilled care like assistance with daily living. Shop for a policy that provides the broadest possible coverage.

Home Health Care

Home health care services can often help you avoid or delay nursing home care. Depending on the agency you work with, it can provide you with basic medical care or skilled nursing care, assistance with dressing, and even house cleaning and shopping.

Although they are regulated, the federal standards that apply to home health care agencies are pretty minimal, and especially if these agencies are not Medicare-certified, they operate with little government oversight. Given that their services are provided behind closed doors, older people using home health care agencies can be easily victimized. This is not to say that there are not good home health care agencies, but before hiring one, you should thoroughly check it out. To locate a good one, get referrals from your doctor, other elderly people, your local or state Agency on Aging, or a social worker at a senior center. After you have some names, here are some questions to ask:

- Are you licensed? Most states require licensing although a license doesn't guarantee quality care.

- Are you accredited? The Community Health Assessment Program (800-847-8480), the National Home Caring Council (202-547-6587), or the Joint Commission on the Accreditation of Health Care Organizations (312-642-6061) all provide accreditation.

- What are your charges? Get estimates for the costs of a medical professional and nonprofessional's time and for drugs, equipment, and supplies.

- Will Medicare, Medicaid, or my private insurance provider pay for your services? Find out exactly what they do and don't cover.

- Are you bonded? Bonding is required in some states. If you sue a bonded agency and win, you stand a better chance of seeing some money.

- Are your nurses, dietitians, therapists, and so on licensed or certified? How much training do your nonprofessionals have?

- How often will your supervisor visit my home?

- Whom do I contact if there's a problem? The agency should have a 24-hours-a-day, seven-days-a-week number you can call.

Call the National Association for Home Health Care, 202-547-7424, or the National Council on Aging, 202-479-1200, for information on how to chose a home health care agency and for a list of home health care agencies in your area.

Medicare provides only minimal coverage of home health care services; long-term care policies may cover them for an additional cost.

All-in-one care

The Continuing Care Community or CCC is a relatively new living option with a lot of appeal. It offers a range of living options on a single "campus," including residential units for older people who are still healthy and active, assisted living, and nursing home care. Some even offer special accommodations for Alzheimer's patients. As your needs change, you can transition from one living arrangement to another without moving far from your spouse or friends.

CCCs require that you pay a one-time entrance fee — the amount of this fee ranges widely from a low of about $20,000 to a high of as much as $300,000! Plus, there's a monthly fee. Often a CCC offers several different types of contractual arrangements.

Although it's easy to be wowed by a CCC's glossy brochures, snazzy facilities, and its promises of life-long comfort and security, don't allow yourself to be overwhelmed by the glitz and promises. Given the costs involved, the complexity of the typical CCC contract, the commitment you're making, and the fact that CCCs are not federally regulated (although about 30 states do regulate them), shop carefully and have an attorney review the CCC's contract. Also, check out a CCC with your local or state Agency on Aging and with the Continuing Care Accreditation Commission. It can be reached at 1129 20th Street, NW, Washington, D.C. 20036 or by calling 202-296-5960.

For those of you interested in learning more about the rights of older people, you can check out two great home pages. The Senior Law Home Page helps you access information about elder law, Medicare, Medicaid, estate planning, and more. It's located at http://www.seniorlaw.com/index.html. The Eldercare Web provides links to countless excellent sources of other elder law information on the Internet. You can find it at http://www.ice.net/~kstevens/ABOUT.HTM.

Chapter 16

Estate Planning

• •

In This Chapter

▶ Writing wills

▶ Exploring alternatives to wills

▶ Toiling with taxes

▶ Planning for incapacitation

• •

*E*state planning. Isn't that just for rich people or really old people?

No. It's for anyone, old or young, who owns property — a home, vehicles, retirement benefits, stocks, bonds, mutual funds, life insurance, and so on — and cares about who will get it when he or she dies.

Estate planning is for people who work hard for what they own, want to protect their assets while they're alive, and who want to be sure that when they die, after-death expenses like probate costs, creditor claims, legal fees, and taxes won't eat up their estate and leave next to nothing for the people they care about.

Estate planning is for business owners who need to plan what will happen to their business or business interests after they die.

Estate planning is for parents with young children who want to choose the person who will raise their children if they both die.

Estate planning is also for anyone who wants to help ensure that if they're near death with no hope of recovery, their estate will not be depleted by unwanted and expensive life-sustaining measures.

 There is something for everyone (estate attorneys and everyday people alike) at FINDLaw's Web site on estate planning, located at http://www.findlaw.com/01topics/31/probate. Among other things, you can download estate-planning software, find answers to many frequently asked questions on subjects such as wills and trusts, access links to other Web sites that deal with estate-planning laws in your state, and read articles on a variety of subjects, including "How to Avoid a Rip-Off Estate Planning Seminar."

What Does Estate Planning Involve and How Do I Do It?

Planning your estate involves preserving and protecting your assets while you're alive with adequate insurance, durable powers of attorney, and a living will. It also involves planning for your death by inventorying and valuing the property you own, deciding who you want to have your property after you die, and at a minimum, writing a will. Depending on the size and complexity of your estate (which is simply all of the property you own), estate planning can include, in addition to a will, the use of inter vivos gifts, trusts, and other legal mechanisms for conveying your property to others. If you want to properly plan your estate, you need to make strategic decisions about minimizing the number of assets in your estate that will be probated after you die, and you need to think about reducing your estate's federal tax liability.

Complex federal and state laws govern much of estate planning, making it a potentially complicated undertaking for all but the smallest, simplest estates. Unless you know the rules and are familiar with the range of estate-planning tools you can use, you may not accomplish what you intended, waste money, and create legal and financial headaches for the people you leave behind. So when it comes to estate planning, my advice is this: Call an estate attorney.

The help of an estate attorney can be particularly valuable to those of you with small to modest estates. When your assets are limited, it's especially important to plan your estate correctly because even minor expenses will have a relatively larger negative impact on the value of your estate than if your estate were substantial.

Even if you're confident about your estate-planning knowledge and know-how, it's a good idea to ask an estate attorney to review your plans before they're final. The attorney can do the following:

- Reassure you that you're on the right track or suggest a better approach.
- Familiarize you with the estate-planning laws you need to know about and tell you how to comply with them.
- Suggest ways you can save your estate expenses with helpful hints about how to cut your probate costs or reduce your estate taxes.
- Point out issues and concerns you might not think about.

Many people procrastinate writing a will. Hiring an estate attorney to do it for you means that you'll actually have one! Expect to pay $500 to $1,000, and maybe more if the cost of living in your area of the country is particularly expensive.

Before I get into some of the specifics of estate planning, a final note about estate planning in general. Always think of it as a "work in progress." Your estate-planning needs will evolve over time as your wealth grows and as the circumstances in your life change. In fact, it's a good idea to review your estate planning annually.

Start with a Will

According to *Consumer Reports,* an estimated 66 percent of all Americans do not have a legally valid will! Yet writing one is the single most important thing most people can do if they want to control who will get their property after they die. The cornerstone of all estate planning, a will gives you a voice after death.

Specifically, a will lets you name your beneficiaries and specify exactly what you're giving to each. Married couples often leave most of their property to one another, but you can also designate as your beneficiaries your children, other family members, your unmarried partner, favorite charities, your college alma mater, or whomever. It's your call.

You also name an estate *executor* in your will, the person who will shepherd your estate through the probate process. (See "Going through the probate process" later in this chapter if you are unfamiliar with the term *probate.*) And you can use your will to designate personal and property guardians for your minor children. In fact, in some states, the only way you can legally designate a personal guardian for a young child is by naming that person in your will.

Dying without a will

Understanding what can happen if you die without a will (which is called dying *intestate)* helps underscore the importance of having one. What follows are some examples of the kinds of problems you may unwittingly create when you die intestate:

- Your state probate court, not you, decides who will inherit your property. The court distributes it to your legal heirs based on the laws of your state. As a result, your spouse may not get all of the property you intended that he or she have when you died, and people you don't like or don't even know may end up with some of what you own. The court gives nothing to your close friends or favorite charities. If you lived with someone in an unmarried relationship, your partner will probably receive nothing.

Your *heirs* are the relatives who are legally entitled to inherit from you. Your *beneficiaries* are the people you choose to leave your property to; they may or may not be your heirs.

✔ Your heirs won't be able to sell or borrow against your assets (real estate, stocks, vehicles, and so on) without first initiating the legal processes necessary to have ownership transferred to them. These processes may be time-consuming and cost money. Here's a real life example: After you die, your spouse needs to cash in some stock to help pay for some unexpected expenses. But because you never transferred ownership of the stock to your spouse, you still own it even though you're dead! Your spouse isn't able to sell it right away.

And here's another example: You and your unmarried partner shared a home for many years. Although you always thought of your home as belonging to both of you, only your name is on the title. Because you died without a will, your partner has no legal claim to the home; therefore, your partner will probably lose the home.

✔ Unless one of your legal heirs offers to act as executor of your estate, your local probate court, not you, will appoint an administrator to play that role. The administrator is paid for his or her services by your estate, leaving less for your heirs.

✔ If you leave minor children behind and if their other parent is not alive, the children may end up being raised by someone you don't like or who doesn't share your values — even by someone you don't know — if no relative or close friend offers to raise them.

✔ If your minor children inherit from your estate and if the value of their inheritance exceeds the amount your state allows a minor to own without active adult supervision, the court will appoint a property guardian to manage what they've inherited until they reach age 18 — age 21 in some states. The cost of the property guardian's services is deducted from your children's inheritance.

Making a will legal

Every state has its own laws regarding what makes a will legally valid. If your will doesn't meet your state's standards, it may be dead on arrival in probate court because it will not be recognized as a legal will. Here are some of the requirements you may have to meet to make your will legally valid:

✔ You must be a legal adult — at least 18 years old in most states — when you write your will or when your attorney prepares it for you.

✔ You must be "of sound mind," which means that you must understand what you're doing: You understand your relationships to the people in your will; you know the nature of the property you own; you realize the significance of a will.

Not all wills are equal

A typed or word-processed will that complies with the laws of your state is always your safest legal choice. Here are some other types of wills that may or may not be valid:

- **Hand-written will:** This type of will may not be legally valid in your state.

- **Fill-in-the-blanks will:** If you don't own very much and your estate-planning goals are extremely simple, this kind of will may meet your needs. Before using one, however, be sure it meets your state's legal requirements. Fill-in-the-blanks wills can either be pre-printed forms or standard wills generated with special computer software.

- **Oral will:** If you're "on your death bed" and it occurs to you that you never wrote a will, your state may accept an oral rather than a written will. Your state may place limits on the dollar amount that you can transfer to others using an oral will, or it may require that your words be put in writing within a certain period of time.

- **Video will:** Although a video of you reading your will won't substitute for a written will, it may help prove that you were of sound mind when you prepared it. This kind of proof can be helpful if, after you die, one or more of your heirs or beneficiaries comes forward to contest the validity of your will.

- You must be preparing your will because you want to, not because anyone is forcing you to or threatening you if you don't.

- Your will must be written, signed by you, dated, and witnessed, usually by two people.

Giving away property

As important as a will is, you can only use it to give away certain kinds of property: property that you own by yourself and your share of property that you own with others as a *tenant in common*.

The list of property that you *can't* give away in your will is a lot longer. It includes the following:

- Property you own as a *joint tenant with the right of survivorship*. This property often includes real estate, stocks, bonds, and bank accounts. When you own property as a joint tenant, your co-owners automatically get your share when you die even if you leave your share to someone else in your will. Married couples often decide to own property as joint tenants.

Joint tenancy can be a useful estate-planning tool for unmarried partners because it allows each unmarried partner to automatically gain full control of the property they own together when one partner dies.

✔ Property you own as a *tenant by the entirety*. Only husbands and wives can own property in this way. When one spouse dies, the other automatically gets the other's share. Only about half the states recognize tenancy by the entirety as a legal form of ownership, and of those that do, many limit the type of assets that can be owned in this way.

✔ Proceeds from life insurance policies, IRAs, pensions, and so on. If you own any of these assets, you've already designated the people who will receive these benefits when you die.

✔ Your spouse's share of your community property. Remember from Chapter 4 that if you live in a community property state, you only own 50 percent of your marital property.

✔ Property you've already given away as an *inter vivos* gift — gifts you make while you are still alive.

✔ Property placed in a trust.

After you die, your will must be probated before your beneficiaries can receive the property you're giving to them. The probate process is explained later in this chapter. Property that you don't give away in your will doesn't get probated and goes directly to your beneficiaries.

Thinking about who gets what

If there's anything fun about writing a will, it's choosing your beneficiaries and deciding what you want to give to each of them. Although an estate attorney can fill you in on all the technical details of gift giving with a will, this section explains a few of the basic things you should know.

Giving to your spouse

If you live in a community property state, you own half of your marital property and your spouse owns the other half, unless you have a prenuptial contract that says otherwise. (See Chapter 4 if you haven't already.) You must say so in your will if you want your spouse to own your half after you die.

Shared or joint wills can create legal problems for the surviving spouse. If you're married, you each need your own will.

Separate property states have laws that prevent one spouse from disinheriting the other. These laws say that when you die, your spouse is entitled to a minimum share of your estate — the *elective share*. Although states can calculate this share differently, most allow a surviving spouse to take a fixed percentage of the dead spouse's property. Some include just the property in the deceased's will; others include everything the dead spouse owned. Regardless of the specifics, if you leave your spouse less than your state's minimum, your spouse can "take against your will" and opt for the elective share.

If you divorce after you've written a will, the provisions in your will relating to your spouse may be automatically canceled.

Ordinarily, if your estate is worth more than $600,000, it will have to pay substantial federal estate taxes after you die. If, however, you're married and you are both U.S. citizens, the IRS allows you to leave your spouse as much property as you want without having to worry about these taxes. This is called the *unlimited marital tax deduction.*

Consult with an estate attorney before using the unlimited marital tax deduction. Without adequate planning, you may be creating future tax problems for your spouse.

To help your surviving spouse and minor children take care of their financial needs while your will is being probated, most states provide for a *family allowance,* which is essentially an advance on what your family will receive once the probate process has been completed. Each state has a different way of calculating the amount of this allowance.

Giving to young children

No matter what state you live in, if you give your minor child property worth more than a certain amount — in the $2,500 to $5,000 range in most states — you must designate in your will an adult who is legally responsible for managing the property until your child turns 18 or 21, depending on your state. This person is a property guardian.

Wills, minors, and property guardians

Although leaving property to your minor children in your will is easy and inexpensive to do, it has some disadvantages. First, your minor child's property guardian has to prepare periodic reports for your state so that it can monitor exactly how the guardian is managing your child's property. Your state also expects the guardian to take an extremely conservative approach to managing your child's assets. These reporting requirements and limitations may be fine with you and even reassuring because you'll know that the guardian is being closely monitored. If, however, you want the value of your child's inheritance to be maximized after you die, including that property in your will is not the way to accomplish that

goal. You may therefore want to consider another option like setting up a custodial account or a trust. These options are discussed later in this chapter under "Alternatives to Wills."

If you're leaving your minor child a substantial amount of property, another drawback of using your will is that when your child turns 18 — or 21 in some states — the property guardian's role ends and your child automatically gains full control of his or her inheritance. The court doesn't care if your child is not a responsible money manager, and what kid is at 18? In the eyes of the law, at age 18, your child has become a legal adult and is entitled to the inheritance.

Giving to charity

Making gifts to IRS-approved charities can help reduce the amount of taxes your estate may have to pay after you die because such gifts are exempt from federal estate taxes. Most states also exempt them from their estate taxes.

Giving to pets

Some people want to remember their pets in their wills; however, many states prohibit leaving property to pets. So if you want to be sure that Spot or Whiskers will be cared for after you die, you should leave property to a friend or family member with the stipulation in your will that it be used to pay for your pet's care.

Appointing an executor

The person you name as executor of your estate will serve as its legal representative after you die during the probate process. Depending on the skills and knowledge of the person you choose for the job and the complexity of your estate, your executor may need the help of an estate attorney during the probate process. Your estate pays the cost of this legal help unless you made other provisions.

If you're like most people, you will probably ask a trusted family member or close friend to be your executor. If you don't feel that anyone in your life is up to the job, or if your estate is especially complicated, a professional executor, usually an attorney or a bank, can be your best bet.

Executors are entitled to be paid a fee for their services, an expense that your estate pays. Most friends and family members who serve as executors waive this fee, but a professional won't. Be forewarned: The professional's services won't come cheap!

Be sure to specify in your will whether or not you want your executor to receive a fee; otherwise, most states automatically provide for payment, usually calculating the executor's fee as a percentage of your estate's value.

Most states require that an executor be bonded, the cost of which is charged to your estate. Usually however, you can waive the bonding requirement in your will. A bond is a financial guarantee that your executor manages the assets in your estate in a responsible, ethical manner. If your executor fails to do so and one or more of your beneficiaries are harmed as a result, the bonding company will compensate your beneficiaries up to a certain amount. The cost of a bond is paid by your estate.

After you die, at a minimum, your executor will do the following:

- ✔ Locate your will.

- ✔ Inventory your assets and determine their worth.

- ✔ Pay any outstanding debts your estate may owe. Unless you've made other provisions, your executor may have to sell assets in your estate to pay your bills.

- ✔ Manage the assets in your will until the court says that they can be distributed to your beneficiaries.

- ✔ Prepare tax returns and pay estate and income taxes if necessary.

- ✔ Prepare reports and budgets for the probate court.

- ✔ Distribute the assets in your will to your beneficiaries after the probate court gives its okay.

All states give executors specific powers. If you want your executor to have other powers, or if you don't want your executor to have the usual powers, say so in your will by specifically detailing the additional powers you're giving or the powers you're taking away.

After you've written your will, take the time to review it with your executor to make sure that he or she understands everything in your will. If your will includes anything unusual — disinheritance of a child, for example — explain why because you won't be there to do so when you're dead. Also, tell your executor where your will will be stored; if you store your will in a home safe or safe deposit box, give your executor the key or combination.

A will is not forever

Your will is most useful when it accurately reflects the current realities of your life; therefore, when things change in your life, it may be time to amend your will. Here are a few examples of the changes I'm talking about:

- ✔ You start a family or add to your family.

- ✔ You get married or divorced or become widowed.

- ✔ You buy or sell your home or another significant asset.

- ✔ One of your beneficiaries dies.

- ✔ You move to a new state — your will may not be valid in your new state.

You can usually amend your will simply by writing a *codicil,* which is a written statement of the change. To make it legal, the codicil should be dated, witnessed, and notarized according to the law of your state. Keep all codicils with your will.

To avoid confusion it's best to limit your codicils to two. If you need more, revoke your current will and write a new one.

Going through the probate process

After you die, your will must be *probated*. In a nutshell, this legal process begins by establishing the validity of your will and ends with the distribution of the property in your will to your designated beneficiaries. Any property in your will must go through probate.

The more assets that must be probated, the longer the process will take and the more it will probably cost your estate. So you may want to minimize your probate assets by using other estate-planning tools besides a will to give your property away. See the following section of this chapter for details.

Whether or not you should be concerned about probate is a subject to discuss with your estate attorney. Depending on the value of your estate and its complexity, the cost of "avoiding" probate may not be worth it.

Some states allow relatively small estates to use an informal alternative to the traditional probate process. This alternative is less time-consuming and less expensive than the traditional probate process.

Alternatives to a Will

You can use other tools in addition to a will to give your property away. Some of these alternatives may even do a better job of meeting your estate-planning goals. Understanding your alternatives is another good reason why working with an estate attorney can be really helpful. Without talking to an estate attorney, you might never know about all of your estate-planning options unless reading estate-planning books is your idea of a good way to unwind after a hard day's work!

Although this chapter cannot begin to tell you all the ins and outs of using these other tools, it can introduce you to some of them. If any sound interesting, talk to your attorney to learn more. Remember, none of the assets you give away using these alternatives will go through probate. Some of these tools also can help you reduce the size of your taxable estate.

Insurance policies, employee benefit plans, and IRAs

Although you may usually think of these things as wealth-building tools, they are also estate-planning tools because each of them will provide a regular income to whomever you named as their beneficiary after you die.

Inter vivos gifts

You may not want to wait until you're dead to give away your money and other property. If you don't, consider making *inter vivos* gifts, a fancy name for gift giving while you're alive. With inter vivos gifts, you gain a number of important benefits. First, you get the pleasure of giving and of watching those you give to enjoy and benefit from your gift. Second, on a much more practical note, you can use inter vivos gifts to help reduce the size of your taxable estate. In fact, if you give enough away while you're alive, you may actually bring the value of your estate down below the $600,000 level so that your estate can avoid paying estate taxes to Uncle Sam entirely!

Federal law allows you to give away every year as much as $10,000 each to an unlimited number of people without paying federal gift taxes. If you're married, you and your spouse can give away up to $20,000 each year to as many people as you want, tax free.

There's a catch to inter vivos gift giving, however. In order for your gift to be considered an inter vivos gift, it must meet certain criteria, namely, it must be a completed and irrevocable gift. In plain language, when you make the gift, you can't retain any ownership rights to it, continue to benefit from it financially, or control it in any way, and you can't take it back once you make it. So if you give your child a share of your vacation home and you own the rest, or if you give your partner a future interest in some stock you own, you're not making an inter vivos gift.

Custodial accounts

All states have adopted some form of the Uniform Gifts to Minors Act or the Uniform Transfers to Minors Act. Depending on what form of these acts your state has adopted, you may be able to give inter vivos gifts of money, securities, insurance policies, annuities, as well as real and tangible property to your minor child by placing the assets in a custodial account that you set up at a bank or brokerage house. This simple and inexpensive alternative to leaving property to your minor child in your will has a number of important advantages. First, the adult you designate as account custodian to manage the account assets for your child does not face the same restrictions and reporting obligations that property guardians face. He or she is therefore more free to maximize the value of the custodial account assets. Second, when you place property in one of these accounts, you gain the tax benefits of an inter vivos gift. Third, depending on your state, you may be able to stipulate that your child not receive the assets in the account until he or she is 25 and presumably more financially mature than he or she will be at 18 or even 21.

You will have to set up a separate custodial account for each minor child to whom you're leaving property.

Consider a trust

Depending on the value of your estate and your estate-planning goals, a trust can be a great alternative to using your will to give away property. When you set up a trust, you create a new legal entity to hold assets for the trust's beneficiaries. To create the trust, you prepare a trust agreement. At a minimum, the agreement should indicate the following:

- The purpose of the trust
- The names of its beneficiary or beneficiaries
- The name of its trustee and substitute trustee
- The trustee's rights and responsibilities
- Your desires regarding how you want the trustee to invest the trust assets
- When and under what conditions you want the trustee to disperse income from the trust to the trust's beneficiaries
- When the trustee should give full control of trust assets to its beneficiaries

A trust is a very complicated legal entity. Do not try to set one up without the help of an estate attorney!

If someone tries to sell you a living or inter vivos trust, check out the salesperson or company very carefully. Bogus salespeople and companies may try to scare you into purchasing a trust or claim that it's a panacea for all your estate-planning needs. Steer clear of anyone who tries to sell you a fill-in-the-blanks living trust. If you want a living trust, your best bet is to work with a reputable estate attorney.

Trusts are popular for many good reasons, especially because they are the most flexible of all estate-planning tools. You can set one up to do just about anything as long as it's legal. No other estate planning tool gives you as much control over the terms of your gift. For example, you can decide if and when the beneficiaries of your trust will receive income from it and when a beneficiary can take possession of the trust assets. You're the boss!

To help illustrate these advantages, here are some examples of why you might set up a trust:

- If you and your spouse were to die, your minor children will end up inheriting a considerable amount of property. You don't want them to automatically take possession of that property when they turn 18 or 21 as they would if you left them the same property in your will (or in a custodial account, depending on your state), nor do you want a property guardian to manage your children's inheritance.

✔ Your husband is a poor money manager and you're concerned that if you were to die first, he would quickly squander the property he will inherit from you.

✔ Your child is profoundly handicapped and unable to earn a living. You want to ensure that after you die, your child's financial needs will be taken care of without jeopardizing any public assistance he or she may be receiving.

✔ You are seriously ill, and although death is not imminent, you know that at some point, you will no longer be able to manage your own financial affairs. You therefore establish a trust naming yourself both trustee and beneficiary and also designating a co-trustee. While you're still able, you manage the trust assets, and when you become too ill, the co-trustee will take over management of the trust property according to the directions you spell out in the trust agreement.

✔ You've just remarried. Although you want to leave most of your property to your new wife, you want to be sure that when she dies, certain property goes to the children from your first marriage, not to the children from her former marriage.

✔ You own a closely-held business and want to do what you can to ensure that when you die, your family won't experience an interruption in the income it provides.

✔ You want to leave all of your property to your spouse. Because your estate is worth more than $600,000, you are concerned with estate taxes and understand the limitations of the unlimited marital tax deduction.

With the help of an experienced attorney, you can set up a trust to address each of these and many, many more situations.

Why you still need a will

As wonderful a legal invention as a trust is, it does not substitute for a will. The following are four important reasons why you still need a will:

✔ To name a personal guardian for your minor child. In some states, writing a will is the only way you can do this.

✔ To designate a property guardian for your minor child.

✔ To convey property you may acquire after you set up a trust, assuming you don't amend the trust to include the new property.

✔ To transfer property that you may have forgotten to place in your trust.

Types of trusts

Two basic kinds of trusts are available: *testamentary* trusts and *living* trusts. Each has its own pros and cons.

Testamentary trust

Easy and relatively inexpensive to set up, this kind of trust is actually part of your will. While you're alive, a testamentary trust exists only on paper. After you die, however, the trust is activated, and after the assets you've earmarked for it go through probate, they are placed in the trust. Because a testamentary trust does not come into existence until you die, it is always irrevocable after that point. But while you're alive, just as you can revoke or change your will, you can revoke or amend any testamentary trusts you include in your will.

Many parents use testamentary trusts to help provide for their young children. Also, people with substantial estates often use testamentary trusts to minimize their estate taxes and to help protect their property from creditor claims.

Living trust

This kind of trust takes effect while you're still alive — thus the name. Any assets you place in it become the property of the person you've designated as trustee. You no longer own them. In some states, however, you can name yourself as trustee. That way, you get to control the trust's assets. There's a trade-off, however: If you're the trustee, the IRS expects you to report any trust income on your personal tax return.

Living trusts can be revocable or irrevocable. Most are revocable, which means that you can add or remove assets from the trust whenever you want, or you can even terminate the trust. Although a revocable living trust does not provide your estate with tax advantages or protect it from your creditors, an irrevocable living trust does. Both kinds of living trusts avoid probate.

In some states, a living trust is assumed to be irrevocable unless the trust agreement states that it is revocable.

The expense of trusts

Given the additional expenses associated with establishing a living trust, it's not a practical estate-planning tool for everyone, and certainly not appropriate if your estate is very small. For example, you have to pay an attorney at least $1,000 to help you set up a living trust, and you incur additional costs transferring ownership of trust assets to the trustee. Also, the trustee of a living trust (and of a testamentary trust) is entitled to receive a fee for his or her services.

Assets you place in an irrevocable trust are treated as inter vivos gifts, so be sure that you don't exceed your annual $10,000-per-person gift maximum. If you do, your estate will have to pay taxes on the excess amount.

Taxes

If your estate is worth less than $600,000 (or less than $1,200,000 if you're married), you're lucky — your estate planning is a little simpler because your estate isn't subject to federal estate taxes. Without proper planning, these taxes can take a big chunk out of your estate. You may still need to be concerned about other taxes, however, including the following:

- ✔ **State estate taxes:** Not all states have these taxes, but the tax rate of those that do is always lower than the federal rate.

- ✔ **Estate income tax:** Your estate has to pay this tax if its income in any tax year exceeds its standard exemptions.

- ✔ **Personal income tax:** If your income is high enough in the year that you die, you will be liable for this tax.

The federal estate tax is a graduated tax based on the current fair market value of all of the assets in your estate, not just those that you give away through your will, as well as on the cumulative value of any inter vivos gifts you may have given away. Every dollar in your estate over $600,000 (or $1,200,000) is taxed at a whopping rate of between 37 and 58 percent! And your estate has to pay these taxes before your beneficiaries can receive what you've left them.

Given the complexity of tax law, it's essential that you get the help of an estate attorney who can help you chose the best tax-minimization strategies for you in the context of your estate plan. Here are a few:

- ✔ Use the unlimited marital tax deduction.

- ✔ Make inter vivos gifts.

- ✔ Set up an irrevocable trust.

If your estate doesn't pay all of the taxes it owes to Uncle Sam, the IRS will use all of its tools to collect.

Planning for Your Incapacitation

Even if you're young and healthy, you may become temporarily or permanently incapacitated and unable to manage your own affairs, including your financial affairs and your medical care. If you don't plan for this possibility and you do become incapacitated, your family may have to petition the court to appoint a conservator to make health care decisions for you or a guardian to make financial decisions on your behalf. These legal actions can be tough on your family as well as expensive. The decisions of a conservator or guardian may not mirror what you would decide if you could speak on your own behalf.

Managing your financial affairs

Give someone you trust with sound financial management skills, or a financial institution, a *durable power of attorney,* which is sometimes called a "poor man's trust." You can create a durable power of attorney by working with an attorney to prepare a written document that meets your state's requirements and that spells out exactly what powers you're granting to this person in legally enforceable terms. You can also specify how you want your incapacity to be determined — after consultation with your doctor or with two doctors, for example. You can cancel a durable power of attorney at any time by sending the person you named as your agent a written notice of the cancellation.

To ensure that a power of attorney will be valid when you become incapacitated, you must set it up as a durable power of attorney.

You can also set up a living trust for your estate. Make yourself the trustee and name a successor trustee who can take over the management of the trust assets before or after you become incapacitated. In the trust agreement, specify when or under what conditions you want the successor to take over. The agreement should also spell out exactly what rights and responsibilities you are and are not giving to the trustee. For example, you may grant the power to make bank deposits, pay bills, and buy and sell investments.

Making decisions about your health care

Prepare a durable power of attorney for health care. It works like a durable power of attorney but for health and medical care decisions when you're unable to make them for yourself due to physical or mental problems that are not life threatening. The person you give a durable power of attorney for health care can also make health and medical care decisions for you when you're dying.

Don't just write down your desires for your health and medical care. Also talk about them with the person to whom you give your durable power of attorney for health care so that the person will feel comfortable carrying out this important and possibly emotionally difficult responsibility.

You should also write a living will. Use this legal document to spell out exactly what life-sustaining health and medical care you do and don't want when you're unable to speak for yourself. A living will not only helps you die with dignity but also helps control the costs of your care so that your estate won't be depleted paying for the "miracles of modern medicine and technology." Living wills are discussed in detail in Chapter 17.

Chapter 17

Death and Dying: Doing It Gracefully

• •

In This Chapter

▶ Living with a living will

▶ Creating a durable power of attorney

▶ Planning for your funeral expenses

▶ Euthanasia, or dying with dignity

• •

*I*f you're like most people, death and dying is not something you enjoy talking about and certainly not something you want to plan for. Yet, as unpleasant a subject as it may be, death is something all of us will face sooner or later. Just as you should prepare for your death through proper estate planning, you should plan for your funeral, burial, or cremation and prepare health care directives such as a living will and a health care power of attorney. Tending to the details of what will happen if you become terminally ill and unable to speak for yourself is the ultimate act of love for your family and the others you care about. You can spare them from having to make difficult and possibly emotionally painful decisions in the midst of their sorrow. So I hope you agree that it's best to stop avoiding the subject and start preparing for the inevitable.

Living Wills

As Chapter 16 emphasizes, if you have assets and care about who will receive them after you die, you must plan your estate, which includes writing a will. Equally important are health care directives such as a living will. A *living will* is a legal document that spells out your wishes regarding the kinds of medical care and treatment you do or don't want should you become terminally ill and unable to communicate your wishes. Without it, your doctor may do whatever is necessary, often regardless of cost, to sustain your life for as long as possible.

You can write your own living will or you can hire an attorney to help you. If you write your own, be sure that it meets the legal requirements of your state (perhaps by having an attorney review it); otherwise, it won't be enforceable when the time comes. To find out what those requirements are, call your state attorney general's office, state office of consumer affairs, local or state agency on aging, or an area hospital. Also, be sure that you express your wishes clearly and without ambiguity. If you don't, your living will may not be enforceable.

Contact Choice in Dying, a nonprofit organization, at 800-989-WILL for a fill-in-the-blanks living will for your state. In addition, the American Association of Retired People (AARP) in Washington publishes *Making Medical Decisions: Questions and Answers about Health Care Powers of Attorney and Living Wills.* This publication can help you think through the issues related to health care directives and enable you to clarify your desires.

Always review your living will with your close family members, your spouse or partner, and your doctor to clarify any questions they may have so that they feel comfortable with your wishes and will respect them when the time comes. Also, be sure that a copy of your living will is a part of your doctor's medical records. And make sure that any nursing home into which you move or hospital to which you are admitted has a copy of your living will too.

Most states require that you inform your doctor that you've written a living will. Even better, you should review its details with your doctor to make certain that he or she feels comfortable with what you're asking. If not, find a more sympathetic doctor.

You can change or revoke your living will whenever you want, but you must do so according to the laws of your state and destroy all copies of the original living will to avoid confusion later. In fact, it's a good idea to review your living will on a regular basis to make certain that you continue to agree with its provisions. Also, if you move to another state, you need to write a new one that complies with your new state's requirements.

If you spend a part of each year in another state, write two living wills — one for each state.

It's easy to write a living will. Unfortunately, getting it activated can be more difficult as recent media stories have made obvious. Officially, at least one doctor (sometimes two doctors) must certify in writing that you are terminally ill or permanently unconscious and unable to make your own decisions before your living will can be activated. It won't be activated just because you're in a lot of pain or don't want to live anymore. You must be close to death.

The Patient Self-Determination Act

With passage of the Patient Self-Determination Act in 1990, Congress began encouraging the use of health care directives: living wills and durable powers of attorney for health care. The law says that when patients are admitted into any facility that receives Medicaid or Medicare funds, they must be given written information about health care directives. If a patient prepares a directive, it must be stored with the patient's medical records.

Doctors are expected to comply with the directives in a living will if they are aware of the living will and if it is legally valid.

In reality, getting doctors to activate your living will may not be quite as straightforward as it sounds. They may disagree about the seriousness of your condition, or they may not want to do what your living will requests, so they may delay completing the necessary paperwork. Or your family may pressure your doctor to ignore the instructions in your living will. Sometimes formal hearings must be scheduled to resolve these problems.

Your family may need to consult with an elder-law attorney if they support your living will but your doctor is balking.

Durable Power of Attorney

Perhaps the best way to help ensure that your living will gets enforced is to give someone you trust a durable power of attorney for health care. This person has the power to push for its activation and to make decisions about your medical care and treatment when you're unable to. Obviously, the decision to give someone this power is a significant one; you should give it to someone you absolutely trust and who is strong and assertive, unlikely to back down or crumble when serious and difficult decisions must be made.

Prepare your living will and durable power of attorney for health care at the same time because the documents go hand in hand.

To give someone a durable power of attorney for health care, you have to prepare a legal document that meets your state's requirements. You can find out what they are by contacting the same resources that can tell you about the legal standards for living wills. In fact, many of them can provide you with a fill-in-the-blanks durable power of attorney for health care together with a sample living will. Again, if you write your own, be sure to have an attorney review it to make certain that it meets the letter of the law in your state and is clearly worded. And again, discuss the details of the power of attorney with the person you're giving it to so that he or she feels completely comfortable with what you're asking for.

Be very clear about what you do and don't want when writing your durable power of attorney for health care document. If your proxy's power is challenged in court, he or she could lose some of those powers.

If You Don't Have a Living Will or Durable Power of Attorney for Health Care

Without a living will or a durable health care power of attorney, you have no direct control over your medical care and treatment when you're close to death with no hope of recovery. Your doctor may work closely with your family to decide what to do, but their decision may or may not reflect your desires.

If your family and your doctor disagree, your family may have to initiate a lawsuit to get its wishes enforced. As you can imagine, doing so takes time and money and puts your family in an emotionally difficult situation. Meanwhile, you are kept alive, possibly against your wishes, for weeks, months, years, or even indefinitely.

Your family can ask the court to appoint someone as your guardian. This person is responsible for making health care decisions on your behalf. Usually, the court appoints a family member as guardian. But if no one wants to assume the responsibility or the court believes that no one is capable of handling the responsibilities of that role, the court may appoint a complete stranger to make critical decisions for you.

Think Ahead: How to Plan Your Funeral and Not Get Ripped Off

To insure that the details of your funeral match your personal tastes and pocketbook, you may want to make the arrangements yourself. Put your desires in writing, arrange for payment, and discuss everything with your loved ones. This kind of planning has several important benefits. First, you have more time to shop for the best deal than your grieving relatives will have after you die. Second, if you do the planning, you will spare your relatives from having to make what may be difficult decisions in the midst of their sorrow. And finally, planning ahead can help prevent your relatives from being victimized by the promises and offers of unscrupulous or greedy funeral home operators.

Paying for a funeral is not an insignificant undertaking. Today, the average cost of a funeral is $4,500. The typical burial costs at least an additional $3,500. So when planning your funeral, research your options, know the laws that govern the funeral industry, and compare prices and services.

If you're living in an unmarried relationship, and especially if you're living with someone of the same sex, make sure that when you write down your funeral plans you name your partner as the responsible party for carrying them out and then sign the document. You may also want to include your instructions in your will, but sometimes wills are not read until after the funeral.

Prepaying your funeral is not necessarily a good idea because after you've paid, you may move to another area, marry, remarry, or change your burial desires and needs for another reason. If you do decide to prepay, be sure that you are working with a reputable funeral home. Before signing a contract, read it carefully and find out under what conditions you can get your money back. Also, be very clear regarding exactly what you're paying for.

The Funeral Rule

The federal Funeral Rule, which is enforced by the FTC, regulates the funeral industry and mandates that funeral homes provide consumers with certain information regarding the options they offer and the cost of those options. The Funeral Rule is intended to help consumers make funeral arrangement and to protect them from funeral scams.

According to the Funeral Rule, you have the right to receive funeral cost information over the telephone and to be provided with a written price list of the services a funeral home can provide. You're also entitled to written information about your legal rights and what your state does and doesn't require when someone is going to be buried or cremated. For example, your state may not require embalming.

All states restrict the location of burial sites, so you are probably barred from burying your spouse under his or her favorite tree in the backyard!

A funeral home should give you printed cost information for the following:

- ✔ Basic services and overhead
- ✔ Transfer of remains to the funeral site
- ✔ Preparation for embalming

- Use of ceremonial or viewing facility and cost of staff
- Equipment
- Hearse or limousine
- Caskets
- Vaults, liners, and other burial containers
- Death certificates
- Music, flowers, and guest books
- Direct cremation and immediate burial

If you're not sure how much something costs, ask. If the funeral home cannot give you an exact price, it should provide you with a good-faith estimate.

Never, ever buy a funeral-related item or service over the telephone. Get it in writing! Steer clear of funeral homes that require you to buy certain packages of services that are not required by your state's laws.

Things to consider if you prepay your funeral

Some people think that it's a good idea to prepay their funeral expenses. They may or may not be right. It depends on their circumstances. To help you decide if prepaying is a wise option for you, here are some of the things to consider:

- Exactly what goods and services are you paying for and what will still have to be paid for?
- What happens to the money you pay in advance? Does your state have a law dictating how prepayments for funeral services must be handled?
- What happens to the interest that's earned on the money you prepay?
- What if you move out of town? Can your funeral plans be transferred to another location, and will this service cost extra?
- If you change your mind about the funeral arrangements you paid for, can you get out of the contract and get your money refunded? What if you just want to change some aspect of your arrangements?
- How are you protected if the funeral home you're doing business with shuts down?

Helpful tips for arranging a funeral

✔ Funeral homes cannot withhold information about the prices of its goods or services.

✔ You should be informed in writing of any special fees or up-front money you may have to pay.

✔ If you opt for direct cremation, the funeral home must make available to you an unfinished wood box or alternative container.

✔ The funeral home cannot refuse to let you use or charge you extra for a casket that it does not sell you.

✔ After you've selected the items and services you want, the funeral home should give you a Statement of Funeral Goods and Services Selected, which lists the price of each item and your total cost.

✔ The funeral home cannot tell you that any type of embalming fluid or process or any particular type of casket can preserve a body forever. Nothing preserves a body forever.

✔ The funeral home cannot falsely claim that particular caskets can keep out water, dirt, or other materials.

Caskets, burial vaults, cremations, and other options

Your religious beliefs, personal preferences, and/or your financial situation all come into play in your decision regarding whether you want to be buried, cremated, donated to medical science, or preserved in liquid nitrogen (yes, you can do this).

If you want to be buried, your body will probably be placed in a casket or coffin. These items can be expensive — as much as $30,000 for a really extravagant one made of expensive materials and with a lot of features. You may, however, be able to buy a very basic casket for as little as $50, depending on where you live.

Save money on your funeral by building your own casket! (Just kidding.)

Depending on the cemetery you will be buried in, you may be required to use a burial vault or a grave liner. Burial vaults are more expensive than grave liners and can cost anywhere from $100 to $5,000.

Some caskets and vaults come with warranties.

For cost and personal reasons, a growing number of people are opting for cremation rather than a traditional burial. If you choose cremation, you purchase a cremation urn, container, or wooden box instead of a casket. An urn is the more expensive option and when purchased from a funeral home costs between $100 to $1,500.

Burial societies

If you want a traditional funeral and burial but can't afford one, you can join a burial or memorial society, which are nonprofit organizations. These societies are able to offer lower-priced funerals and burials because they buy and sell funeral services and goods in large quantities and in turn, pass some of their savings on to their members. To join a burial or memorial society, you have to pay about $15 to $30 per year. In exchange, you may be able to save as much as 75 percent on your funeral costs.

If you decide to donate your body to medical science, your donation may be used to help train new doctors or to advance medical research purposes. Also, you can donate your organs to others. Unless you expressly prohibit it, in most states, your family has the right to donate your body or body parts.

Not all bodies that are donated to medical science are accepted, so you should have back-up arrangements in the event that yours is rejected.

If your body is refused by medical science and you still want to aid the medical field, try donating your gray matter to the Harvard Medical School. It is conducting research on Alzheimer's disease and other brain disorders.

Viatical settlements

If you have a terminal illness and need cash fairly quickly to pay your medical bills or finance your funeral, you may be able to sell your life insurance policy to a viatical settlement company for a lump sum of cash; the company continues making your premium payments until you die. Usually the company pays you a percentage of the total value of your life insurance policy, sometimes as much as 80 percent. This means that if you have a $100,000 policy, the viatical settlement can be as much as $80,000 in cash.

If you sell your life insurance policy to a viatical settlement company, it becomes the sole beneficiary of that policy; the person you originally named as beneficiary will no longer stand to benefit from it after your death; therefore, before selling your policy, consider your beneficiary's financial needs.

Viatical settlement companies will only buy your policy if you're terminally ill — have less than 2 years to live — and if your policy has a substantial face value. And although it may sound pretty heartless, the shorter your life expectancy, the more the company will pay you.

If your insurance policy is provided by your employer, the viatical company will not purchase the policy unless it can be converted to an individual policy or some other arrangement can be guaranteed.

What follows are some tips for getting the best deal from a viatical settlement company:

- ✔ Comparison shop.
- ✔ Find out whether your state licenses these companies, and if it does, make sure that the one you deal with is licensed.
- ✔ Check to see if you have to pay taxes on the settlement you receive. In many states, it is tax-free money; however, you may have to pay federal capital gains tax on the difference between the amount of your settlement and what you paid into your policy.
- ✔ Check with your state attorney general's office or state consumer protection office, your local Better Business Bureau, and the FTC to find out if the company you're considering doing business with has had any complaints filed against it.
- ✔ Steer clear of any company that pressures you. You need time to think about this important decision.
- ✔ Ask an attorney to review the agreement. These agreements are quite complex.

Don't expect to see cash from a deal with a viatical settlement company within days or even weeks. A reasonable time frame is three months.

Accelerated benefits

Another way to get money to pay for your medical care or funeral if you're terminally ill is with accelerated life insurance benefits. With this option, instead of selling your insurance policy, your insurance company pays you between 25 and 100 percent of your policy's proceeds.

Generally, accelerated benefits are not part of a standard policy but instead are offered as extras or attachments to new or existing policies. If your policy does not include accelerated benefits, call your insurance company to find out if you can add this feature for an additional premium. If not, some insurance companies are willing to loan you money instead, depending on the kind of insurance policy you have.

Collecting accelerated benefits or a viatical settlement can affect your eligibility for financial assistance from public programs such as Medicaid.

Euthanasia and Your Right to Die

When a doctor gives a patient a medication or provides a certain treatment that is known to result in death, that action is called *euthanasia*. Although you have the right to refuse any medical treatment, including those that are life-sustaining, you do not have the right to euthanasia, and the doctor who performs this act is breaking the law in all states.

Thirty two states specifically outlaw doctor-assisted suicides while others outlaw them through their general homicide laws. Assisted suicide occurs when someone plays a passive role in another person's death by providing him or her with the means to commit suicide.

The right to end your own life when you're terminally or chronically ill, or to have help doing so, is at the core of today's right-to-die debate, and both the courts and public opinion are beginning to believe that death is a very private decision that government should stay out of. A growing number of state and federal courts have therefore ruled that terminally ill patients have a Constitutional right to suicide, and the doctors who help them end their lives are not being prosecuted. Assisted suicide is being viewed as a legitimate way to end suffering, not as murder. It is expected that the U.S. Supreme Court will take up the issue of doctor-assisted suicide in late 1996 or in 1997.

The most famous advocate of assisted suicide is Dr. Jack Kevorkian, a retired pathologist. On May 14, 1996, he was acquitted at his third trial after being charged with assisting in the deaths of two women, one with multiple sclerosis and the other in chronic pain from a series of unsuccessful surgeries. Kevorkian openly admits that he has assisted and been present at over 30 suicides, but he has never been convicted for any of these deaths.

Part IV
Other Legal Stuff

In this part . . .

The chapters in this part deal with legal issues that are in the media spotlight these days — complex problems for which the law may need refining. I devote chapters to immigration, juvenile and criminal law, and privacy law.

Chapter 18

Getting Here and Staying Here: Playing by the INS Rules

In This Chapter

▶ Finagling your way to permanent residence

▶ Living in the U.S. as an alien

▶ Becoming a citizen

*A*merica, Land of Opportunity. Where the streets are paved with gold and everyone is a millionaire. Although the reality of living and working in the U.S. usually doesn't live up to the hype, for many foreigners, the United States offers the opportunity to make relatively good money and to live a lifestyle that is the envy of many countries. Also, many foreigners want to come to the U.S. for a relatively short period of time in order to benefit from its educational opportunities, to participate in cultural and business exchange opportunities, or just to vacation. Who can and can't come to this country and under what conditions are all responsibilities of the United States Immigration and Naturalization Service (INS) and are governed by federal law.

How to Get Here

Generally, people who want to come to the United States, regardless of the purpose of their visit and the length of their stay, must get permission by applying at the American Consulate or U.S. Embassy in their country for a *visa*. A visa is actually a stamp that is placed on the foreigner's passport.

The visa process can be quick and perfunctory, or it can be time-consuming and take many years; it depends on the kind of visa you're applying for, your country, your skills, whether you have close family members already living here, and so on.

Two basic types of visas are available:

- ✔ People who want to come to the U.S. for a relatively short period of time — usually six months to a year — apply for non-immigrant visas. They're just visiting.

- ✔ Foreigners who want to work and live here must apply for immigrant visas. If they get one, they become *permanent lawful residents*.

Tourists from certain countries including Canada, most European countries, and Japan can come to the U.S. for up to 90 days without visas as long as they have valid passports.

Foreigners can apply for more than 25 different non-immigrant visas, depending on the purpose of their visit. They can obtain visas for doing business in the U.S., vacationing here, attending school as a full-time student at an educational institution on a list approved by the INS, working here temporarily in certain types of jobs, and participating in exchange programs approved by the U.S. Information Agency. Each different type of visa has its own application process.

Who can and who can't come to the United States

In the vernacular of the government, any non-citizen who wants to come here or who is already visiting or living and working is considered an *alien*.

Because so many aliens want to come to the U.S., this country tends to be pretty picky about who it lets in, even if it's just for a short visit. The INS has certain criteria that it uses to screen aliens applying for visas. They use some of these criteria to help protect the physical safety and health of Americans and to preserve and protect our national security. Other criteria help ensure that an alien contributes to, and is not a drain on, the U.S. For example, an alien must

- ✔ Be able to support him or herself financially. An alien's capacity to do this is judged on the basis of such things as income, work history, and whether an individual has ever been on public assistance.

- ✔ Not have a history of potentially harmful emotional problems like schizophrenia, pyromania, and pedophilia. Also, aliens with an addiction to drugs or alcohol or who have a communicable disease that may create or contribute to a public health problem can be denied visas.

- ✔ Not have a history of certain kinds of criminal activity such as murder, rape, arson, robbery, and assault. Also, those who have participated in prostitution within the past ten years or who are suspected of having done so can be barred from entering the U.S.

- ✔ Not have a history of being (or suspected of being or wanting to be) a spy or terrorist. Members of the Communist Party can visit; they just can't live here.

- ✔ Be able to provide proper documentation and prove that he or she hasn't been deported or excluded from the U.S. in the past.

Staying Here Permanently

To live and work permanently in the United States, an alien must have an immigrant visa or *green card*. (The term *green card* is a misnomer because the cards actually come in a variety of colors.) Having one entitles the holder to remain and work in the U.S. indefinitely, come and go from the U.S., and bring his or her spouse and children to the U.S. A green card does not, however, entitle the cardholder to U.S. citizenship. A complex system of quotas and preferences determines who can and cannot immigrate to the U.S.

The processes of immigration and naturalization can be confusing and time-consuming. Working with an attorney familiar with the federal laws governing these processes can help cut through bureaucratic red tape and ensure that all paperwork is completed and filed correctly. The cost of this help can range from a few hundred dollars to as much as $5,000 depending on your needs and the complexity of your problem.

Because the INS makes extensive use of voice mail, finding an actual INS employee to talk with can be challenging, and even then, it's unlikely that the person you speak with will be able to answer complicated questions — another reason to seek the help of a qualified attorney.

To order INS forms, call 800-870-36767. Yes, this number is longer than most.

If you're engaged to a foreigner, you can bring your fiancé to the U.S. on a non-immigrant visa, assuming you've met in person within the past two years. Once here, your marriage must occur within 90 days, and you can fill out the necessary paperwork to make your spouse a permanent resident. In essence, by virtue of marriage, your spouse gets on the "fast track."

Sorry, That Slot Has Already Been Filled

Once per month, the U.S. Department of State issues a printed bulletin listing the availability of immigrant visas for every country for that particular month. The U.S. maintains *quotas* that allot more visas to foreigners born in some countries than to those born in other countries. Within these quotas are preferences that are essentially quotas within quotas. You'll understand better after you read the next couple of sections in this chapter — I promise!

The quota system is based on an alien's country of birth, not country of citizenship. So if someone were born in one country but is a citizen of another country to which he or she has moved, he or she must apply for a visa under the quota allotted to his or her birth country. As with all things legal, however, there are exceptions.

The immigration preference system has two parts: family-sponsored preferences and employment-based preferences. Each part has its own set of requirements and waiting periods. Most aliens who want to immigrate must be sponsored by a relative or U.S. employer.

Sponsorship by a family member is usually the quickest way to get an immigration visa. The family-based preference system allows a certain number of visas every year to be issued to relatives of U.S. citizens and to aliens who are already permanent residents. Presently, there are four major categories of family-based visas, and each has its own annual quota. Those categories with the greatest preference have the largest quotas.

To sponsor a relative, you must file a petition with the INS, provide certain documentation, and pay a filing fee. After all of the paperwork has been completed and the INS has received your petition, the petition is stamped with a date, and your relative is placed on the immigration waiting list.

As a U.S. citizen, you can sponsor your spouse, unmarried children under age 21, and your parents, assuming you're at least 21. You can also try to get green cards for your married children and your siblings, but they may have to wait years to immigrate to the U.S. The wait can be as long as 15 years depending on any number of factors, and there is no guarantee that someone on a list will actually get to the U.S. If you're a green card holder, you can sponsor your spouse and unmarried children.

Assuming the INS approves your petition, your relative must apply for an immigrant visa. Some time later, the INS will call your relative for a final interview, and he or she will have to meet certain requirements such as passing a medical exam.

If the INS approves your relative for an immigrant visa, he or she must come to the U.S. within four months of the approval. Your relative's passport is stamped with a *permanent resident* visa, and he or she is free to travel in and out of the U.S. as long as the visa is in effect. A couple months later, your relative should receive his or her green card.

An alien can also immigrate to the U.S. by locating an employer willing to sponsor him or her. Sponsorship generally requires that a worker have an offer of permanent employment from the sponsoring employer and be certified by the Department of Labor. As with the family-based preference system, there are several different categories of employer-based preferences and an annual quota of visas for each. The more preferable a category of employee by INS standards, the bigger the quota. For example, employer-based preferences give highest priority to the "best and the brightest" from other countries. Also, individuals in the arts, sciences, education, business, and athletics whom the INS regards as "extraordinary" can immigrate here even if they don't have an offer of employment in the U.S. — so long as they promise that they will continue to work in the field in which they are extraordinary.

Labor certification

The formal term for certification of an alien worker by the Department of Labor is *Alien Employment Certification.* An alien's future employer must initiate the certification process by completing certain paperwork. The employer has to prove to the DOL that no U.S. citizen is able or willing to do the job that the alien will be doing, and that once employed here, the alien's wages and other conditions of employment won't harm similar U.S. workers in any way. The certification process can take as little as six months or as long as a couple years, depending on the state in which the employer is located.

Professional nurses and certain other health professionals with very special credentials are another category of alien worker who may be able to immigrate to the U.S. without labor certification.

Professionals with advanced degrees and individuals with "special merit" are the next most preferred group of alien workers within the employer-based preference system. Skilled workers and less-educated professionals are next in line. Unskilled workers with less than two years of work experience or training face the greatest challenge if they want to immigrate to the U.S. because they're generally viewed as having the least to offer the U.S. and are also considered most likely to end up needing government assistance. Relatively few visas are therefore available to this group of workers, and they may have to wait at least six years before they can move here.

Special priority aliens

Some aliens are not subject to the usual quota system, even though they still have to follow the application process:

- ✔ Certain relatives of U.S. citizens, including their spouses, their children (assuming the children are younger than 21), and their parents (assuming the U.S. citizen is over 21).

- ✔ Refugees. These individuals cannot or don't want to return to their own country because they fear persecution based on their race, religion, nationality, political views, and so on.

Alien Rights

All aliens living in this country have certain rights. But exactly what those rights are depends on whether an alien is here legally or illegally. Aliens with green cards — legal aliens — have the most rights. Some of their rights are established by the U.S. Constitution; others by federal and state laws or by court rulings. For example, legal aliens have the right to

- Participate in certain federal programs, including Medicaid, federal housing, food stamps, and unemployment insurance
- Seek employment
- A public school education
- A lawyer if arrested

Undocumented aliens — aliens who are in this country illegally — have a legal right to

- Receive emergency medical care and some welfare benefits
- A public education
- Legal representation if arrested for a crime

The rights of aliens, especially illegal aliens, have become a hot political issue in some parts of the country and on Capitol Hill. For example, some politicians and citizens groups want to deny all legal rights to illegal aliens or scale them back dramatically. At the time this book was written, legislation to do such things has been introduced in both the House and Senate.

Becoming a U.S. Citizen

Many immigrants want to become naturalized U.S. citizens so that they can enjoy the benefits of citizenship and/or so that they can have an easier time bringing their relatives to the U.S.

If you have immigrated to the U.S., you have to wait five years before you can begin the naturalization process. After you've reached this milestone, you can begin the process by completing an application, filing it with the INS office in your state, and paying a filing fee. You also have to provide fingerprints, photographs, and additional documentation.

If your immigrant visa was based on your marriage to a U.S. citizen, you can apply to become a citizen after just three years of permanent residence, assuming you also meet other criteria.

Sometime later, the INS will call you for an interview. The purpose of this interview is to help ensure that you have a basic grasp of English, that you intend to continue living in the U.S., and that you're of good moral character. The INS also tests you on your knowledge of U.S. history and government. Don't sweat it! If you fail any part of the test, you can always take it again.

Citizenship classes offered by local community groups and correspondence courses can help you bone up for the English language and citizenship tests. The INS office closest to you can tell you about some of these resources. In addition, the federal government publishes special textbooks. Order Form M-132, "Information Concerning Citizenship Education to Meet Naturalization Requirements," from the INS for information about these federal textbooks and correspondence courses.

If you're age 55 or over and you've been living in the U.S. for at least 15 years, or if you're age 50 or more and you've been living here for at least 20 years, the English proficiency requirement can be waived.

If your application for citizenship is denied, you can appeal in federal court. Get legal help.

You should learn whether or not you've been approved to become an American citizen within four months of your interview. A swearing-in ceremony will be held at which you take the oath of allegiance to the U.S. and sign it. You are also given a Certificate of Naturalization, which you can use to obtain a U.S. Passport.

The American Immigration Resources on the Internet Web site (`http://www.wave.net/upg/immigration/resource.html`) offers the text of immigration laws, regulations, and procedures, and it also gives you links to immigration lawyers, consultants, and organizations. The Immigration Home Page, located at `http://www.panix.com/~rmadison/`, is another helpful Web site for those concerned about the immigration process. Its offers detailed information about waiting lists and visas as well as updates on changes in immigration law.

Chapter 19

Juvenile Law: The Times Are Changing

• •

In This Chapter

▶ The differences between adult and juvenile law

▶ Juvenile hearings and sentencing

▶ Your child's record

▶ Juveniles tried as adults

▶ Parental responsibility

• •

*W*hether its from reading the daily paper, watching the local nightly news, or from personal experience, most of us are aware of the high crime rate in America and the fact that more children are turning to violence and crime. Sad to say, but some kids make the "juvenile delinquents" of the 1950s look downright innocent.

A soaring juvenile crime rate means that a greater number of parents are going to be dealing with the juvenile court system in the years to come. So if you're a parent, it's in your best interest to prepare for the worst by educating yourself about juvenile law, including what to do if your child is arrested, how a juvenile hearing works, what happens if your child is found guilty, and how the laws dealing with parents and child delinquency are changing.

Juveniles and the Law

Although state laws dealing with crimes committed by children vary, most recognize that children under a certain age, usually eight or nine, do not have the mental capacity to commit a crime. For example, at one time or another when you were still quite young, you may have taken a piece of candy without paying for it even though you knew it was wrong. But as a second or third grader, did you really think, "I'm committing a crime against the laws of the state by taking this candy?" Probably not. You were more worried about getting "busted" by your parents! Even though you may have realized that stealing the candy was wrong, it's unlikely that you understood the legal consequences of your behavior at such a young age.

Generally, a juvenile, or minor, is legally defined as a child under the age of 18 who still lives with or is supported by his or her parents. Fortunately, the courts realize that most young children have not yet developed the ability to reason like adults; therefore, special laws pertain to juveniles who commit crimes. If your child participates in delinquent behavior and the judge believes that he or she is capable of distinguishing between right and wrong and knows the consequences of his or her actions, then the child will be accused of a crime.

The legal term for a child charged with a crime is an *adjudicated delinquent*.

When Your Child Gets Arrested

If you're a parent, you no doubt pray that your child will never get into legal trouble for committing a crime. Technically, most states call a crime committed by a juvenile an "act of delinquency." If the worst happens, you need to know that your child has the same rights as any adult who is arrested. (If you're not sure how the criminal justice system works, see the next chapter.) For example, your child cannot be exposed to an unreasonable search or seizure, and when arrested, should be read his or her Miranda rights, including the right to remain silent and to obtain a state-appointed lawyer.

Financial need is a factor in determining whether or not a child can have a court-appointed lawyer. Some states consider the income and assets of the child's parents in making this determination.

Don't assume that because you're the parent that you can do a good job of representing your child in court. Even if the crime your child is accused of is relatively minor, you should hire an attorney familiar with the juvenile court system in your area.

For your child to be charged with a crime or act of delinquency, a prosecutor must convince the juvenile court judge that your child knew or had the ability to know that he or she was committing a crime. Obviously, your child's age and mental capacity play a significant role in making this determination. If the judge believes that your child can discern right from wrong, legal from illegal, a juvenile hearing will take place. And like an adult charged with a crime, if your child is charged, he or she has the right to be released on bail until the date of the hearing.

If your child is accused of a nonviolent crime or a first offense, you don't have to post bail to get your child released.

Juvenile Hearings

Of the important differences between a juvenile criminal case and a regular criminal case, perhaps the most important is that children are subject to the juvenile justice system in their state and not to the standard adult criminal justice system. A second key difference is that juvenile court proceedings are called *hearings,* not *trials,* and that they are usually closed to the public. Just like a trial, however, evidence is presented, witnesses are called, and so on.

Another important difference is that most states have laws that require a child's name and offense be kept from the media in order to help protect his or her privacy. But a growing number of these states are naming names when a juvenile commits a felony.

Although your child's name and offense should be reasonably safe from the press, in most states, that's not always the case. For an especially dramatic example of what can happen when the media does get wind of your child's crime — actual or alleged — see the sidebar about Harvard and Gina Grant later in this chapter.

Most juvenile hearings are held before a judge specially trained to hear children's cases and to make decisions based on the fact that the accused is a child, both mentally and emotionally. There is no jury; your child's fate is in the hands of the judge.

In most states, depending on the crime your child is alleged to have commited, after this initial hearing, the judge may determine whether or not your child will be tried as an adult. In some states though, older juveniles and ones who have committed especially serious crimes such as rape or murder may go directly to an adult court.

When Your Child Is Found Guilty: Probation or Prison?

Unlike the role of the judge in a regular criminal trial, the task of a judge in a juvenile hearing is to decide what's in "the best interest of the child," not to punish the child. The court's focus tends to be on rehabilitating juvenile offenders so that they don't go on to commit other crimes. It's not surprising then that many judges sentence juveniles to probation instead of sending them to a detention center or juvenile prison.

A judge is much more likely to give your child probation if you show up at the hearing and are obviously involved in your child's life.

If your child is sentenced to probation, he or she is required to visit a juvenile probation officer on a regular basis. (The officer is trained to work with children.) In some ways, a juvenile probation officer functions much like a guidance counselor, helping children stay out of trouble, teaching them about acceptable behavior, and sometimes even becoming a role model for juveniles in trouble.

Probation also involves following certain rules such as attending school, obeying a curfew, working a steady job for older teens — the kinds of things we ordinarily expect of most kids. No big deal. But if your child breaks the rules, he or she may end up in a juvenile detention center — the equivalent of an adult prison. A much bigger deal! Your child can also end up in a juvenile detention center if he or she has been in trouble with the law before or if the judge feels that your child's offense is especially serious.

Although the age varies from state to state, generally children as young as 12 and as old as 18 can be sent to juvenile detention centers.

No two juvenile institutions are alike; they vary in strictness and security. The court therefore tries to place a juvenile found guilty of a crime in the facility most appropriate to his or her crime and past behavior. If your child is a repeat or a violent offender, like the two boys from Chicago mentioned in the following sidebar, he or she is more likely to end up in a strict, maximum-security juvenile detention facility.

The Juvenile Justice Home Page (http://home.earthlink.net/~ehumes/homejuv.htm) is an interesting Web site. It provides a fascinating history of the juvenile justice system in general; highlights resources for parents, families, and kids; and offers links to other criminal justice Web sites. This site also features excerpts from *No Matter How Loud I Shout: A Year in the Life of Juvenile Court* by Pulitzer Prize-winning author Edward Humes. Focusing on the Los Angeles Juvenile Court, the book follows five children through that court in order to illustrate the failings of the juvenile justice system.

Juveniles brutally murder 5-year-old

On January 29, 1996, two boys, ages 12 and 13, were sentenced to juvenile prisons for dropping Eric Morse, a 5-year-old child, out of a 14th floor window at a Chicago public housing project because he refused to steal candy for them.

At the time the crime was committed, Illinois law stated that children under the age of 13 could not be sent to a juvenile prison. But the law was changed as a result of Eric's death. The 12-year-old who actually dropped the 5-year-old out the window became the youngest child in the country to be sentenced to a maximum-security juvenile prison. Because the 13-year-old only aided in the crime, he received a lighter sentence. The new law allows both boys to be released and legally free of their crime on their 21st birthdays.

Your Child's Record: Will the Slate Be Clean?

Because the goal of the juvenile justice system is to rehabilitate, not to punish, juvenile offenders, and because no one wants a child who has been rehabilitated to go through life fearful that an important opportunity will be lost because someone somewhere will find out that he or she had once been arrested, all states protect the privacy of juvenile offenders. Some do so by keeping a juvenile's record of juvenile delinquency confidential; others seal these records; and a few states actually destroy them. Regardless of how your state deals with these records, the general public, including colleges, your child's employers, and the media cannot have access to them. Also, many states have laws prohibiting the release of juveniles' names to the media or to the public in general.

Only government agencies like the state police and F.B.I. can access your child's criminal record.

Juveniles Tried as Adults

Whether it's the best response or not is certainly debatable, but recently, many children have been tried as adults. Many experts believe that we will see more juveniles tried as adults as the juvenile population grows, the crime rate increases, and as juveniles commit more adult crimes. Trying children as adults is not altogether new, however. Some states have permitted it since the early 1920s. Also, many states have laws that exclude certain serious crimes from being tried in juvenile court — for example, murder and robbery, especially those that are gang-related.

One estimate indicates that by the year 2005, we will see a 23-percent increase in the portion of the juvenile population that is violence-prone.

Today, nearly every state allows a judge to transfer a juvenile case to a criminal court when the juvenile commits a heinous crime or has a history of criminal behavior and a lengthy record of prior offenses. And believe it or not, sometimes a juvenile's parents request that their child be tried as an adult!

Harvard revokes acceptance due to past juvenile record

Even though laws exist to protect juveniles from their past mistakes, sometimes those mistakes can come back to haunt them. Take Gina Grant as an example, a young woman from South Carolina. An exceptional high school student, Gina had tutored underprivileged children in her spare time and had served as the co-captain of her school's tennis team. Accepted at such top flight colleges as Harvard, Columbia, Barnard, and Tufts, Gina was looking forward to a bright future. It appeared as though everything was going her way!

But Gina had one not-so-minor problem: She had been arrested and charged with her mother's murder when she was in high school. According to Gina, after she and her mother had a fight, her mother, who was inebriated at the time of death, committed suicide by stabbing herself in the throat. But investigators didn't buy Gina's story especially because the coroner's report showed that her mother's head had been struck several times with a crystal candlestick, which coincidentally was found with some bloody towels in Gina's bedroom closet. So Gina was arrested for the murder of her mother. This information should have remained confidential because of a state law that protects the identity of juvenile offenders. Unfortunately, the sheriff in Gina's town told

the media that Gina had been arrested for the murder.

Ultimately, Gina pleaded "no contest" to manslaughter and was punished for her crime. Later, believing that she'd paid her dues, Gina assumed that her slate was clean and that her juvenile record was confidential; therefore, when she completed her college applications, she naturally did not mention her past record. After she completed the college application process, however, her past unexpectedly caught up with her.

After Gina had been accepted at Harvard, an anonymous person delivered the college a letter regarding juvenile crime together with South Carolina newspaper clippings about Gina's case. Suddenly, Gina's admission to Harvard was revoked and her future was in jeopardy. Harvard's response triggered a national debate about juveniles' criminal records and their right to confidentiality. And despite pressure to the contrary, Harvard stuck by its decision, saying that Gina misrepresented herself. Adding insult to injury, many of the other universities that had accepted Gina announced that they too were reconsidering their decisions. Tufts, however, eventually stood by its decision to admit her, and Gina accepted the school's offer.

Transfer methods vary from state to state but can be done in one of three ways:

✔ **Judicial waiver:** This method is the most common. Transfer depends on the child's age and offense. Most of the time, such transfers are initiated in response to the request of a prosecuting attorney. A judge is expected, however, to consider what's in the child's best interest in making the decision.

✔ **Prosecutorial discretion:** In many instances, states have given prosecutors the freedom to charge certain crimes committed by juveniles in criminal courts. The prosecuting attorney must show that the child understood that he or she was breaking the law.

✔ **Statutory exclusion:** More than half the states have enacted laws that exclude specific offenses from juvenile court. Furthermore, states continue to expand the range of excluded offenses, which means that more crimes committed by juveniles must be tried in criminal court.

Although presently less than half of all juvenile cases are transferred to adult criminal courts, if a juvenile is tried as an adult, he or she is subject to the same trial process faced by an adult charged with a crime, including trial by jury. If a jury hears your child's case, his or her fate is not decided by a juvenile judge accustomed to dealing with juvenile offenders; it's in the hands of everyday people — many of whom may hold very different views than a judge when it comes to crime and punishment.

If your child is found guilty, he or she can be sentenced to an adult prison, which tends to be more crowded and dangerous than a juvenile facility. It's unlikely that your child will get much rehabilitation there. Or your child may be sent to a juvenile home until he or she turns 18, at which time he or she may be transferred to an adult prison.

Parents Beware: The Laws May Hold You Accountable

As a strategy for reducing juvenile crime, a growing number of states and some cities as well are beginning to practice "tough love" or "tough law" on both parents and children. They're enacting *parental responsibility* laws, which try to force parents to exert more control over their children's behavior by holding the parents at least partially responsible for their children's crimes. Parents who violate these laws can be fined or even imprisoned. To some, parental responsibility laws might seem unfair. After all, single-parent homes are more common today than ever before, and even when there are two parents in the home, both are usually trying to juggle the demands of full-time careers with their parental responsibilities. But proponents of parental responsibility laws point to the following: Most juvenile delinquents don't receive the emotional support they need, putting them at risk for criminality. (Chapter 5 has more information on parents' rights and responsibilities.) For example, the two boys from Chicago who murdered Eric Morse had continually run away from home, slept in abandoned buildings, and failed school subjects including gym class. One of the boy's fathers was serving time in prison. Obviously, these children's lives lacked something — maybe supervision, maybe support, maybe love, and maybe all three.

In several states, courts now require parents to pay institutional costs for their child when he or she commits a crime. And parents may also be subject to imprisonment and fines, under certain conditions. For example, Louisiana's parental responsibility law says that parents can be found guilty of "improper supervision of a minor." If a child even associates with a drug dealer, gang member, or convicted felon, a parent can be imprisoned for up to six months and fined up to $1,000.

Currently, a federal Parental Rights and Responsibility Act is under discussion. If enacted, it will protect parents from being punished for their children's behavior.

In some states . . .

✔ Parents can be fined when their children vandalize public buildings.

✔ Courts can send parents to counseling or classes when their children commit crimes.

✔ Parents can be jailed if their child skips school.

✔ Parents who are found guilty of "improper supervision" can be fined and imprisoned.

✔ Child executions are permitted (in 24 states), but only in extreme cases. The minimum age that a child can be put to death varies in these states (from 14 to 17). According to the Supreme Court, subjecting children to capital punishment does not violate the Eighth Amendment, which prohibits the infliction of "cruel or unusual punishment?" In reality, states rarely execute children. The state of Illinois did not even execute the two boys responsible for the brutal death of Eric Morse.

Chapter 20
Crime and Punishment

. . . .

In This Chapter

▶ Types of crimes

▶ The whole process of getting arrested and going to jail

▶ The trial process

▶ Your rights as a prisoner

▶ Being the victim of a crime

. . . .

Most of you will never see the inside of a jail, so you'll be spared the considerable anxiety and expense that being arrested for a crime can bring. Bad things do happen, however, and sometimes they have legal consequences that involve the criminal justice system. So if you or someone you know is arrested, or if you become a crime victim, it's helpful to have an understanding of how the criminal justice process works, as well as the rights of defendants and victims. Having this information can help you cope with what may be a frightening and overwhelming experience.

What Is a Crime?

Although you probably think you know a crime when you see one, in reality, the definition of a "crime" is not always straightforward. Officially, a crime is a wrongful act that violates your state, the United States, or your community. But in plain English, a crime is an act that breaks the law and that causes injury or harm to people or to society in general.

If you're incarcerated in a county or municipal facility, you're in a jail. If you're in a state facility, you may be in a jail or a prison, in a restitution center, or a rehabilitation center, and if you're in a federal facility, you're in a prison.

Sometimes, *not* doing something is considered a crime. For example, if you're a pediatrician and believe that one of your young patients is being abused, if you don't report your suspicions, you can be accused of a crime, depending on your state.

Civil cases are initiated by individuals, businesses, or organizations and tried in a civil court. Ordinarily, if the defendant in a civil case is found guilty, punishment is payment of money; however, criminal lawsuits are brought by a state government or by the federal government — they're actually initiated by a prosecuting attorney acting on the government's behalf — and are tried in a criminal court. A criminal defendant can be an individual or an organization. Those convicted of committing a crime may be given probation, fined, sentenced to jail or prison, or a combination. You can also be sentenced to death. O.J. Simpson's past and current legal difficulties offer a good example of the distinction between a civil and a criminal case. The State of California charged Simpson with the double murders of Nicole Brown-Simpson and Ronald Goldman, and he was tried in a California criminal court. After his acquittal, the Simpson and Goldman families sued Simpson in civil court.

The laws and the court processes and procedures governing civil and criminal cases are quite different.

Types of Crimes

States' governments, not the federal government, have jurisdiction over most crimes, and each state has its own penal code, which categorizes particular crimes, usually as petty offenses, misdemeanors, or felonies. Although states can differ in how they categorize crimes, in general, the categories are as follows:

- ✔ **Petty offenses or citations** are relatively minor crimes like littering, running a stop sign, speeding, illegally parking, jaywalking, trespassing, disturbing the peace, and so on. Usually, when you commit a petty offense, you are ticketed, not arrested. In fact, many states have decriminalized certain petty offenses.

    Although a petty offense may be minor, don't ignore it! If you do, you are committing another crime.

- ✔ **Misdemeanors** are more serious crimes such as assault, battery, shoplifting inexpensive items, vandalism, writing a hot check for a small amount, and so on. Depending on the seriousness of the misdemeanor you're convicted of, you can be fined or sentenced to jail, usually for a year or less.

- ✔ **Felonies** include kidnapping, rape, arson, burglary, murder, and manslaughter — the most serious types of crimes. If you're convicted of a felony, you can be punished by a year or more in prison in some states. Some felonies, like capital murder, are punishable by death. You can also lose some of your civil rights — your right to vote, to possess a firearm, and to serve on a jury, for example.

Some misdemeanors may be treated as felonies. For example, if you're arrested for drunk driving and you've been arrested and convicted for the same crime before, you may be accused of committing a felony instead of a misdemeanor. How many times before depends on your state.

If you're charged with a crime and you're not sure of how it's categorized by your state, ask your attorney.

To be convicted of committing a serious crime, the prosecuting attorney usually has to prove two things beyond a reasonable doubt to a judge or jury: that you did what you are accused of and that you intended to do it (that you had a specific motive or reason to commit the crime). If, however, you're accused of a relatively minor offense, like a traffic violation, the prosecuting attorney doesn't have to prove specific intent because negligence is assumed. In other words, if you're caught speeding, you're charged with criminally negligent driving because the law assumes that you didn't intend to exceed the speed limit, but rather, that you didn't use reasonable care while you were driving. You were negligent.

An increasing number of crimes are being *federalized.* In other words, rather than allow individual states to adjudicate the crimes according to their own penal codes, the federal government is making them federal crimes and trying those accused of committing them in federal court.

Getting Arrested

There is no way to provide in a single chapter a comprehensive discussion of the various roads down which a criminal case might travel. This chapter therefore presents a general overview of what is most likely to happen if you're arrested. Also, it focuses on what happens when you're arrested for a misdemeanor or felony, not when you're charged with a petty violation, because the court system treats these minor crimes much differently than more serious ones.

Being arrested means that you're suspected of having committed a crime but doesn't mean that you're necessarily guilty. In fact, our legal system is based on the assumption that you're innocent until proven guilty. To be found guilty, you either have to admit your guilt or go through the trial process.

There are a couple ways that you can be arrested. If you commit a crime in front of a police officer, you can be arrested on the spot. But if you're suspected of committing a crime or assisting with a crime, ordinarily to be arrested, a judge must issue a warrant giving the police or another law enforcement agency the right to arrest you.

Federal cases vs. state cases

Although states prosecute most crimes, the Constitution gives the federal government jurisdiction over certain types of crimes, and those crimes are ordinarily tried in federal court.

If your case is heard in federal court, a federal magistrate sets your bail, not a judge, assuming bail is an option, and a judge, instead of attorneys for the defense and prosecution, performs the *voir dire* (French for "to speak the truth"), which involves interviewing prospective jurors. Also, in federal cases, a judge can comment to the jury about the evidence, and when it's time for sentencing, the federal judge must normally adhere to strict guidelines that don't apply in state courts. Parole is not an option for those in federal prisons.

Although it doesn't happen often, sometimes the jurisdictions of the state and federal courts overlap in regard to a crime. When this situation occurs, the federal and state prosecutors have to decide which jurisdiction will hear the case.

If you're arrested, the arresting officer will probably tell you why. But you don't have a legal right to be told. It's a courtesy.

You can also be arrested without a warrant if the police believe that they have *probable cause;* that is, they have evidence that causes them to believe that you've committed a crime or are going to. Some states also permit warrantless arrests if the police have *reasonable suspicion.* Warrantless arrests most often occur when the police need to make an arrest on the spot, and the delay involved in getting a warrant can prevent the arrest from taking place. For example, if a police officer sees you wearing a mask, holding a flashlight, and prying open the window of a home in your neighborhood, the police officer most likely has probable cause to arrest you.

If you're arrested without a warrant, you're entitled to a prompt hearing to determine whether there is sufficient probable cause to formally charge you with a crime. If you're released, however, you can later be rearrested for the same crime, and the second arrest does not violate the double jeopardy rule.

Ordinarily, to arrest you in your home, the police either need a warrant or your consent. The same rule applies if the police want to search your home.

In states that use grand juries, you can also be arrested if a grand jury indicts you for a crime, which means that it formally accuses you of committing a crime based on a review of the evidence.

Can't my case be dismissed if the police forget to read me the Miranda warning?

Contrary to popular belief, when you're arrested for a crime, the police don't have to read you the Miranda warning unless they intend to interrogate you. The Miranda warning says that you have the right to remain silent and that anything you say can be used in a court of law; that you have the right to speak with an attorney and to have your attorney present when you're questioned by the police; and that if you can't afford to pay an attorney, the government will provide one for you. The Miranda warning helps protect your Fifth Amendment right not to incriminate yourself. Prior to getting an attorney, don't volunteer any information to the police, and after you have one, always exercise your right to remain silent unless your attorney tells you to do otherwise.

Search warrants and search and seizure

If you're arrested, the police can search you for evidence related to your alleged crime. They can also search the area immediately surrounding you — essentially the area that is at your arms length. Anything the police find that they think may be evidence of your crime, they can take. Ordinarily, however, if the police stop you but don't arrest you, they will need a warrant to search you, but there are exceptions.

The law presumes that a warrantless search is invalid; therefore, it can be challenged in court.

If a judge believes that there is probable cause or a reasonable belief that a crime has been committed, he or she will issue a search warrant that states exactly what the police are looking for. After the judge issues the warrant, the police must conduct their search soon after, and they must conduct it in a reasonable manner, which means, for example, that if the warrant says that the police are looking for a shotgun because they believe you used it to murder someone, they should not search through your jewelry box because a shotgun doesn't fit in most jewelry boxes.

If the police want to search you and/or your property without a warrant, don't consent to it, even if you're innocent and anxious to vindicate yourself. If you do consent, the police can take what they consider to be evidence and use it to build a case against you.

Getting booked

After you're arrested, the police will take you to the local police station to be booked. At the station, you are fingerprinted, and you may have to provide a sample of your handwriting or your voice, depending on what you're accused of.

Legal help

Yes, lawyers are expensive, but when you're charged with a crime, not hiring one is penny wise and pound foolish. Certainly, you can represent yourself in court, but usually, you'll be doing yourself a serious disservice. Here are some reasons why:

- ✔ The prosecuting attorney you'll be up against has completed law school and passed the bar. In other words, he or she knows more about the law and legal procedures than you do.

- ✔ The prosecuting attorney has tried other criminal cases before and is more comfortable in the courtroom than you.

- ✔ The judge or jury cannot consider the fact that you're representing yourself when deciding your case, which means that trying to play on their sympathies by acting as your own attorney does not work as a defense strategy.

Even if you're an attorney, representing yourself is not advisable. It will be tough for you to separate the facts from your emotions and perform well in court.

If you don't have enough money to pay an attorney, you can ask for a court-appointed lawyer (a private attorney who is paid a very small amount of money to represent you) or a public defender (a lawyer who works for you but is paid by the county or state), but only if conviction for the crime you are accused of can result in a jail sentence. To prove your financial situation, you may have to provide the court with copies of your tax returns, bank statements, or other financial documents.

The downside of asking the court to give you an attorney is that you have to take what you can get, and the skills and experience level of the lawyer you end up with may not be what you need to win your case; however, if you're dissatisfied with your attorney and can convince the court that you should have a different one, the court may agree to give you a new lawyer.

After the court provides you with a court-appointed attorney or public defender, he or she can petition the court to have a private investigator or expert assigned to help with your case. This additional assistance is typically requested to help "level the playing field" for an indigent defendant. The court is most apt to okay such a request if you've been accused of a very serious felony.

Honesty is the best policy when you're working with your lawyer — even if you're guilty of what you've been charged with. To provide the best defense possible, your lawyer needs to know all the facts. Think of your attorney as a doctor trying to cure your legal problem. In order to have a fighting chance of doing so, your attorney must know all of your "symptoms." If you withhold information from your doctor, he or she may not have all the facts necessary to determine the best way to cure your health problem.

What you tell your lawyer is confidential information. It cannot be used against you in court.

The law views your blood, urine, breath, handwriting, and the sound of your voice as physical traits — parts of your identity; therefore, your Fifth Amendment rights are not being violated when you're asked to provide samples of them, and you're not incriminating yourself when you do. You should always, however, speak to an attorney before providing such samples.

After you're arrested, the arresting officer will write up a report detailing the circumstances surrounding your arrest and why you were arrested. He or she may write a longer report later or supplement the original report with new or additional information. The officer will also fill out a property report listing everything you had in your possession at the time you were booked, including your personal effects and anything the police take as evidence.

You have to turn over to the police all of your personal effects such as your watch, jewelry, wallet, and so on. Make certain that the police list all of the items you turn over, or you may have trouble later getting them back.

Depending on the nature of the crime you've been accused of, a state or federal detective or investigator may be assigned to your case. He or she will begin searching for additional evidence and talking to witnesses in an effort to build a solid case against you.

Going to jail (Do not pass go; do not collect $200)

If going to jail was as inconsequential as it is in the game of Monopoly, being arrested would be taken a lot less seriously. After you're booked, unless you're immediately released on bail, you will spend some time in jail waiting to be arraigned or formally charged with a crime. Usually this period is quite brief — just a day or two or maybe less, depending on your crime — but when you're in a crowded, smelly jail with a lot of strangers, a brief time is probably an oxymoron.

You don't have a Constitutional right to make a phone call from jail, but you may be allowed to make one call. Don't forget that the call has to be collect, as any money you had in your pocket was taken from you when you were booked. Because your calls from jail are limited, make yours count. For example, if bail is an option, call a relative or a friend who can help you arrange your bail.

Phone conversations in jail are not necessarily confidential; yours may be recorded, and anything you say can be used against you! The only exception is any phone conversations you have with your attorney. Even so, don't discuss your case in detail — your guilt or innocence especially — whenever you're on the phone. Do it in person.

You may be videotaped while you're being arrested and from the minute you go to jail. So watch what you say and how you behave!

Some states void the privileged nature of conversations with people like doctors, therapists, religious advisers, and spouses. In those states, anything you say to anyone can be used against you if your case goes to trial. So hold your tongue!

Being formally charged

After you're booked, you must be formally charged with a crime in order for your case to move forward. How you're charged depends on whether you've been arrested for a misdemeanor or a felony and also depends on the particular criminal process in your state.

Regardless of the crime you're accused of, you must appear in court at an *initial appearance.* (Depending on your state, this appearance may be called something else.) The judge will tell you what you've been charged with and read you your rights, and it is at this point that the judicial system begins to examine the merits of your case to determine whether or not to move forward. If you've been arrested for a misdemeanor, unless all charges against you are dismissed, you enter your plea at this time — guilty, not guilty, or *nolo contendere* (no contest). Depending on the crime you've been accused of and your state's legal system, you may even be convicted at this point if you plead guilty; otherwise, your trial date will probably be scheduled.

Arrangements for your release on bail or on personal recognizance may be initiated at the initial appearance.

If you've been arrested for committing a felony, unless the judge dismisses your case at the initial hearing, the evidence regarding your guilt or innocence will either be sent to a grand jury or will be considered at a preliminary hearing. If you've been charged with a federal crime, a grand jury is always involved.

A grand jury is a group of so-called "everyday people" who review the evidence in your case to determine whether or not enough evidence exists to pursue a case against you and issue an indictment. During a grand jury hearing, the prosecuting attorney presents the case and may call witnesses. If the grand jury thinks that the prosecutor has presented sufficient evidence, it issues an indictment; otherwise, your case is dropped. If new or additional evidence turns up, your case can be considered by a grand jury again and you could be indicted.

In some states, you have limited rights to have your side of the story explained to a grand jury, and the process can be pretty much a one-sided affair. In fact, typically, you can't even sit in on the grand jury's deliberations. You may, however, be called as a witness to answer questions. If this happens, you are not entitled to have your lawyer represent you, but your lawyer may be able to watch and listen. Also, depending on your state, you may be able to testify in person before a grand jury or submit your testimony in a letter. But you should be aware that anything you say or write to the grand jury can be used against you later!

If a preliminary hearing is held, the prosecution presents its case against you to a judge. Unlike a grand jury hearing, your attorney can present certain types of evidence in your favor. The formal legal term for this is *information*. You attend the hearing, but you can't say anything. If the judge believes that there is sufficient probable cause, your case moves forward; otherwise, the case against you is dropped. Some states allow a prosecuting attorney to try to get a grand jury indictment when a judge dismisses a case.

If you're indicted by a grand jury, or if the judge at the preliminary hearing decides that the police had enough probable cause to pursue the case against you, the next step is arraignment. At the arraignment, the judge reads the charges against you, informs you of your legal rights, and asks how you plead. How to plead is something you and your lawyer should already have discussed because it can be a critical decision.

Pleading guilty

This plea is an admission of guilt. You're saying, "Yep, I did it," and you're giving up your right to a defense. If you plead guilty, usually, there's no going back; you can't change your mind later. And depending on what you've admitted to, you may be sent to prison immediately.

The only time you should plead guilty is when your attorney tells you to and when you understand why it's a good idea. For example, you may plead guilty as part of a plea bargain agreement.

Pleading nolo contendere

Depending on your state, you may have the right to enter a plea of no contest. If you do, you aren't admitting your innocence or guilt; you're saying that you're not contesting the charge.

Many states view a plea of no contest as an admission of guilt, and you are sentenced as though you are guilty of the crime you've been charged with. The judge or your attorney should explain the implication of a no contest plea.

Pleading not guilty

If this is your plea, a trial date is set.

Your defense

If you plead not guilty to a misdemeanor or felony, you and your lawyer have to determine what the basis of your defense will be now that your case will be going to trial. You have several possibilities, the most common of which are an alibi, entrapment, self-defense, or insanity. You and your lawyer should discuss your defense early in your case.

Alibi

If you can prove that you were someplace else or with someone else when the crime you've been accused of was committed, or that there is another reason why you could not have committed the crime, you have an alibi. In most states, if you want to use an alibi defense, you have to do so at the start of your trial; in other words, you can't introduce an alibi midway through it.

Entrapment

When you claim entrapment, you're not denying that you committed a crime; instead, you're claiming that you were induced or lured into the crime by a police officer or another agent of the law. Entrapment is a common defense in drug cases involving undercover cops; in some states it's also used in prostitution cases. To make the defense work, however, your attorney must be able to show that the crime probably would not have occurred if you had not been entrapped.

Self-defense

To use self-defense successfully, your attorney must convince the court that you committed a crime because you believed that your life was in danger and that you had to protect yourself and/or your property. For example, if you're arrested for killing someone who broke into your home, self-defense may be a good argument.

Insanity

Pleading insanity works if your attorney is able to convince the court that at the time you committed the crime, you were unable to discern between right and wrong because of your mental state. The insanity defense is usually reserved for very serious crimes, and at least one medical expert has to testify about your mental state. Also, in some states, you must let the court know ahead of time of your intent to use the insanity defense.

If you're not convicted of a crime by reason of insanity, you are likely to be sentenced to a maximum security mental institution, which is really not much better than being in prison.

During the days or months leading up to your trial

After your attorney knows that your case is going to trial, he or she begins planning the pretrial motions that he or she will introduce as part of the strategy for helping win your case. These motions can include motions to suppress evidence, to change the location of your trial, or to learn the names of the witnesses that the prosecution plans to call. The prosecuting attorney can also introduce motions. Both attorneys present arguments for or against each motion.

What is bail?

At the time of your arraignment, if not before, the judge usually gives you the opportunity to post bail, which means that you are allowed to pay a certain amount of money to get out of jail. Bail is something you're legally entitled to for certain types of offenses, but not all. It depends on your state and the circumstances.

The amount of your bail is intended to help ensure the court that you will show up for subsequent court dates. If you show up, you may eventually get back the amount of your bail minus any fees and fines you may owe.

According to the Eighth Amendment, the amount of bail you have to pay cannot be unreasonably high given the crime you are charged with. For example, if the police charge you with shoplifting $100 worth of clothing from a department store, your bail should not be set at something outrageous like $250,000.

To decide whether to let you out on bail and how much bail you have to pay, the judge considers the following:

- The likelihood that you will show up for future court dates

- Whether you have steady employment

- If any of your family lives in the area and whether you have strong ties with them

- Whether you're a long-time resident of the area

- If you have a criminal history

- The severity of your alleged crime

- The possibility that you may harm your alleged victim or a witness

Both your attorney and the prosecuting attorney can suggest what they think is fair, but the judge has the final say.

In some states, if you can't afford to pay your bail, you can *borrow* it from a bail bondsman. Working with a bondsman is expensive, however, because you have to pay the bondsman a non-refundable premium of about 10 percent to 15 percent of the total bail bond, and you may also have to use your house, car, or bank account, as loan collateral.

If you work with a bondsman and you don't show up in court when you're supposed to, the bondsman may hire a bounty hunter to track you down and bring you to court or jail. Sometimes in such a situation, a bondsman will ask the court to *go off* your bond, which essentially means that the bondsman wants to be released from being financially responsible for you're showing up. If the court grants the bondsman's request, a warrant will be issued for your arrest.

Instead of posting bail to get out of jail, the judge may decide to release you on your own recognizance, and you'll have to sign a written promise to appear at the next scheduled court date. This situation is most likely if the crime you've been accused of is not extremely serious and you have no criminal record.

If you're out on bail or on personal recognizance and you don't show up for your court date, a warrant is issued for your arrest. After you've been arrested and are back in jail again, it's unlikely that you will get released on your own recognizance for a second time because you've shown that you can't be trusted; also, your original bail amount may be raised. In addition, you may lose all the money you paid for your bail.

Although the discovery phase is a basic part of most civil cases, interrogatories, depositions, and other common tools of discovery are rarely used in criminal cases in most states. When discovery does take place in a criminal case, it's quite limited because a criminal defendant has a Constitutional right to be protected from self-incrimination, and to participate in discovery can lead to self-incrimination.

Prior to your trial date, the attorneys may also discuss the possibility of a plea bargain and begin working one out. In fact, at least 90 percent of all criminal cases never go to trial. Usually, a plea bargain results in a less severe punishment than the maximum associated with what you've been charged with. The judge hearing your case must approve your plea bargain.

Why the large number of plea bargains? One reason is that mounting a defense costs a lot of money, and most defendants want to minimize their legal costs. Also, prosecuting attorneys often have very heavy case loads, so frequently, they're amenable to a plea bargain as a way to lighten their load. A third reason for the number of plea bargains is that defendants typically want to pay as small a price as possible for their crimes. So if being exonerated of the crime they've been accused of doesn't appear to be a realistic possibility, they're apt to go with a plea bargain.

The Trial

If your criminal case goes to trial, it may be heard by a judge (a bench trial) or a jury. If you've been charged with committing a felony, you have the right to choose who you want to decide your fate. But if you're accused of a misdemeanor, your state may not give you that option, and your case will automatically be heard by a judge.

Although the Sixth Amendment entitles you to a speedy trial, which means that you cannot be detained in jail for a long time due to "unreasonable delays," in reality, some court schedules are so crowded that you can literally spend years in jail for a serious offense, if you're not out on bail, waiting for your trial date.

If your case is heard by a judge, he or she hears all the evidence and decides whether you're guilty or innocent. A bench trial is almost always cheaper and faster than a jury trial. Also, if your crime has received a lot of negative publicity, a bench trial may be preferable because the jurors hearing your case may have been prejudiced against you by the media.

Despite the advantages of a bench trial, history has shown that jurors are twice as likely to find you not guilty (acquit you) than a judge.

Jury selection

If you're going to be tried by a jury, when your day in court comes, the first thing on the agenda is selecting the people who make up your jury. They are chosen from a list called a *venire*. The names on that list come from lists of registered voters, lists of people with driver's licenses, and/or tax assessment rolls. People in certain important occupations, such as doctors, lawyers, teachers, and firefighters, may be exempt from jury duty.

The individuals on the venire are screened during the voir dire process, which is essentially an interview process. Either your attorney or the prosecuting attorney can oppose or reject some of the jurors. To do that, they can use two different types of challenges: *for cause* and *peremptory*.

- ✔ **For Cause:** Both attorneys have an unlimited number of *for cause* challenges. They can use them to reject potential jurors whom they believe may be potentially prejudiced, unsympathetic, or biased against their side of the case, but they have to provide a basis for that opinion.

- ✔ **Peremptory Challenge:** Neither attorney has to provide any reason or justification when they dismiss a juror using a peremptory challenge. (A juror's race or gender cannot be the basis for a dismissal.) The number of peremptory challenges they can use is limited, however; different states set different limits.

Alternate jurors will also be selected should a jury member need to be replaced during the trial. The alternates hear the case but do not participate in the jury's deliberations.

Opening statements

Your trial typically begins with the prosecuting attorney's opening statements. The attorney presents the facts and the evidence of the case to the jury but does not argue points or draw conclusions. Your attorney can also make an opening statement at this point or can wait until the prosecution has rested its case.

The right to testify . . . or not to

If you're a defendant, the Fifth Amendment of the Constitution protects you from self-incrimination; therefore, you don't have to take the stand in your trial and testify, but you can if you want to and if your attorney feels that doing so can help your defense. Although the final decision regarding whether or not to testify is yours to make, you should take your attorney's advice very seriously.

Although you may be able to help your case by testifying, there have been many instances when a defendant's testimony and ability to hold up under the prosecution's cross-examination have had disastrous results, especially when the defendant said things damaging to his or her case that the jurors might not have heard otherwise.

If you testify in your trial, you have to answer all questions truthfully or risk being charged with perjury. Also, if you decide not to testify, your decision cannot be considered an admission of guilt and cannot be used against you in the courtroom or taken into account by the jury during its deliberations.

After opening statements, the prosecution presents its case using physical evidence, direct testimony, and sometimes circumstantial evidence. Your attorney has the right to cross-examine any witnesses that the prosecution puts on the stand and to object to statements that the prosecution makes in the courtroom.

After the prosecution has called all of its witnesses, the defense takes center stage. Although your attorney is not obligated to call witnesses, he or she probably will, and the prosecuting attorney has the right to cross-examine them.

Closing arguments

After both sides have argued their cases and examined witnesses, closing arguments begin. First, the prosecution sums up its case, argues the facts, and comments again on the evidence. Then your attorney presents his or her closing arguments and also responds to the prosecution's statements. Because the state bears the burden of proof, it is allowed to make one last closing statement — its final chance to convince the jury of your guilt.

Jury deliberations

After both sides have their says and close their cases, your fate is in the hands of the jury. The judge gives the jury instructions regarding their deliberations, and jury members then retire to the jury room to begin considering your guilt or innocence. But first, they have to select a foreperson or presiding juror to act as their spokesperson.

While the jury is deliberating, no one can make contact with them. If they have a question for the judge or want to reexamine evidence, they have to give a note to this effect to the court bailiff who then delivers it to the judge.

Typically, the jury in a criminal case must reach a unanimous decision about a case, although in some states, the decision can be 10–2 or 11–1. If the jury can't reach a decision, the jury is *hung,* and the trial ends in a mistrial. When this happens, you can be tried again for the same crime by a new jury.

The decision

If the jury comes to a unanimous decision, it informs the bailiff who in turn notifies the judge. Anyone who has ever watched *Perry Mason* knows that the jury can reach one of two decisions — "guilty" or "not guilty." If you're found not guilty, you are released, and in most cases, you cannot be charged for that same crime again, as you're protected by the double jeopardy rule. But if the jury decides that you're guilty, either attorney (but usually the lawyer for the losing side) can ask that the jury be polled, which means that each juror is asked to state his or her verdict aloud. Then the judge sets a sentencing date.

The Fifth Amendment protects you from being prosecuted twice for the same offense — the double jeopardy rule. But there are exceptions. For example, although it rarely happens, you can be tried twice for the same crime — once in your state court system and once in the federal system. And you can be tried again for the same crime if your case results in a mistrial or if you appeal your case and your conviction is overturned.

The sentence

Generally, a judge determines your sentence, but in some states, jurors play a role. Regardless, your attorney can present evidence of mitigating factors that can help lessen your sentence. The prosecuting attorney can object to your attorney's arguments and present evidence.

As an outgrowth of the victim's rights movement, it's also becoming more common for victims to play a role in the sentencing process. They may be allowed to make statements regarding what they feel is fair punishment for your crime, and the judge may take those recommendations into consideration. If, however, your state has "mandatory sentences" (minimums or maximums) for certain crimes and you're convicted of one of those crimes, the judge's decision-making powers regarding the most appropriate sentence is limited no matter what anyone has to say.

Although mandatory sentences limit a judge's sentencing power, they ensure that criminals committing the same crime receive equal punishment.

Probation

If your sentence is probation, you avoid jail time as long as you comply with the terms of your probation. In addition, you will have to live under the supervision of a probation officer for a certain period of time. You're most apt to receive probation if you're a first-time offender and have committed a nonviolent crime. While you're on probation, you have to report to your probation officer on a regular basis so that he or she can make sure that you're meeting the conditions of your sentence. Those conditions can include such requirements as finding steady employment, performing a certain number of hours of community service, quitting drinking, supplying urine samples for drug testing, staying away from people with a criminal record, or attending meetings that can help you address the root cause of your crime — Alcoholics Anonymous or Gamblers Anonymous, for example.

Pardons

Pardons are rare occurrences. Usually governors can pardon people whose cases were tried in state court, and the President can pardon federal cases. If you're granted a pardon, all of the legal consequences of your conviction are wiped out. Your punishment is set aside and any civil rights you lost as a result of your crime are restored.

Appeals

Although there is no Constitutional right to an appeal, if you're unhappy with the outcome of your trial, you may be able to appeal to a higher court if there is a legal basis for the appeal. When you appeal, you're asking the higher court to overturn or throw out the lower court's decision. Most appeals are based on technical error; that is, a procedure wasn't followed properly, and it affected the trial's outcome. After your attorney has filed your appeal and prepared a legal brief, the prosecuting attorney will respond with an answering brief, and your attorney may respond with yet another brief. Sometime later, the court can make its decision regarding your appeal, and you'll be notified in writing.

If you're found guilty and your case is under appeal, you may be able to stay out of jail while the appeals process is going on if the court allows you to post an appeals bond.

Writ of habeas corpus

If you're imprisoned, in addition to filing an appeal, you can also file what's called a petition for a writ of *habeas corpus,* which is a request that the judge review the legality of your imprisonment. Typically, your petition argues the legality of your incarceration based on certain legal technicalities or procedural violations. Although most habeas corpus petitions are rejected, if yours is accepted, you may be released from jail, or the violations you're alleging will be addressed.

Although most state courts allow any prisoner to file a writ of habeas corpus, federal courts have begun limiting prisoners' rights to file them.

Your Rights as a Prisoner

Being incarcerated means you lose many of the things you take for granted — your right to drive a car, to take a walk in the park, to go out to dinner with your family or friends, and so on. That's why being in jail or prison is such difficult punishment for most people; however, as a prisoner, you still have legal rights. For example, you're legally entitled to be treated fairly and not be subjected to brutality or cruelty. Also, you're entitled to food, water, medical attention, and access to the legal system, including access to a law library where you can research the law and prepare motions in order to end your imprisonment.

Depending on your sentence, you may not have the right to parole. If you are eligible for parole, after serving a certain amount of your sentence, you can apply for an early but supervised release from prison. A parole board reviews your case and listens to you explain why you should be released. If your request is rejected, you have the right to know why and the right to be heard by the parole board. If you are approved for parole, you have to meet certain conditions once you're free, including regular meetings with your parole officer.

Due to prison overcrowding, some prisoners are being released early, not paroled.

If You're the Victim of a Crime

Being the victim of a crime, especially a violent crime, can be frightening and emotionally scarring. Over the years, therefore, victims' rights advocates have pressured states and the federal government into enacting laws that better define and protect the rights of crime victims.

If you're a crime victim, the police must make a reasonable effort to find the person who committed the crime. If they find that person, you have the right to press charges. In some state cases and in all federal cases, you have the right to be paid for damaged or stolen items and any medical expenses you may have incurred due to the crime. If the person who harmed you or your property is found and convicted, the judge may make restitution or reimbursement part of the convicted person's probation. You can also sue that person for reimbursement, and in some states, you can apply for compensation from its Victim's Compensation Fund.

Some courts have assistance programs that counsel victims.

You also have the right to testify in court against the person accused of the crime, and ordinarily, you can be present throughout the criminal proceedings. At sentencing, you may even be allowed to make a statement before the judge about how the crime has affected your life and what kind of punishment you would like for the criminal. Although the judge doesn't have to consider your statement, many judges do.

It's almost always a good idea to become actively involved in the criminal process when you're the victim of a crime. At the very least, you should stay in touch with the prosecuting attorney and ask the attorney any questions you may have about the proceedings or the status of the case. Sometimes, becoming involved in the criminal process can help you work through the emotions you may be feeling as a victim.

If a suspect accused of committing a crime against you gets out of jail on bail, you have the right to be protected by the police if that person threatens you. For example, a restraining order may be issued ordering that person to stay away from you, but realistically, these measures are of limited value. Also, depending on your state, you may be notified if the person who committed a crime against you is being considered for parole, and you can participate in parole hearings. Also, about half the states let a crime victim know if the person who committed the crime has escaped from prison.

Chapter 21

Privacy: Do You Really Have Any?

● ●

In This Chapter

▶ The federal Privacy Act

▶ The Right to Financial Privacy Act

▶ Things you should know to protect your privacy

● ●

As Americans, we cherish our privacy. We value the right to lead our lives with a minimum of government interference and to keep the details of our private lives to ourselves. Privacy is central to our concept of freedom. But often without our knowledge or permission, information about some of the most personal aspects of our lives — our financial data, demographic characteristics, buying habits, and medical history — is collected by the government, private companies, and high-tech snoops. Much of this information is uncorroborated, which means that it may be incorrect. Yet it may be used to make decisions that can affect our lives in important ways. For example, we may be denied the job we want, the insurance we need, or we may even be arrested because of erroneous information in a database somewhere.

Ironically, as much as we value our privacy, few federal laws specifically address the issue of privacy. And those that do tend to be narrowly focused, outdated, and full of loopholes. Most were written before personal computers became ubiquitous and before technology facilitated the creation of the sophisticated databases that exist today. What follows are just some of the ways that your private information is being collected, shared, and sold:

✔ Companies comprising the billion-dollar information industry are making big bucks collecting consumer data from the Census Bureau, credit applications, product warranty cards, magazine subscription cards, and public records to create detailed consumer profiles. They sell this data to marketers. These companies are virtually unregulated.

✔ Some companies specialize in selling information to employers. For example, to help them make hiring decisions, an employer may query a database company to find out if a job applicant has ever filed claims for on-the-job injuries. If the applicant has, he or she may be labeled a potential troublemaker and not get hired, even though the individual may have had a good reason for filing the claim. As another example, an employer may ask a private database company to tell it whether an applicant has ever been arrested. Most likely, if the applicant has been, he or she will be denied a job — even though the database may not show that the applicant was acquitted!

✔ Federal agencies regularly collect, store, manipulate, and share massive amounts of data about us — our medical histories, educational backgrounds, financial status, employment histories, criminal histories, and so on. Sometimes they enhance their information with information from private databases.

✔ Many federal agencies create detailed *profiles* of certain groups of people — tax evaders and welfare cheaters, for example. Then they compare the consumers in their databases to these *profiles* in order to identify the people they're looking for. *Profiling* has been widely criticized by privacy advocates because the technique is not foolproof and therefore has disrupted the lives of innocent people.

✔ High-tech snoops can use computers to access our Social Security numbers and other identifying information and in turn can use that data to create new identities for themselves and others. They can also use this information to tap into your bank accounts, and charge on your credit accounts.

According to the federal Fair Credit Reporting Act, anyone with a "legitimate reason" can get information about you from a credit bureau.

✔ States are selling motor vehicle registration and home ownership data to private businesses. However, in 1997, a federal law will go into effect banning state motor vehicle departments from disclosing personal information about license holders, including their address, social security number, and the kind of car they drive. But the law includes many exceptions.

The Medical Information Bureau (MIB) is a repository of medical information about many consumers. This information may affect your ability to get adequate health, life, and disability insurance, and may even affect your employment opportunities.

Depending on your state, you may have certain privacy rights in the workplace. Also, the federal government bars employers from deliberately tapping your phone conversations or listening to your private conversations at work without telling you ahead of time.

In light of these modern-day challenges to our privacy, it may surprise you to know that the word "privacy" isn't even mentioned in the Constitution! Perhaps the explanation is a simple one — in the 18th century, our privacy could only be threatened in few ways, and the Founding Fathers believed that Amendment Four of the Constitution, which protects Americans from "unreasonable searches and seizures," pretty much took care of any potential problems.

So far, legislators have shown considerable reluctance to help us protect our private lives by passing new laws or by strengthening existing ones. The burden therefore is on each of us to do what we can to protect our privacy. Although you won't find a foolproof way to maintain your privacy, you can start by being aware of the laws that do exist and of the steps you can take to limit who has access to your personal information.

The Federal Privacy Act

The federal government is this country's biggest collector of information about us. Just stop to think about the kinds of personal data you share with it when you fill out your income tax return every year; apply for Social Security, Medicare, or other government benefit programs; fill out an application for a student loan; or participate in a Census Bureau survey!

The federal Privacy Act was passed in 1974 to limit the personal information that federal agencies collect on us. The law says that when practical, agencies must collect only "necessary" information, and that when you provide information about yourself, the agency must tell you how it will use it. The Privacy Act also says that before an agency can share your information with another agency, it must get your written permission. The law gives you some other rights as well, including the right to

- Obtain a copy of the data file that a federal agency is maintaining on you
- Dispute the accuracy and completeness of the information in that file
- Have file information corrected, updated, or deleted

How to find out what's in your information file

To find out whether or not a federal agency is maintaining a file on you and what's in that file, write a letter to the agency's Privacy Act Officer or to the head of the agency. Clearly stipulate in your letter that you're making your request pursuant to the federal Privacy Act, and describe as best you can exactly what records you're asking for. Your request can be as general as "all records you are maintaining on me." Also, write "Privacy Act Request" on the outside of your envelope.

Be sure your letter includes your full name, address, and Social Security number, and attach to it a copy of your driver's license. If your request is too vague, the agency will notify you, and agency personnel should be able to help you restate your request with greater specificity.

Some agencies have very specific procedures for making record requests. For example, your signature may have to be notarized. So before you make your request, it's a good idea to write to the agency for a copy of its request requirements.

Depending on what you're asking for, loopholes in the Privacy Act may allow a federal agency to deny you the information.

Although the law does not specify how quickly an agency must respond to your request to know what's in your data file, most agencies have a ten-day response policy. If a month goes by and you've not heard anything, you may want to write the agency another letter and enclose with it a copy of your first letter.

How to amend your file

When the agency sends you the information you've requested, it should also include instructions for how to challenge the information if you believe it's out-of-date, incorrect, or incomplete. Typically, you are instructed to do the following:

- ✔ Write to the agency official who released the information to you.
- ✔ Clearly spell out the problem you've identified and how you want it corrected or what you want added.
- ✔ Include copies of documentation that justifies your request for an amendment to your data file.

If an agency allows you to request a change in your file by phone or in person, put your request in writing too. A written request can be helpful if your request ends in an appeal.

After you make your request for an amendment, the agency should respond within ten days of receiving it. The agency may respond by telling you about any additional information it needs. It may agree to your request or deny it. If your request is denied, you must be told why and be provided with instructions for appealing the agency's decision.

If your request is denied, you have the right to prepare a short statement regarding what you disagree with in your file and to have it made a permanent part of your the agency's record on you.

The Privacy Act does not spell out a specific procedure that agencies must use when an agency's decision is appealed. The law, however, does require that each agency establish an appeals process. (You use the same process if the agency denies your request for information and if the agency denies your amendment request.)

If the agency denies your appeal, you can sue the agency in federal district court. If you win your lawsuit, you may be able to recover court costs and attorney's fees.

You must file your lawsuit within two years of an agency's final denial.

Privacy Act shortcomings

The federal Privacy Act falls far short of protecting consumer privacy. Here are some reasons why:

✔ The law is worded vaguely and therefore is open to interpretation.

✔ The law includes many exemptions to the ban on agencies sharing information about you without your written consent. A particularly problematic exemption is one that allows a federal agency to share consumer data with another agency when it's done for "routine use." Just about anything can be justified as routine!

✔ The Office of Management and Budget (OMB) has responsibility for monitoring and enforcing this law. Its powers to do so are extremely limited, however, and as a consequence, agencies tend to ignore and abuse the provisions of the Privacy Act.

The Right to Financial Privacy Act

The federal Right to Financial Privacy Act (RFPA) was written to help balance the need of federal law-enforcement agencies (the FBI, Department of Justice investigators, Treasury Department investigators, and Social Security Administration officials, for example) to review a consumer's bank records as part of a criminal investigation and a consumer's desire that his or her financial information be kept private. The law does not apply to state law-enforcement agencies.

The Supreme Court has ruled that consumers' bank records are the property of the financial institution that they bank with and that consumers do not have a Constitutional right to privacy when it comes to these records. So in the absence of a state law to the contrary, banks are free to provide both government entities and private companies information about your financial transactions.

According to the RFPA, federal law-enforcement officials can gain access to your bank records by obtaining your written permission (if you provide your permission, it's good for up to three months) or by getting an administrative or judicial subpoena, court order, or search warrant.

If officials try to gain access to your bank records via a written request, subpoena, court order, or summons, they must serve or mail you a copy at your last known address on or before the day that the bank is served with the request and then wait ten or fourteen days, depending on how you've been notified, before they can look at the information. The officials must also give you a written explanation of why the information is being sought and of your legal right to challenge the information request. (If law-enforcement officials use a search warrant to get access to your bank records, the law allows them to notify you after the fact — as much as 90 days after the bank has been served. Also, under broadly defined conditions, the agency can get extensions of this notification deadline in 90-day increments.)

The RFPA gives you the right to challenge in court a federal law-enforcement agency's efforts to access your bank records. To win your challenge, you have to demonstrate that the agency doesn't need the information or that it has violated the provisions of the RFPA. You need an attorney's help to take this action.

The RFPA does not apply to state or local law-enforcement officials. So in the absence of a state law prohibiting access entirely or one that limits access, state and local law-enforcement officials can go to your bank, present appropriate identification, explain the purpose of their visit, and review your records!

Other Federal Privacy Laws You Should Know About

A few other privacy-related federal laws you should know about include the following:

- ✔ The Computer Matching and Privacy Protection Act regulates the freedom of federal agencies to compare consumer information in one database to information in another to reduce waste, fraud, and abuse. The law says that if the computer matching reveals something negative about you, before an agency can take action, it must notify you and give you a chance to respond. This law does not affect computer matching done for tax and law-enforcement purposes.

- ✔ The Video Privacy Protection Act prevents retailers who rent videos from disclosing or selling their customer's video-rental records without obtaining their prior approval or unless there's a court order requiring them to do so.

Chapter 8 discusses the strengths and weaknesses of another important federal privacy law — The Fair Credit Reporting Act.

Other Things You Should Know about Protecting Your Privacy

With the exception of the Fair Credit Reporting Act, most federal privacy laws do not apply to the private sector, individual snoops, or electronic criminals. Consequently, you must be vigilant in protecting your personal information, and here are some practical suggestions for doing so:

- ✔ Don't give out your Social Security number unless doing so is absolutely necessary. (Your bank, employer, and brokerage house need it because they report your income to the IRS.) Your Social Security number is the key to accessing information that taxing authorities, employers, financial institutions, universities, motor vehicle departments, and others may be maintaining on you.

- ✔ Don't put your Social Security number on your checks, and whenever possible, keep it off your driver's license too.

  More than 40 states let you request a license number that does not include your Social Security number.

- ✔ Minimize your paper trail by paying with cash whenever you can.

- ✔ When you pay with MasterCard, Visa, or American Express, don't put your phone number, home address, or other personal information on the credit card sales slip, and don't provide the merchant with your driver's license number. All three bankcard companies prohibit merchants from refusing to sell to you if you want to pay with their cards and you refuse to provide this information.

  Some state laws prohibit merchants from writing your phone number, address, and other information on your sales slip when you pay with a bankcard. These laws also apply to retail store charges and to gas cards.

- ✔ Don't participate in phone and mail surveys unless you really want to. And if you do, understand that the information you provide may be bought and sold many times and become part of numerous private and possibly government databases.

- ✔ Review your monthly bank and credit card statements carefully for transactions that you don't understand. Doing so helps alert you to the possibility that someone has gained access to your account or to your credit card account numbers. If you think either has happened, contact your bank and/or your credit card company immediately.

  To activate the protections of the Fair Credit Billing Act (see Chapter 8), you must contact your credit card company in writing about any unauthorized charges.

- ✔ Write your bank and your bankcard companies and ask them not to give any of your personal information to third parties.

✔ Contact the Direct Marketing Association (DMA) to get your name removed from mailing and telemarketing lists. Here are the addresses to write to: Mail Preference Service, P.O. Box 9008, Farmingdale, N.Y. 11735-9008; and Telephone Preference Service, P.O. Box 9014, Farmingdale, NY 11735-9014. Although you may still get some direct marketing mail and calls, contacting the DMA cuts them way back.

✔ Actively lobby your state and federal elected officials to close the loopholes on existing legislation intended to protect some aspect of your privacy. Ask them to write new legislation that provides consumers with more protection from both governmental and private sector invasions of your privacy.

Protecting your privacy in cyberspace

You won't find any sure ways yet to protect your privacy in cyberspace, but the following practical and easy-to-use tips can help ensure that your personal information doesn't get into the wrong hands:

✔ Be careful what information you send via e-mail, especially in regard to credit card and bank account numbers, PIN numbers, your Social Security number, and so on, as well as sensitive communications. When you send a message online, although it may seem like it's transmitted faster than you can say "e-mail," and although you may be under the impression that your message bounces directly from your computer to the computer of the person you're writing to, in fact, your message actually makes several lightning-fast stops at computerized "post offices" along the way. A skilled cybersnoop can intercept your message at any point. Also, a record of whatever you send can exist on your computer and on the computer system of the online company that transmitted your message (America Online, CompuServe, an Internet service provider, and so on). Current law allows a government agency like the IRS to gain access to that information if necessary.

✔ If you make purchases or conduct other financial transactions online, before you share any personal data, ask the vendor if your transaction will be *encrypted* — put into a code — so that your personal information is protected from others. Although encryption is not a guarantee that your private information will stay private, it does make illegal snooping more difficult.

✔ If you use an online service provider other than one of the major national companies, find out how it protects the privacy of its customers' credit card account numbers and other personal information.

✔ When choosing a password to get online, avoid the obvious ones. They are easier for cybersnoops to figure out. Also, change your password on a regular basis.

Part V
The Part of Tens

"Oops."

In this part . . .

The last part of every *Dummies* book presents stuff in the form of top-ten lists. I use this part to provide you with succinct tips and tricks, and I also point out some of my favorite resources, where you're likely to find more information.

Chapter 22

More Than Ten Ways to Avoid Legal Problems

In This Chapter

▶ Thirteen pieces of advice that will keep you out of trouble

You can never completely avoid legal problems, but you can keep them to a minimum, especially if you follow the advice in this chapter.

Increase Your Legal IQ

When it comes to the law, ignorance is no excuse if you end up on the wrong side of it. So bone up on the basic laws that affect your life; know your rights and responsibilities where they're concerned; and one last thing, be sure to obey the law!

You can take advantage of several low-cost and even free ways to get a legal education. You're already on your way if you're reading this book. Other resources include visiting the Web sites highlighted throughout the book, ordering free brochures from the FTC on subjects of concern or interest to you, and contacting your state attorney general's office to obtain publications explaining your state's laws.

Think Before You Act

A good offense is always the best defense; therefore, before you take an important action in your business or personal life, be aware of the potential legal risks and what you can do to minimize them.

In addition to consulting the resources I mentioned in the previous section to help you understand potential risks and how to deal with them, you also may want to talk with an attorney. For example, if you're going into business for yourself, you can save both money and heartache, not to mention improve your chances for success, if you consult an attorney at the outset about such things as different legal structures, employment law basics, and your state and federal tax obligations as a business owner.

An estimated 63 percent of all new businesses fail within six years of being established. Some of these businesses would no doubt have survived if their owners had sought legal advice at the start, not at the end, when it was time to file for bankruptcy.

Use Common Sense

Some people seem to attract trouble like honey attracts flies! Their proclivity for legal problems is not because they walk around with a dark cloud hovering over them or because a black cat crossed their path. It's usually because they apply little or no common sense to the way they live their lives.

I'm sure you know at least a few people like this. They regularly exceed the speed limit and then bemoan the fact that they've lost their license. They're a sucker for every get-rich scheme they hear about and then wonder why they have no money. They do little or nothing to check out a used car before they buy it and inevitably end up with a clunker. They don't get warranties in writing and then are angry when the product they bought doesn't live up to its claims and the business who sold it to them refuses to make good on it. They get involved in important business deals without written contracts and then rant and rave about being taken. They inevitably fall for deals and offers that are simply too good to be true. And if their lives weren't complicated enough already, these people are always quick to sue, to right the so-called wrongs that have been done to them! If they spent even half as much time and energy evaluating their actions and transactions with at least a modicum of common sense and skepticism, their legal hassles would be fewer, their lives would be happier, and I bet they'd have more money in their bank accounts too.

Commit Important Agreements to Writing

I can't say it enough: Get all important agreements in writing, especially those that involve money. A handshake is not enough, even if you're dealing with a friend or relative. If problems develop later, it's a lot easier to resolve them when your agreement is spelled out on paper than if you and whoever else is party to the agreement have to try to reconcile what may be dramatically different memories of what you agreed to.

Writing things down in a contract can help you think through and address many if not most of the issues and problems that may arise during the duration of your agreement. It also helps minimize the likelihood that legal problems will develop down the road and can provide mechanisms for resolving them outside of the courtroom.

Never sign anything without reading it first. If you don't understand a provision in a contract you're being asked to sign, get an explanation or have your attorney review it.

Purchase Adequate Insurance

Although having adequate insurance won't insulate you from legal problems no matter how honest and cautious you are, insurance does provide you with a financial safety net should things go wrong. Without appropriate liability insurance for your home, your business, and your car, if you're sued, you could lose everything you've worked hard to accumulate.

Keep Your Debt to a Minimum and Save on a Regular Basis

Now that long-term job security appears to be a thing of the past, if you want to avoid trouble with creditors and even bankruptcy, keep your debt to a minimum and save as much as you can. That way, if you do lose your job or if you're forced to take a cut in pay, you'll have a shot at keeping your credit record trouble free.

In the past, staying with a single employer and working one's way up the corporate ladder was often the safest way to maximize your earnings. Now however, many experts believe that our economy is in the midst of a paradigm shift. They contend that now and in the immediate future, you must be ready and willing to move from employer to employer and to accept periods of unemployment along the way in order to maximize your career opportunities and earnings power. In such an environment, the less debt you have, the easier it will be for you to cope successfully with such changes in your job situation.

Use credit only when you absolutely have to, and only use it to purchase the things that you really need or that are extremely important to you, such as a home, a car, or a college education for your child.

Be Forgiving in Your Dealings with Others

Not every social or business exchange with an unsatisfactory outcome merits a lawsuit. In fact, most don't. And most things that end badly are not the result of malfeasance or deception.

Although many problems do merit legal action, before you hire an attorney, give yourself time to get over your initial anger, hurt, or disappointment about what went wrong. Talk about the situation with a dispassionate friend. You may be surprised to find how just a few days or weeks can put something in a whole new light!

Don't Argue with a Law Enforcement Official

An infraction that may have resulted in little more than a warning or a slap on the wrist can become a much more serious legal problem if you make a law enforcement officer angry. And on a more serious note, there's an old saying in the legal world that "you can beat the rap but you can't beat the ride." In other words, although the courts may find you innocent of whatever you're charged with (the rap), if you do something to anger the arresting officer during the arrest process, you may find yourself the victim of police brutality. Videotapes in recent years have provided dramatic documentation of this sort of treatment.

Don't Thumb Your Nose at the IRS

You're asking for legal trouble if you ignore your tax obligations to the IRS. It doesn't matter whether you're an individual or a business, the IRS *will* get what's coming to it sooner or later, even if the agency has to force you or your business into bankruptcy to get it.

Don't Mix Flirtation with Business

If you tell off-color jokes on the job, flirt, or make sexual advances to a fellow worker, you not only risk losing your job but you can also be sued for sexual harassment. What you may view as innocent fun someone else may see as offensive and disrespectful.

Even if the person you flirt with doesn't object to your behavior at the time or laughs at your jokes, your actions may legally be viewed as sexual harassment.

Meet Your Child Support Obligations

Not meeting your legal obligations to your children not only speaks volumes about you as an individual but also is almost certain to get you in legal trouble sooner or later. Federal and state governments have become very serious about tracking down deadbeat Dads and Moms to make them pay what they owe, and they are developing new and more effective means of doing so.

If you have a child with a man that you're no longer living with, most states expect the child's father to assume all the legal responsibilities of paternity, whether you were married to the man or not.

If you have failed to meet your child support obligations, depending on where you live, your state may have posted your photo on a special Web site as a deadbeat parent. As a growing number of people use the Internet, some states are using these Web sites as a way to track down parents seriously behind in their child support payments.

Don't Set Up Your Business as a Partnership

There ought to be a warning on partnership agreements like the one on cigarette packages. Only this warning would say *WARNING: Partnerships can be hazardous to your business.*

Based on my work as an attorney and on my own experience in two different partnerships, I've come to the conclusion that when you go into a partnership, you're almost always asking for legal trouble. Sure, some partnerships work well and make money for all concerned, but most, sooner or later, become legal quagmires, even if you've got the best agreement money can buy. For example, one of you may begin feeling as though the other isn't working hard enough or is taking too much out of the business. Or you may discover that your partner lied about his or her professional abilities or resources or that your partner is stealing from the business. Even if your partnership provides you with a legal means of dealing with these and other potential problems, doing so isn't easy. When you are joined at the pocketbook as you are in a mutually-dependent relationship like a partnership, breaking up is always hard to do.

The actions of one partner legally obligates all other partners, which means that if your partner incurs a financial obligation on behalf of the business against your wishes or without your knowledge, it's your debt as much as it is your partner's in the eyes of the law, and if your business can't make good on the debt, your creditor can try to collect directly from you or from your partner — whoever has the money.

Plan Your Estate

No, *you* won't have to deal with the repercussions that you may create for your loved ones if you don't plan your estate. But if you own property and other assets and you die without a will, or if your will isn't legally valid, your bequest to those you leave behind may be legal and financial headaches and expenses. The greatest gift you can leave your loved ones is good estate planning.

Depending on the size of your estate and the needs of your spouse or unmarried partner and any children you have, you may need to do more estate planning than just writing a will. See Chapter 16 for details.

Chapter 23

The Ten Most Common Mistakes Consumers Make When Hiring an Attorney

· ·

In This Chapter

▶ Advice for hiring the attorney that's right for you

· ·

*H*iring an attorney can be intimidating, especially if you've never used one before and your legal problem is serious. What should you expect from an attorney? How can you tell a good one from one who's not so good? Will you be able to afford the legal help you need? By reading this book, you can arm yourself with facts and tips that you can use to hire the best attorney your money can buy, but knowing the kinds of mistakes consumers most often make when hiring an attorney can make you an extra-confident consumer of legal help.

Not Asking an Attorney to Come Down in Price

With law schools graduating about 30,000 new lawyers every year and thousands of them already in practice, there is obviously no shortage of attorneys in the marketplace. In fact, when it comes to getting legal help, it's a buyer's, not a seller's, market. You're in the driver's seat. Believe it or not, you may find that attorneys are actually eager for your business and are willing to negotiate on price to get it!

When an attorney proposes charging you on an hourly basis, suggest that he or she bill you instead on a flat-fee basis. If an attorney is willing to take your case on contingency, find out if he or she will accept a lower percentage of the settlement.

If an attorney won't negotiate on price, don't automatically scratch him or her off your list. You may be making a penny-wise and pound-foolish decision if the attorney has unique skills or abilities that can increase the chances of resolving your legal problem in your favor.

Thinking That Lawyers Who Advertise Should Be Avoided

Attorney advertising has developed a bad reputation — no doubt about it. But don't be so shortsighted that you automatically assume that if an attorney advertises, he or she must be desperate for business or somehow inferior. Some good attorneys advertise and some bad ones don't. Highly qualified attorneys who specialize in certain areas of the law, including consumer bankruptcy, wills, and personal injury, often use advertising to market their legal services.

Attorneys who advertise often provide their services for a lower than usual cost.

Hiring an Attorney You Don't Feel Comfortable With

Have you ever sat across from someone whose manner intimidated you? Have your instincts ever told you that someone is not trustworthy? Or how about someone who seems bored with what you're saying? If your answer is "yes," you probably found that you had a tough time talking honestly with that person and that you felt uncomfortable with him or her. Maybe you even felt a little angry that you weren't being taken seriously enough.

If an attorney triggers any of these feelings in you, even if the attorney comes highly recommended, follow your instincts and look elsewhere for legal help. When the legal issue you're dealing with is serious and you've got a lot at stake, you need an attorney you can trust, an attorney you can talk to, and one who listens with sympathy, not boredom. Although money-hungry attorneys who view clients as little more than contributions to their bottom lines have certainly helped give the legal profession a bad name, many lawyers are truly interested in helping others.

Steer clear of attorneys who don't give you their full attention when you're explaining your legal problem to them; who don't ask questions; or who spend a lot of time bragging about themselves.

Not Avoiding Attorneys Who Win by Intimidation

Attorneys who try to intimidate the other side or try to grind people down until they yell "Uncle!" rarely serve their client's best interests. More often than not, such tactics make the other side so angry that they dig in their heels and swear off compromising. Worse yet, lawyers who think they're Rambo have a habit of turning a relatively minor legal problem into a more serious, not to mention more expensive, one. Ordinarily, you want a problem solver as an attorney, not a pit bull!

To find a problem-solving attorney, consider asking other attorneys you may know about the reputation of the attorney you're considering. Rambo attorneys usually have a well-known reputation in their legal community for playing hardball. Also, pay attention to how the attorney describes the likely progress of your case. If he or she never raises the possibility of compromise and never suggests that you think about what you'd be willing to settle for, the attorney is giving you some pretty strong clues that legal problem solving is not his or her strong suit.

If you hire an attorney and subsequently become unhappy with his or her approach to your legal problem, you can always fire that one and hire another one.

Hiring an Attorney Because You're Angry and Want to Get Even

Using the legal system to get revenge or to assuage your hurt feelings is an awfully expensive way to deal with problems! Far better responses involve using mediation or arbitration, talking to a therapist, or simply forgetting about what got you upset in the first place. Using the courts to pursue grudges, to hurt others because you think that they hurt you, or to pursue claims for minimal actual damages is little more than a waste of your time and money and of the legal system's already overtaxed resources. Furthermore, such tactics reinforce America's image as a country full of lawsuit-crazy people. But if you insist on using the courts to make yourself feel better, I can guarantee that you'll find an attorney who will be perfectly willing to take your case — as long as you've got the money!

Not Telling Your Attorney Everything about Your Case

Attorneys *hate* to hear the phrase, "By the way, I forgot to tell you. . . ." Those words make us want to tear our hair out! Not to mention that when you fail to tell your attorney the whole story, warts and all, right from the start, you do yourself a serious disservice. The information you keep to yourself can derail your attorney's entire legal strategy. So tell the truth, the whole truth, and nothing but the truth, not only on the witness stand but in your attorney's office too!

Information you withhold from your attorney is likely to come to light sooner or later. Your attorney may discover it in the course of working on your case, or the other side may unearth it. When the information does come to the surface, your attorney may not be able to do anything to minimize its negative impact, and you may even lose what would otherwise have been a winnable case.

Hiring Someone You Know to Represent You

Hiring an attorney friend or an attorney you're dating to represent you is a prescription for disaster, and if you do, you risk destroying the relationship. For one thing, you may find it difficult, if not impossible, to tell an attorney with whom you have a personal relationship the whole truth about your legal problem. Also, because attorneys often have to tell their clients sobering and serious things — things clients may not want to hear — you may put your attorney friend or loved one in an unfair position if you ask him or her to represent you. And if you're unhappy with something that your attorney does or doesn't do, you're likely to find it difficult to express your displeasure if that attorney's relationship with you involves more than just business.

Finally, losing your case can put a damper on a friendship and squelch a relationship that might have developed into a beautiful thing.

Not Checking Your Attorney's Courtroom Track Record

Contrary to what you might think, many attorneys rarely if ever step foot into a courtroom. Some are just great at negotiating solutions to legal problems and are at their best when they're dealing with legal problems that can be resolved in the calm and comfort of their office — and most legal problems can be. Often, these lawyers studiously avoid cases likely to end up in the courtroom because they don't like the stress and are not cut out for courtroom drama.

So if you're facing a legal problem that may very well end up in court, you need someone who enjoys courtroom action and who has a successful track record trying cases like yours; otherwise, if it looks like your case may be headed for a trial, your lawyer may pressure you to settle for something that may not be in your best interest simply because he or she wants to avoid going to court.

Not Getting a Written Contract or Agreement of Representation

Doing business with an attorney is no different from doing business with anyone else. You need a written agreement. It should spell out in specific terms the services that the lawyer will provide you and all financial arrangements, and it should also state what will happen if you or your lawyer want to get out of the agreement.

Not Making Certain That Your Attorney Doesn't Have a Conflict of Interest

Always avoid working with an attorney who has represented the individual, business, or organization that you're having a legal problem with; otherwise, given your attorney's past relationship with the defendant in your case, you may find yourself in the uncomfortable position of wondering whether or not your attorney is really trying to settle your problem in a manner that represents your best interests.

Although it's the duty of an attorney to check for conflict of interest situations, an attorney who really wants your business may rationalize away such a conflict; therefore, be sure to bring up the issue at your initial meeting and certainly before you sign an agreement of representation.

Not Interviewing More Than One Attorney

As the saying goes, "There is more than one way to skin a cat," and the same holds true for resolving legal problems. You may be surprised by the number of different approaches to the same legal issue you'll hear when you talk to more than one attorney, not to mention the differences in their costs! So shop around to find an attorney who's willing to work with you on price and whose approach to your problem makes you feel comfortable.

Chapter 24

Ten Great Free and Almost-Free Sources of Information and Legal Help

* *

* *

Many free and low-cost sources of information can help you understand your rights, avoid legal problems, and deal with problems when they do develop. Accessing these resources is usually just a matter of knowing where to look and whom to call. Although many of the ones listed in this chapter have already been mentioned in earlier chapters, I think they're so important that it's worth calling them to your attention one more time.

An Attorney Who Practices in the Area of Law That You Need Information About

It may seem like a paradox (because this chapter is about free or almost-free sources of information, which doesn't usually describe attorneys), but a lawyer can actually be a great free source of legal information and advice, assuming that you find one who offers potential clients a free initial consultation. If you come to that first meeting well-prepared, you may in fact learn everything you need to know to deal with your legal problem yourself if it's relatively simple and straightforward.

Most ethical attorneys will be honest and will tell you up front whether or not you really need their help. After they understand the nature of your problem, many will even provide you with an overview of what to do and what not to do on your own.

To get the most out of a free consultation, spend time thinking about what you want to know. Write down your questions and bring them to the meeting. At the meeting, be prepared to take notes. When you talk with the attorney, explain your problem as succinctly as possible, without editorializing or bringing in a lot of extraneous information. Remember, you have a limited amount of free time with the attorney — an hour at best — and you're not in his or her office to hear the sound of your own voice!

Ask the lawyer straightforward questions:

- ✔ How would you define my legal problem?

- ✔ Given my concerns or plans, what do I need to do to minimize the possibility of legal entanglements?

- ✔ If I sue, what do you think are my chances of winning?

- ✔ If I hired you as my attorney, exactly what would you do for me?

- ✔ Can I do those things myself? (You may want to be up-front about the fact that you don't have a lot of money to spend.)

- ✔ If I do things myself, what are the potential pitfalls?

- ✔ How long do you think it will it take to resolve my legal problem, and how much will it cost if I were to hire you?

If an attorney is anxious for your business, he or she may try to convince you that you need his or her help by focusing on worst-case scenarios.

Consumer Credit Counseling Services (CCCS)

If you're having serious trouble paying your bills or you want to become a better money manager so that you can stay out of financial difficulty, a Consumer Credit Counseling Services (CCCS) office is the place for you.

A national nonprofit organization, local CCCS staff can help financially-troubled consumers negotiate affordable debt repayment plans with their creditors. Many offices also offer money management seminars, such as how to develop and live on a budget. If you're being hounded by debt collectors, losing sleep over your financial situation, or thinking about bankruptcy, schedule an appointment with the CCCS office closest to you immediately. Unless your financial situation is too far gone, the services of CCCS can help you avoid having to file for bankruptcy.

CCCS offices are in every state. To find the one closest to you, look in your yellow pages or call 1-800-388-2227.

Bankcard Holders of America (BHA)

To become a more informed user of credit, get in touch with the nonprofit Bankcard Holders of America (BHA).

One of the best ways to avoid having to step across the threshold of a CCCS office is to educate yourself about your rights and responsibilities as a credit consumer before you ever say "Charge it." BHA can help you do that. It publishes many excellent, inexpensive pamphlets on such topics as these:

- ✔ Your rights at the cash register or when you're dealing with creditors
- ✔ What to do when there's a problem with your bankcard bill or when you're being hassled by a debt collector
- ✔ Which banks are offering the best deals on national bankcards

You can become a member of the organization for an annual cost of $24. Membership benefits include discounts on BHA pamphlets and other publications and a bimonthly newsletter, which presents up-to-date news and tips that can help consumers make smart choices when they shop for and use all types of credit, not just bankcards. For more information, call 540-389-5445.

The Government

Find out what Uncle Sam has to offer. It's a little-known fact (because the federal government does relatively little to promote its publications), but your tax dollars help pay for hundreds of wonderful, highly informative brochures, handbooks, and pamphlets on just about every consumer-related subject you might want to know about! Take advantage of these great resources.

Here's a rundown on some of the best sources:

The Consumer Information Center

Contact the Consumer Information Center in Pueblo, Colorado, for a copy of its catalog. I bet you'll be surprised to discover the scope of subjects covered by the publications that you can order from it. Here are just a few sample titles: *Nine Ways to Lower Your Auto Insurance, Handy Reference Guide to the Fair Labor Standards Act, Guide to Choosing a Nursing Home, Questions to Ask Your Doctor Before You Have Surgery, How to Buy a Manufactured Home,* and *How to Solve Credit Problems.*

The majority of these publications are free, but those that aren't are priced at no more than $4, and most are available for a mere $.50. A real deal! Order your catalog by writing to the Consumer Information Center at P.O. Box 100, Pueblo, CO 81009.

You can read online versions of the publications in the Consumer Information Center as well as other consumer news and updates by checking out the Center's Web site at `http://www.pueblo.gsa.gov`.

The Consumer's Resource Handbook

Order a copy of *The Consumer's Resource Handbook.* Produced by the U.S. Office of Consumer Affairs, I think every home in America should have a copy of this. Updated annually, it provides practical information for being a smart consumer, including tips for getting the most for your money, reviews of some of the most important consumer laws, suggestions for how to handle your own legal complaints, advice for writing a complaint letter, and even a sample letter. It also lists the addresses and phone numbers of the offices you can contact to get help resolving your consumer problems, including national consumer organizations; corporate consumer contacts; car manufacturers; better business bureaus; trade associations and other dispute resolution programs; state, county, and city consumer offices; many federal agencies; and much more. To order a copy for your home, contact the Consumer Information Center, P.O. Box 100, Pueblo, CO 81009.

The U.S. Office of Consumer Affairs maintains a National Consumer HELPLINE at 1-800-664-4435. Call it for information you don't find in the handbook.

The Federal Trade Commission

The Federal Trade Commission (FTC) produces many helpful brochures on the consumer- and business-protection laws that it enforces. Here are the titles of some of its "best-sellers": *Work-at-Home Schemes; A Consumer Guide to Car Leasing; Women and Credit Histories; Buying and Borrowing; Home Equity Credit Lines; Warranties; Choosing a Career or Vocational School; Scams by Phone; Using Plastic: A Young Adult's Guide to Credit Cards; Credit Reports: What Employers Should Know about Using Them; Getting Business Credit;* and *Complying with the Credit Practices Rule.*

Some of its consumer brochures are available in Spanish. To get a complete list of the FTC's brochures, write to Office of Consumer and Business Education, Federal Trade Commission, Washington, D.C. 20580-0001.

The FTC is on the Internet. Many of its publications are available at `http://www.ftc.gov`.

Federal Elected Officials

Your federal elected officials are often overlooked sources of information and assistance. They're called public servants, right? And they wouldn't be in office if you and others didn't put them there. So make them work for their money! I'm talking about your U.S. senators and representatives. Their staff can help you find the information you need, help you deal with problems you may be having with a government agency or program, provide explanations of laws or updates on pending legislation, and refer you to additional resources. To connect with the office of your U.S. elected officials, call 202-225-3121. That's the number of the Capitol Hill operator, who can put you through to the right office.

If your legal issue or question concerns a state or local law or program, call the office of your state or local elected officials or the appropriate government agency. If you don't know exactly whom to call, start at the top with the office of your state's governor or your community's mayor, for example. The person you talk to should be able to point you in the right direction.

Community-Based Legal Services

Depending on your annual income and the size and makeup of your community, you may be eligible to use the services of a free legal clinic. Although these clinics are not usually the place for you if your legal problem is especially complicated or involves a lot of money, they can be an excellent resource if your concern is relatively straightforward.

- **Legal clinics sponsored by state or local bar associations:** In every state, attorneys are being asked by their bar associations to do more *pro bono* or free legal work for consumers who lack the financial resources to access quality legal help.

    Call your local or state bar association to find out if a legal clinic is in your area. You can also learn the criteria for qualifying to use its services and how to schedule an appointment.

- **Law school legal clinics:** To give their students real-world experience working on legal problems, many law schools sponsor free legal clinics. The students who provide this service work under the supervision of law school attorneys.

- **Legal Aid offices:** These offices provide free or low-cost legal assistance to consumers whose annual income qualifies them for this assistance. Their services are funded by federal, state, and local governments as well as by private donations. Call your local or state bar association or a private attorney to get the number of the Legal Aid office closest to you.

To qualify for help from these resources, you may have to provide proof that you can't afford to pay for an attorney's help.

A Business Veteran

Entrepreneurs or aspiring entrepreneurs should know about one of the best free business resources available: SCORE, which stands for "Service Corps of Retired Executives." Sponsored by the federal Small Business Administration, retired small business owners in communities around the country volunteer their time to share their knowledge and information with others. Many have dealt with the very same problems you may be facing, so they can tell you what worked for them and what didn't, what to avoid and what to try. Why reinvent the wheel or learn the hard way by making costly legal mistakes when you can talk to a SCORE representative? SCORE is another federal program that your tax dollars are helping to pay for, so make your tax dollars work for you!

Chapter 25

Ventura's Top Ten Law-Related Home Pages on the Internet

In This Chapter

▶ Several cool Web sites

*Y*es, you *can* get lost on the Internet. I did many times in researching this chapter. Cruising the Net was like peeling an onion; each click of my mouse uncovered more and more layers of information and resources on just about any legal subject I looked for.

My experience was somewhat overwhelming, but I found it exciting to discover just how much legal information is available. If you have enough time and use the right search engines (I especially like Lycos and Magellan), you can learn more than you ever thought possible about nearly every aspect of the law and our legal system. You can also read the actual text of laws that have been proposed or passed, download legal forms, participate in online discussions about the law, get referrals to attorneys in your area, and a whole lot more.

To help you zero in on some of the very best sources of legal information available via the Internet, I've picked my own top ten law-related home pages. If you visit them, you too will quickly begin to appreciate both the breadth and depth of information and resources available to you with a quick click of your mouse.

By the way, for those of you who aren't very experienced with computers, in order to access the Internet, you need a computer made within the last couple of years, a fast modem, Web browser software (I like Netscape), and either a subscription to a major online service or direct access to the Internet via an Internet service provider.

The American Bar Association

`http://www.aba.net.org`

The American Bar Association (ABA) is a national organization for attorneys. From its home page, you can access a world of helpful information and resources. Here's just a sampling of what you'll find:

- ✔ Click on the ABA's online lawyer referral service if you think you need an attorney and want help finding one. The service refers you to lawyers in your area who handle your type of legal problem, and what's more, you either get a free half-hour initial legal consultation with the lawyer you meet with, or you are asked to pay a nominal fee for that meeting, which in turn is used to help fund the ABA's referral service.

  Don't assume that, just because a lawyer is part of an online lawyer referral service, he or she is the attorney for you. Screen that attorney just as you would screen any other attorney you're considering. See Chapter 3 for more on hiring an attorney.

- ✔ From ABA's home page, you can also get to a state-by-state directory of *pro bono* legal service programs for low-income people. And if you're not low income but you don't have much money to spend on legal advice — which probably describes most of us — you can read about some of the innovative legal help programs around the country that are designed to help people of modest means but who make too much money to qualify for *pro bono* or subsidized legal services. These programs include nonprofit initiatives, legal help lines, court-based and bar-sponsored programs, military-sponsored programs, and entrepreneurial initiatives. One of these legal help programs may be in your neighborhood!

- ✔ Another ABA-sponsored resource you get to from its home page is LAWlink, which can help you link up with many, many other legal research and information resources on the Internet, everything from the legislative, executive, and judicial branches of the federal government to selected law school libraries and other legal research sites.

The Legal Information Institute

`http://www.law.cornell.edu`

This Web site is sponsored by Cornell University's law school. (Other law schools on the Internet include those from Indiana University, the University of Chicago, and Stanford University.) From its easy-to-use home page, you can get to a wide variety of legal subjects, such as family law, contracts, business law, consumer law, landlord-tenant issues, financial issues, real estate transactions, employment law, and criminal law. You can also find information about the courts and courtroom procedures.

The 'lectric Law Library

http://www.lectlaw.com

This fun, iconoclastic home page offers referrals to a wealth of legal information and resources. In fact, CNN calls it "Quite simply the best legal resource that we have on the Web." Whether or not it lives up to that accolade is for you to judge, but I certainly count it as one of the best.

To explore what the 'lectric Law Library has to offer, you must enter the library's "rotunda," from which you can move into any number of other "rooms," including The Laypeople's Lounge and The Law for Business Lounge, where you can access information on just about any legal issue. If you want to read about current legal issues and news, check out The Newsroom, and if you want to delve more deeply into various legal issues, current or past, go to The Periodical Reading Room, which is full of law-related journals, newspapers, and other publications.

The Reference Room is home to the 'lectric lawcopedia; you use it to access legal information by subject area and to get legal terms and phrases defined. In this room, you can also find links to some of the Net's best legal resources and search engines. And if you want to download sample legal and business forms, such as leases, wills, and contracts, go to the Forms Room. Incidentally, the 'lectric Law Library brags that it's got "the Net's biggest collection of legal forms." Finally, after spending hours reading all of the information available to you in the 'lectric Law Library, unwind in The Rubber Room, where you can yuk it up by reading lawyer jokes, anecdotes, and bloopers.

Court TV Law Center

http://www.courttv.com

Court TV, the cable network that lets you watch real people deal with real legal problems from the comfort of your own home, has produced an attractive and easy-to-use home page that is not only a promotional tool for the network's programming but also a source of good legal information and assistance. Click on Get Legal Help or go to Court TV's Small Business, Family Law, or Elder Law Centers for information on specific legal subjects that fall under each heading.

Or go to Lawyer Search, where you can locate (by city, legal specialty, or law firm) an attorney who can help with your legal problem. And if you want to make certain that the lawyer you find hasn't been disciplined or been in trouble, click on Lawyer Check. There, you can e-mail the attorney's name and address to the Law Center. Its staff will contact the appropriate state authority about the lawyer and get back to you with any negative information it may find.

LEGI•SLATE

http://www.legislate.com

LEGI•SLATE is a subsidiary of *The Washington Post* and claims to be the nation's premier provider of online congressional and regulatory information, providing "behind-the-scenes maneuvering, current political gossip, [and] inside information" on recently introduced Congressional legislation. Its public access Gopher helps you read the actual text of bills and regulations, and if you go to its Inside the Capitol Web page, you can get informative lessons on the Constitution and the Declaration of Independence, an overview of how the government works, and explanations of legislative and regulatory processes.

Hieros Gamos, A Comprehensive Site to the Legal Profession

http://www.hg.orghghome.html

This home page claims to be "the largest and only comprehensive site with over 12,000 original pages and more than 10,000 links" to other sources of legal information on the Internet. Assuming that bigger is better, this is the place for you if you want to get the scoop on more than 6,000 legal organizations or search for law firms, private investigators, alternative dispute resolution professionals, and much, much more.

FindLaw

http://www.findlaw.com/

At the FindLaw home page, you can search an index of legal resources by subject or by specific statute or law. You can access some of these topics through the Legal Subject Index: library information, legal associations and organizations, news and reference materials, and law schools. The Statute and Law index helps you pinpoint information on judicial opinions and case law, federal and state government resources, lawyers, and sample legal forms. To make your search for legal information easier, test-drive FindLaw's LawCrawler.

Cecil Greek's Criminal Justice Page

http://www.stpt.usf.edu/~greek/cj.html

I don't know who Cecil Greek is, but I can tell you that his home page links you up with some of the most eclectic and fascinating law-related information resources on the Internet. Here is just a sampling of the major topic categories (and there are also a myriad of subcategories) that you can get to from this home page: juvenile delinquency, the courts, police agencies and resources, prisons and the death penalty, crime and crime prevention, date rape, husband battering, victims rights, unsolved crimes and fugitives, missing children, militias, cults, and white-collar and computer crimes. It even has a link to a Web page titled "The Bureau of Missing Socks," which is described as "the first organization devoted to solving the question of what happens to missing socks." If you're looking to get lost in cyberspace, you can do it here!

Nolo Press

http://www.nolo.com

Nolo Press is one of this country's premier publishers of self-help legal books and software. Although I am not as enthusiastic a proponent as Nolo is of people handling their own legal problems, I do think that the company's books and software offer consumers and small business owners a lot of valuable information that can help them become more informed consumers of legal help. From Nolo's home page, you can access excerpts from many of the books it has published. Major subjects covered include estate planning, business and workplace issues, family matters and the legal concerns of seniors, home owner and landlord/tenant issues, immigration, intellectual property, money and consumer matters, and small claims court. Those of you who are independent contractors or who make use of independent contractors may want to go from Nolo's home page to its Independent Contractor Law Web site, where you can get questions answered, access information about new developments in laws that affect independent contractors, and find out about other Internet resources that you can use.

THOMAS

`http://thomas.loc.gov/home/thomas.html`

With THOMAS (as in Jefferson), you no longer have an excuse to claim that you don't know what your federal elected officials are up to — as long as you can get online. You can read the full text as well as summaries of bills that have been introduced and get periodic updates on their status. And if you have an opinion about any of them, click on the House and Senate Web sites to get the e-mail addresses of your elected officials and send them a message. You can also access committee reports and historical documents, including the Constitution, the Federalist Papers, and the Declaration of Independence. THOMAS also has links to many Congressional and legislative support agencies' services like the Library of Congress.

Your elected official may not be a member of the Information Age yet. At the time this book was researched, some U.S. senators and representatives had not yet gone online.

Appendix
Sample Letters

• •

I make it very clear in Chapter 8 that you need to keep tabs on the information in your credit report. But before you can evaluate that information, you need to obtain a copy of your report from the credit bureaus that are maintaining records on you. Use the first sample letter to do just that.

The second sample letter shows you what information you need to provide should you find any inaccurate information in your credit report.

The third sample letter is a simple complaint letter. As discussed in Chapter 2, you can resolve many everyday legal problems yourself, without the help of an attorney. This complaint letter can be a great first step, depending on the nature of your problem.

Sample Letter Requesting a Copy of Your Credit Report from a Credit Reporting Agency

You don't have to use this exact letter when requesting a copy of your credit history, but to avoid delays, be sure that your letter includes all of the same information as this one. Also, don't forget that if you've been denied credit, employment, or insurance due to information in your credit record, you are entitled to a free report if you request it within 30 days of the denial. Attach a copy of your denial letter to your request letter.

The addresses for the major credit reporting agencies are listed in Chapter 8.

Date
Dear Sir or Madam:

I would like a copy of my credit report. A check for $XX.XX is enclosed to cover the cost of my report.

My full name is: (Don't forget to indicate if you're a Junior, Senior, the III, and so on.)
My Social Security number is:
My date of birth is:
My current address is: (no P.O. boxes)

My previous addresses are: (This information is necessary only if you've not lived at your current address for at least five years; otherwise, provide all previous addresses for that time period.)

My spouse's full name is:
My spouse's Social Security number is:

If you have any questions about this request, you can reach me during the day at (your daytime number including area code) and in the evenings at (your nighttime number with area code).

Please send my credit report to the following address:

Thank you for your prompt attention to my request.

Sincerely,
Your signature

Sample Letter Asking That a Credit Reporting Agency Correct a Problem in Your Credit Report

Date
Dear Sir or Madam:

In reviewing the credit report I recently received from your company, I noted the following problem/s: (Describe the error/s in your report clearly and succinctly.)

The enclosed documentation provides proof of the error/s. (Depending on the error, you might include copies of receipts, credit card bills, canceled checks, letters, and so on.)

Please look into this matter and make all necessary corrections in my credit record. Once you do, I would like you to send me a corrected version of my credit record. You can send it to the following address:

I would also like you to send a corrected version of my credit record to anyone who has reviewed it over the past six months for credit purposes. I would like written confirmation that you have done this.

If you have any questions, I can be reached during the day at (your phone number including area code). Thank you for your help.

Sincerely,
Your signature

My full name is: (Don't forget to mention if you're a Junior, Senior, the III, and so on.)
My Social Security number is:
My date of birth is:
My current address is: (no P.O. boxes)

My previous addresses are: (This information is necessary only if you've not lived at your current address for at least five years; otherwise, provide all previous addresses during that time period.)

My spouse's full name is:
My spouse's Social Security number is:

Sample Complaint Letter

Your Street Address
Your City, State, ZIP code
Date

Name of the Contact Person , if available
Title, if available
Company Name
Consumer Complaint Division, if you have no contact person
Street Address
City, State, ZIP code

Dear (Contact Person):

On (date), I (bought, leased, rented, or had repaired) a (name of the product with serial or model number or service performed) at (location, date, and other important details of the transaction).

Unfortunately, your product (or service) has not performed well (or the service was inadequate) because (state the problem). I am disappointed because (explain the problem: for example, the product does not work properly, the service was not performed correctly, I was billed the wrong amount, something was not disclosed clearly or was misrepresented, and so on).

To resolve the problem, I would appreciate that you (state the specific action you want — money back, charge card credit, repair, exchange, and so on). Enclosed are copies (do not send originals) of my records (include receipts, guarantees, warranties, canceled checks, contracts, model and serial numbers, and any other documents).

I look forward to your reply and a resolution to my problem, and I will wait until (set a time limit) before seeking help from a consumer protection agency or the Better Business Bureau. Please contact me at the above address or by phone at (home and/or office numbers with area codes).

Sincerely,
Your name

Enclosure(s)

cc: (reference to whom you are sending a copy of this letter, if anyone)

Index